Why We Kneel, How We Rise

Why We Kneel,
How We Rise

Michael Holding

With Ed Hawkins

**SIMON &
SCHUSTER**

London · New York · Sydney · Toronto · New Delhi

First published in Great Britain by Simon & Schuster UK Ltd, 2021

1 3 5 7 9 10 8 6 4 2

Simon & Schuster UK Ltd
1st Floor
222 Gray's Inn Road
London WC1X 8HB

www.simonandschuster.co.uk
www.simonandschuster.com.au
www.simonandschuster.co.in

Simon & Schuster Australia, Sydney
Simon & Schuster India, New Delhi

A CIP catalogue record for this book
is available from the British Library

Hardback ISBN: 978-1-3985-0323-6
Trade Paperback ISBN: 978-1-3985-0324-3
eBook ISBN: 978-1-3985-0325-0

Typeset in Bembo by M Rules
Printed and bound by CPI Group (UK) Ltd, Croydon, CR0 4YY

To Mom — who lived her life quietly hoping for race equality

CONTENTS

Preface   1

Speaking Up

1 Black Clouds   9
2 A Sheltered Start   22
   With Usain Bolt

3 Black Lives Matter, Too   35
   With Naomi Osaka

4 Living It   53
   With Hope Powell

Why We Kneel

5 Dehumanisation   75
   Slavery by a different name
   The lynchings
   The virus

6 Show of Strength   113
   With Ibtihaj Muhammad

7   History Lesson   124
Whitewash
How do we teach?
And who by?

8   Fear   160
With Michael Johnson

9   Acceptance   173
The ultimate sacrifice
The forgotten
The beat goes on
On the shoulders of giants

How We Rise

10   Progress   221
With Thierry Henry

11   The Blueprint?   237
With Makhaya Ntini

12   A New Generation   252
With Adam Goodes

13   We've Got a Chance   267

A *Why We Kneel, How We Rise* Black
History Timeline   283

Sources   297

PREFACE

After my last book was published in 2010, entitled *No Holding Back*, I thought my writing days had ended. But I was inspired to put pen to paper once again by a sequence of events coming together at, for the want of a better term, 'the right time'. Although these events should never be termed 'right' in any fashion as they involved the loss of human life, the reaction to George Floyd's murder, and the much later recognition of the loss of Breonna Taylor's life, meant all over the world there was debate and discussion about ending the mistreatment of people of colour. Hopefully their deaths – and hundreds of others – will not be in vain.

The graphic display of George's life, that of a Black man in America, slowly ebbing away under the pressure of a white police officer's knee on his neck led to millions of people taking to the streets in protest, to say 'this cannot continue'. This book is my way of saying 'this cannot continue'.

If you look up racism in the *Oxford English Dictionary*, you will find these words:

The belief that different races possess distinct characteristics, abilities or qualities, especially so as to distinguish them as inferior or superior to one another.

I thought long and hard about the best way to communicate how people of colour have been dehumanised for centuries. I want to educate about why racism exists, how it works and what it is like to be treated differently just because of the colour of your skin. What does it *feel* like when you walk into the room as the only Black guy? What does it *feel* like to be eyed with suspicion? To be followed when you go into a shop? To know that your life is valued less?

I want to show how the dehumanisation of a race of people began and was then encouraged in order to satisfy the narrative of inferiority and superiority. I wanted to educate people about the true history of mankind, which should dispel the myth of one or another race being inferior or superior.

And I am very fortunate that, as a former international sportsman – I played 162 times for the West Indies cricket team between 1975 and 1987 – and, dare I say, respected television commentator, I have enough contacts in the world of sports to bring together a collection of Black icons to help tell that story. How better to get people to sit up and take notice than if some of the most iconic athletes in the world tell their story, about how racism has affected them?

So you will hear from my compatriot Usain Bolt, the fastest man who has ever lived, about the sheltered upbringing we both had in Jamaica; and how the fierce tennis champion Naomi Osaka is using her status as the most sought-after athlete in the world to inspire change.

The great American Olympic athlete Michael Johnson talks to me about the fear that underpins the entire system of racial inequality, and Ibtihaj Muhammad, the groundbreaking Olympian, reveals what it's like to be Black, Muslim and a woman in the present-day Land of the Free.

Thierry Henry, one of the greatest footballers of all time, opens up about how only worldwide fame can help to protect you from racism. The story of how racism ended the career of Adam Goodes, legendary Aussie Rules star, may well move you to tears. Trailblazers are here too – Makhaya Ntini, the first Black African to play cricket for South Africa, and Hope Powell, England's first Black soccer coach.

Through the last days of summer 2020 and into the winter, I spoke with each of them. All of the interviews were conducted over Zoom as the Covid pandemic raged and rules on social distancing and international travel made meeting up in person impossible. I am hugely grateful for their time, generosity and support. And, I should add, none of them was 'hand-picked' because they had a good, emotive story to tell that fitted the narrative. They had a story to tell because of who they are perceived to be, because – just like any person of colour – they have suffered from centuries-old stigma.

My experience of racism will be intertwined with theirs and I hope this combination will amplify the messages and engage as many people as possible. I largely focus on race in America and Britain. Why? Because I have lived in both countries and, in my opinion, the two nations' role in the past, present and future are most relevant to the quest for equality.

I would like to thank my immediate boss at Sky, Bryan Henderson, the executive producer of Sky Sports Cricket, whose idea it was to allow Ebony Rainford-Brent and myself to express our feelings on the BLM movement and racism in general. Thanks also to my overall employer Sky UK Ltd for the support and encouragement throughout the entire process.

I have mentioned in the pages of the book some folks who

encouraged me to go further than just what I said on that July morning, but I would like to additionally give a huge shout-out and thanks to my ghostwriter Ed Hawkins, who also did my last cricket book. He was invaluable and did a brilliant job in converting my ramblings and WhatsApp-messaged stories into something readable and, ultimately, the production of this book. Not to mention the research he did to make sure the stories and illustrations we used were factual and accurate. Kudos to Joe Citrone for efficient transcription work.

A book can always be written but without a publisher it goes nowhere and so I would like to thank my literary agents, Charlie Campbell and Charlotte Atyeo, who handled all the groundwork to get the right publisher, Simon & Schuster, who I must also thank for having the confidence in the writer and the subject to commit themselves to publishing the work. Thanks to Ian Marshall and Frances Jessop for the advice and editing.

Lastly, but by no means least, I would like to thank the personalities who agreed to be interviewed and give us a bit of a look into their lives and share their opinions on matters discussed. I will be eternally grateful to them for taking time out of their busy schedules and being so committed to the cause, as their presence in these pages has enhanced the story and the teaching we're trying to do.

They are, in alphabetical order:

Usain Bolt
Adam Goodes
Jeffrey Harriott
Thierry Henry
Michael Johnson

Ibtihaj Muhammad
Makhaya Ntini
Naomi Osaka
Hope Powell

Just finally, before we get started, I want to be clear: this is not a book of complaints. It is a book of facts. I hope it will enlighten, inspire, surprise, shock, move. And, above all, help to bring about real change.

SPEAKING UP

CHAPTER 1

Black Clouds

Thank goodness it rained.

It was the morning of 8 July 2020 in Southampton. I was supposed to be commentating on live television for Sky Sports as England played West Indies. But the sky was heavy and dark and full of rain, meaning no play was possible. Without on-field action to discuss, there was only one subject to talk about.

George Floyd had been murdered in Minneapolis only six weeks previously. A police officer called Derek Chauvin had forced him to the concrete ground and put a knee on his neck. 'I can't breathe,' George said. We know that because passers-by were filming what was happening on their mobile phones. He said it more than twenty times. George pleaded for his life. He called out for his mother. 'Momma, momma, momma.' 'He must be high,' said another policeman. Onlookers pleaded for Chauvin to get off his neck. That knee was on George's neck for eight minutes and forty-six seconds.

The footage was seen all around the world. Those who could watch until the bitter, tragic end were shocked and appalled at the senseless brutality. We saw a person being killed in front of our eyes. Someone's father, husband, brother. If you were Black, you probably watched it and thought: *Could have been me, could have been a member of my family.* But you also knew it was not an aberration, it was not the first time a Black man had been senselessly killed by a police officer. This time the whole world was able to see.

And it couldn't be ignored. Everybody, it seemed, was talking about racism, the Black Lives Matter movement, and asking how and why this was still happening in 2020.

With no cricket and the rain still falling, Sky showed a short film involving me and my commentary colleague, Ebony Rainford-Brent, talking about the Black Lives Matter movement, protests and our personal experiences of racism. When it was over, I was asked to speak again. And it was live. Ian Ward, the anchor of the show, asked me how hard it was to make that film and speak about such things. Well, I didn't hold back. And from what I said, and the way that I said it, I think people saw anger, frustration and emotion. I just about managed to hold back tears.

In those minutes I wanted to help people to understand how and why Black people like George Floyd were being killed. George Floyd was not an isolated case. In March of that year Breonna Taylor, a hospital worker, was shot by police while in bed at her home in Kentucky during a drugs raid. Only one of the three white policemen, who fired up to thirty-two shots between them, was charged. And it wasn't with murder. Instead 'wanton endangerment' was the charge because bullets from his gun ended up in a neighbouring apartment. In 2020 alone in America there were 226 fatal shootings of Black people by police. Harvard research showed that, in some parts of the country, if you are Black you are six times more likely than white people to be shot to death by those who are supposed to protect you. In the United States, according to data provider Statista, the rate of fatal shootings (per million of the population) from 2015 to June 2020 was as follows: 30 Black, 23 Hispanic, 12 white, 4 other.

It is not just an American problem. Let's get that straight early on. I've heard people in the UK say that it is. For George Floyd read Christopher Alder, who died in a police station in Hull, England, in 1998. CCTV footage showed Alder lying face down on the floor, not moving and with his trousers around his ankles. Police officers are standing around laughing for ten minutes while Alder, unable to breathe, dies. Five officers were prosecuted for manslaughter and misconduct but all were acquitted. For Christopher read Sean Rigg, Ricky Bishop, Mark Duggan, Leon Briggs, Kingsley Burrell, Mikey Powell, Sheku Bayoh, Darren Cumberbatch, Simeon Francis. According to the BBC, Black people account for 8 per cent of deaths in custody but only 3 per cent of the population.

Black people suffer. Our lives are worth less. And the statistics don't lie. In the US and UK our children are more likely to leave school without qualifications, we are more likely to go to jail, more likely to live in poverty, more likely to live in social housing, less likely to own a home. We earn less, our women die in childbirth at a higher rate, our infant mortality is higher. And, not surprisingly, our life expectancy is lower.

All of these things happen because we live by a system that tolerates and enforces deeply entrenched ideas that Black people, or people of colour, are inferior. From a seed of an idea hundreds of years ago that Black people were 'different' and 'other' has grown a belief system that has led to the consistent dehumanisation of Black people. It has given us the transatlantic slave trade, 'science' that ranked Black people as the lowest of the low, governments enforcing segregation of races, economic policies that deprived Black people of houses and jobs, and, of course, police brutality.

Underpinning all of that is education. Or the lack of it. And that was the main thrust of what I said on Sky Sports.

I want to expand on education. When I say education, I mean going back in history. What people need to understand is that this thing stems from a long time ago, hundreds of years ago. The dehumanisation of the Black race is where it started. People will tell you, 'That's a long time ago, get over it.' No. You don't get over things like that. Society has not gotten over something like that, so how can individuals?

I didn't quite understand as a young man what brainwashing meant – I now understand. People – Black people and white people – have been brainwashed in different ways.

Everything should be taught. In my schooldays, I was never taught anything good about Black people and you cannot have a society that is brought up like that, where you only teach what is convenient to the teacher. History is written by the conqueror, not those who are conquered. History is written by the people who do the harm, not by the people who are harmed. We need to go back and teach both sides of history.

Until we do that and educate the entire human race, this thing will not stop. We need to teach and re-educate, as a lot of Black people in this world are growing up believing that they are lesser than other people and that cannot be right.

At the time I had no idea what impact my words would have. But as soon as I was off-air and saw the messages and emails coming through on my phone, I realised that people had taken notice. Job done, I thought. The clips of the speech were being passed on through social media. I think the phrase they use these days is 'gone viral' (it has now been watched almost 7 million times). The next evening, I was asked to talk again on Sky News. I agreed, thinking that it would be the last interview I did on the subject. I had made my views clear so I didn't see any reason to keep repeating the same stuff – if people didn't get what I was talking about from what I'd already said, I thought, then they wouldn't ever get it and perhaps didn't want to understand.

I almost made it through this time without crying. It was the last question that got me.

Mark Austin, the interviewer, asked about the emotion I had held back. And I told him it was because I was thinking about my parents. And what they had been through. And, as I started explaining it to him, that emotion came again. And it was too much for me. I was overcome. I wiped the tears from my eyes. I struggled to find my voice.

My mother's family stopped talking to her because my father was too dark. He was dark-skinned but I have seen so many others much darker than my father; however, her family didn't want her marrying him. All she wanted was to build a family with the man she loved. And she sacrificed her relationship with her family for that. Because of that, she barely existed to them.

When I was a young man growing up, her siblings were always around, along with her mother, but no one else from the older generation. It was much later that I found out the reason for that. Of course, at the time, I had no idea why; I just enjoyed the relationship with her brothers, Eric and Henry, and her sisters, Norma and Etta.

I was looking up at those dark Southampton skies again, wiping my face, as the interview came to an end, thinking about my mom and dad who are no longer alive. Thinking about how, as a family, we had never talked about it. Soon after that interview my sisters, Rheima and Marjorie, messaged me, asking: 'How did you know that about Momma and Daddy?' They didn't even know that I knew, as it had never been discussed as a family. It had been swept under the carpet, a family secret that had been ignored.

And, to be honest, I was ready and willing to do the same as this thing blew up. Not quite sweep it under the carpet but move on and put it behind me. As I had said to Jason Holder, the West Indies captain, during a discussion live on Sky, and to use a cricket analogy: I had bowled the ball and found the edge; it was up to others to now take the catch to complete the job.

I felt exposed and vulnerable. And, unsurprisingly, I didn't like those feelings. Who would? I was inundated with requests from the media to talk more about my experiences and my family. And I wanted nothing to do with it.

My collaborator on this book, Ed Hawkins, who helped me write my autobiography in 2010, messaged me. He thought it would be a good idea to keep spreading the word. To produce something that would do exactly what I had demanded: to re-educate, to tell the true history of the world and how Black people had been dehumanised. But I was unsure. I didn't want to be appearing here, there and everywhere. I felt people needed to absorb it, rather than having it shouted at them every which way. 'I will leave people to use what I've said already,' I told him, 'although I could have said much more.'

Then two things happened. The morning after the discussion with Mark Austin, my Sky colleague Ian Ward came up to me.

'So, what happens next?' he asked.

'Next?' I said. 'I've nothing to add, Wardy. It's there for anyone who wants to see it.'

'Are you sure?' he said.

Then, I got a call from a number I didn't recognise. It was Thierry Henry, the football star. He said two words: 'I understand.' We spoke for some time, and later exchanged messages. And he encouraged me to keep talking. He said that I could reach out, help influence people and bring about some change, however small. 'When I saw you on television I thought, *I have to call you,*' he said. 'Wow, it was emotional. Here is a Black guy saying it is okay to cry. To show people what this means. You know Black men aren't supposed to cry, right? Well, it changed me.'

I spoke to my colleague Ebony Rainford-Brent, who was the first Black female cricketer to play for England, in 2007, and won a World Cup. She endured racist abuse throughout her career. Truly appalling abuse that, if I put it in black and white on these pages, it would turn your stomach. She has suffered. It has affected her health and it had a profound impact on her career. It is such a tragedy that Black people can't even go to their jobs, where they excel, where they want to achieve and want to thrive, without having to put up with this. And since doing that film with Sky she has withdrawn from the conversation, fearing a backlash because she dared to say something. She is afraid. Women, whatever the context, always seem to suffer more. They are considered targets for particularly vile abuse. And I don't blame her or judge her for taking a step back. She was brave to say anything at all at her age or stage in life. Should I speak for her and people like her, to help?

I started thinking. I thought about my 6-year-old grandson who lives in America. I mentioned him in my interview with Mark Austin, saying that I hoped there would be change by the time he was my age. And I also thought how, when he gets a bit older, his parents will have to tell him not to walk around wearing a hoodie, never to say anything to a policeman apart from 'yes, sir' and 'no, sir', and to be completely compliant. And how, if I had been given such instructions when living in a country riven by racism as a young man, I'm not sure I could have done it.

We will never forget the story of George Floyd, in the same way that we will not forget the story of Tamir Rice, the 12-year-old boy from Cleveland, Ohio, who was shot by a white police officer, two seconds after he arrived at the scene, for carrying a toy gun. Parents are now having conversations with their kids about how they should and should not play.

My two daughters live in America. And I am lucky that I've not had to have those same conversations with them because they know, and I know, that if they were ever unfortunate enough to have interaction with a police officer, they would do exactly what they were told. Every day the mothers and fathers of Black kids in America are having to sit them down and tell them what to expect. 'Now, if you're stopped by the police, this is what you need to do.' I understand the need to be respectful, but why should any kid growing up in any country have to be told exactly what to do and what not to do because of the colour of their skin? And why should their lives depend on it?

I also thought of my own early experiences of race and colour. Very, very early memories. Things that happened which I hadn't thought about for years.

New York City in the sixties. I was in my early teens. I had gone there from Jamaica with my mother to visit an old family friend. I must have been on an outing with this friend. And she was holding my hand, showing me the sights in Manhattan. And I see a guy in the gutter. A homeless person, poor, broke and begging. And my eyes are on stalks and my mouth is open wide. And she yanks me by the hand and says in our Jamaican way: 'What happen? You don't know white people can be poor too?' I had never seen a poor white person.

New York again. But this time we're visiting a relative in upstate New York, Rochester. It's early morning and my mom, as usual, is up before me. Our bedroom is on the second floor of the house and my mom's at the window. She says: 'Mikey, come over here and look at this.' And she points out a white kid and a Black kid, playing together in the neighbour's yard below. She shows me and says, 'Mikey, we've got a chance.' That was the only time I ever heard her speak about anything to do with racism. I never even heard her use the word. And it shows how much it had to be on her mind all the time for her to call to her youngest child, who she had never discussed such things with before, and make such a remark.

And here's the thing. When I said what I said, a lot of people who know me got in touch to say: 'Mikey, we had no idea you felt like that.' Well, that's pretty much how I've lived my life. I mostly keep my thoughts to myself but if you ask me, I'll tell you. And that's what Sky Sports did. They asked me the question.

The truth is, though, I've been running away from this issue my whole life.

My family – and I understand perfectly why they did it and apportion no blame – pretended there wasn't a problem. As my sister Marjorie said to me a few years ago, and we were laughing about it: 'Momma didn't really prepare us for what this world was really like.' And I never knew what racism truly was until I left Jamaica to play cricket all around the world and commentate on it. England, Australia, South Africa. And yet, I chose to keep my head down and do my best to ignore it. It was far easier for me to do that instead of make a fuss. That's not an easy thing to admit.

As a person with a platform and a reputation, I could have done more. I could have campaigned and been vocal. Then, when I did say what I said, it wouldn't have been a shock. And by shock, I mean to *me*. I was taken aback by the reaction and thought, *I'm not sure I like all this attention . . . gonna shut up now.* That is in part due to how I am perceived to be. I tend not to get overexcited. I think as a commentator I am mostly known, or at least I hope, for being fair-minded and rational. A lot of people were saying, 'Well, if Mikey reckons it's a problem . . .'

That was good to hear, for sure. But after Ian Ward spoke to me, then Thierry Henry called me up, I thought long and hard about my life and I realised it was time to speak. Maybe

my voice could make a difference an.
even-handed could be of benefit. I th.
the occasions when I could and should have
But didn't. Inside I grimaced. It was time not tv
mistake again. Time to become unselfish. So I spok.
again. 'Let's do it,' I said.

You see, I have been fortunate. I have travelled the world because, simply, I was good at playing a sport. It has been a privileged life. And one of the big privileges was that it gave me life experiences that educated me. As soon as I left Jamaica I started to become aware of racism. I listened to people tell their stories. I heard their problems. I saw them. And the more I experienced, the more I wanted to learn. This is over several years. Thankfully, because of all the time spent on aeroplanes and in hotels, I was able to read. And I educated myself as to what had happened in the world and what was happening in the world. That is darn lucky. Not everyone gets that time. So an opportunity to try to pass on some of that knowledge, I felt, shouldn't be ignored.

There was not one 'lightbulb' moment when I suddenly realised that something was not right, although I would say that my trips to England in the 1970s and 1980s proved to be a particularly rich – and troubling – education. So apologies if you were hoping for some one-off dramatic moment of awakening. But I guess that's what life is, a constant lesson. I know more now than I did in my twenties, thirties and so on. I know more than I did yesterday.

This story, in many ways, aims to right some wrongs. Perhaps chief among them the way my mother's family reacted to my father. And this brings me to probably the most important point of the whole book, and I know some of you thinking it: how can Black people be racist like that? Well, racism is not a white-only issue. This thing affects everybody. We all live under the same system, are affected by its skewed rules and education system.

That is why my mother's family didn't want her marrying someone with darker skin. My mother was relatively light-skinned. And let me tell you, a lot of Black people covet that. They want to be as light-skinned as possible, or their offspring to be as light as possible, so it can help them to get on in life. The perception is that the lighter skin you have, the less likely you are to be affected by racism, whether that's being abused in the street, or your chances of being offered a job or shot at by a cop. The darker you are? Bad luck. That's what the system has done to people.

On the same point, this is not a story about hating white people. The word I used on Sky Sports was 'brainwashed'. White or Black, pink or green, we have all been indoctri-nated to believe that one colour is the purest and best. The further down the colour chart you go, the lazier the person, the more aggressive, untrustworthy, less intelligent. Of course it is ridiculous to blame 'white people' for that. They don't know any better and have been to the same schools and col-leges and lived in the same societies and cultures as the rest of us. You are a product of your environment. As I said on Sky that morning, this thing gets into your head and psyche almost by osmosis. It happens without you being aware.

And, for that reason, you are likely to find some parts of this book difficult to read. The savage treatment of Black people is hard to stomach and I guarantee that you will turn a page in this book and say to yourself, 'Huh, I didn't know that.' If your mind is open, I really hope you will learn something.

And maybe by the end of it you will realise, Black or white, why George Floyd was murdered. Not in a way designed to make whites feel guilty or ashamed, or for Blacks or people of colour to feel angry, but just to make you recognise that, for hundreds of years, people of colour have been treated like sub-humans. And now it's time they got some equality.

But it is also not a gloomy book. I want it to be a story about positivity. And that's why you will learn about brilliant Black minds and bodies and the incredible life-changing, life-saving things they have achieved. About how we can fix the education system so that everybody, regardless of their colour, benefits. If we have a fairer system, or start to move towards equality, nobody will lose out. There's enough to go around, folks.

So it's about hope. It's about why we kneel, and how we rise.

CHAPTER 2

A Sheltered Start

With Usain Bolt

When Usain Bolt was around twenty years old, making his way as a sprinter, he was in London for an athletics meet. He had some time off so thought he'd go to do some shopping. He walked into a mall. After a while he noticed a security guard was following him. *Strange*, he thought, but maybe it was coincidence. He went into a jewellery store because he was interested in buying a watch. 'I said to the woman behind the counter, "I like this one ... how much?" She tells me. And she says, "Are you sure you can afford it?" I was thinking, *Why is she assuming I can't afford the watch?'*

'That wouldn't happen now.' Well, he's right about that.

When I was a similar age, the exact same thing happened to me. I asked to see a watch that was in the showcase and, before the lady took it out, she told me the price with a tone suggesting I could not afford it. It was as if she wanted to save herself the effort. I detected the attitude immediately and just said, 'I'll take it' before she even took it out, just to mentally give her a jolt. It cost more than I'd wanted to spend but there was no way I was going to give her the pleasure of saying in her mind, 'I knew it.'

Coincidence? I don't think so.

In Usain's case, it is a ridiculous and shocking story because he is now one of the most famous people in the world. He is probably the most famous Black man in the world. Everywhere he goes people know who he is. The fastest man in history. Some might say he is one of the finest physical specimens ever. And yet, back then, he was made to feel like he was nothing.

'I just remember thinking, *Could you show me the watch?* I didn't understand,' he says. 'And I didn't think back then, "This is racist", because it was new to me in that moment. But remembering racism, in a sense, is an education and a learning experience. And you might tell that story and someone else goes, "That happened to me." So as an experience it was unpleasant but good comes from telling it. And it was a shock for that first time coming from Jamaica.'

Usain remembers that story – and I remember mine – because of the way it made us feel. It hurt. And it still does. That's because we were both made out to be sub-human. Dehumanisation. There are a lot of stories like that in this book. They are not coincidences, either.

I got the chance to fire some questions at Usain just after he recovered from a bout of Covid. He was a cool customer, exactly like his reputation. But that demeanour was at odds with what he was saying, because he told of the pain and anguish about what was happening to Black people. I was very keen to compare notes on life growing up in Jamaica.

What was his upbringing like? What were his views of racism at the time? What was he taught at school? But first of all, I sensed a real desire to make his voice heard about race because he has so rarely been asked about it.

'It hurts to see it. My heart bleeds to see the atrocities still happening. In this day and age, why would it still exist? We're all bleeding emotionally and psychologically.'

As we know, Usain (eight Olympic golds) is one of the finest athletes of all time and the greatest ever sprinter. His fame, his athleticism, his character make him stand out. He is proud of his Blackness. And Black people are proud of him. As a man of almost superhuman quality, he personifies what Black people can achieve if they are just given the chance. But does that superhuman quality mean he is almost 'protected' from the everyday racism that his brethren experience? He doesn't like the word 'protected'.

'I'm not sure "protected" is right. Okay, I don't get followed by security guards any more. You might not be in a situation to be abused on the streets or to be kneeled on or choked. But you see it around you and, as a Black man, you'd be like, "Whoa, those things are still happening today." It's affecting you mentally like anybody else. The things that you're seeing of late, nobody's thinking, *Oh, I'm protected.*'

But we were protected in another way. For two young men from Jamaica those stories about the watch are early experiences of racism. What is significant about what happened to us might not seem too obvious. But we had grown up in a country where there was very little racism by the time we came along. Jamaica was, and is, a predominantly Black country. It wasn't always that way, of course. When Jamaica became a British colony, it was 82 per cent white. As a slave plantation producing tobacco, cotton and then sugar, the population began to change quickly. But although Black people would outnumber whites, you've got to remember who was in charge. And it wasn't Black people.

Jamaicans resented British rule, racism, and the all-powerful Colonial Office. But from 1944 the country underwent what was called 'constitutional decolonisation', which means that we as a people started to be able to make our own decisions. Total independence from Britain came in 1962. And the days of white rule, segregated areas and white-on-Black racism were becoming only memories. I was born in 1954. A decade earlier Jamaica was a totally different country. Twenty years before that even more so. The 1960 census reported a white population of 0.7 per cent and that had fallen to 0.18 per cent by 2001. So you can see why racism would disappear and has disappeared. And in those moments Usain and I have described it was disturbing and upsetting to suddenly be confronted with the reality of life. I guess you could say I had enjoyed a sheltered upbringing until that point.

And this is one of the main reasons I wanted to talk to Usain. Maybe I was seeking some sort of reassurance. Was he naive like me about the hard, brutal reality of what was happening away from our island home?

'We grew up in a rural area; we didn't know racism,' he says. 'You didn't know that thing existed. It was very community-based, very loving, very community-centric. We weren't aware of racism at such a tender age. We were just kids having fun, playing cricket, playing football. So in the context of the rural community, we just would not have experienced that.'

Snap. Usain and I had the same upbringing, despite us growing up a generation apart. We were the sort of boys to be out at play all day, kicking a football around, playing marbles, riding bikes or making a ball out of tape and string to play Catchy Shubby – a version of cricket which was chaotic because there seemed to be about twenty or thirty people taking part. We used an old bin for the 'stumps'; Usain used to carve three stumps into a tree. Matches would last hours. Moms would be calling out to come in for supper as the sun went down.

The kids we were playing with? They almost all looked pretty much the same as me but the few who didn't, we didn't notice. We were kids having fun.

Usain lived in Sherwood, a small village among the trees and bush. So he had his circle of friends and they were Black. There was no 'otherness' to make him question differences in culture or identity. I grew up on Dunrobin Avenue in Kingston, which was a small residential area on the outskirts of the city and completely underdeveloped when my parents moved there. By the time I came along, there were some white and Chinese families living on the road but they didn't mix with us. At least the seniors didn't. The kids would play a bit with us sometimes but would rush home before their parents came back home from work. But I didn't give it a second thought. I just guessed that they had their own things to do or own games to play, or maybe their parents were just very strict and they didn't want them to know they had left the yard when they weren't there. I didn't think, *Oh, they're not supposed to be mixing with us because they have different skin colour.*

'The only thing I experienced in Jamaica close to racism was classism,' Usain says. 'I remember living in a certain apartment complex and the neighbours weren't pleased that a young guy from my background – and I guess that means coming from a small village – was living next to them. Some people don't like to see young people doing well.'

In school, there was no education around racism save for what happened during the slave trade. 'Jamaica's an ex-colony,' Usain says. 'So we were taught with that colonial influence. You would never be taught about racism.'

If you wanted to find out, though, you educated yourself. When you go round the world you want to understand more. You see how different cultures work and so a natural curiosity kicks in. That happened to me, eventually, although I spent a long time putting that re-education off. Without it, though, I wouldn't be writing this book.

Usain, at the same age, is further ahead. He tells me that when he was in high school he started to take an interest in what was actually happening outside of the Caribbean, in places like America and the UK. When he wasn't running, playing football or playing cricket, he would talk with his friend Nugent, who he has known since he was four, about Black history. Nugent, a history graduate, is now his manager.

'We spent a lot of time discussing great achievements in Africa,' Usain says. 'And people don't know that Africa used to be a major centre for worldwide trade before slavery destroyed that. We talked about how there was a civilisation in the Caribbean long before Christopher Columbus came to these islands. And the great mathematical and scientific achievements of Africa. There's plenty to show Black pride in. It's important that our schools also teach about the brilliance of our ancestors and not just being slaves on the plantation. Maybe they could teach about the great Muhammad Ali, too.' You could add Marcus Garvey, among others, to that list. Garvey was Jamaica's first national hero and he helped to inspire America's civil rights movement by arguing for Black economic independence and for African-Americans to show pride in their heritage.

There was no real education about racism at home, either, or what was happening to Black people elsewhere in the world. I am sure I never even heard my mother use the word 'racism'. Family life, or parents instilling discipline and passing on knowledge, was instead all about being polite, looking smart and working hard.

'Yeah, those sorts of negative things or feelings ... we wouldn't have dwelled on them. My parents wanted me to be happy and positive. They wanted to encourage me to push on and achieve. Don't give room to the naysayers. Maybe they thought if they had talked about such things it could have made me worried about the future. I'm not an athlete who is angry and trying to say, "You were wrong." God blessed me with a talent and I tried to make the best out of it.'

I guess you could argue that with minimal racism in a country, why does anyone need to talk about it? People are not being denied opportunities because of the colour of their skin. They are not being abused on every other day they leave the house or treated differently.

But I have briefly spoken about it with my children when they were making their way in the world. My youngest daughter, Tiana, she never really understood racism. She couldn't quite comprehend the attitude of some African-Americans she came across in her early days after moving to America. Why? Because she was born and spent her early years in Jamaica, too. And when she moved to the United

States she grew up in a West Indian-dominated community. So she was shielded from it. She only truly got it when the Black Lives Matter movement began. When she saw my Sky Sports speech she posted on Facebook. Here's a section of what she wrote:

> What people have missed, including me for a long time, is that Black people are not just angry, Black people are sad and Black people are tired. Black people are not trying to say Black lives are worth more than others. We Black and brown people just want to be able to have the same rights white people have had for centuries. That's all.

A dad finally getting a daughter to listen and pay attention? I think those who know how tough that can be will forgive me for feeling a sense of pride when I saw it. Tiana didn't come to the realisation until she moved to America because there would have been no reason for me to talk to her about the problem while she was growing up in Jamaica. But, as we know, Black folks in America, and to a lesser degree in the UK, have to be coaching their kids, and in particular their boys, in how to deal with life every day in a society where they are 'other', and especially in their interaction with the police.

Usain has that all to come. He became a dad to baby Olympia in May 2020. He knows that with the world the way it is, he is going to have to (all in good time) probably teach his daughter about its harsher side.

'As a father now I want to protect. Every decent human being is worried and concerned that the colour of a person's skin can determine if they're getting opportunity or if they're being scrutinised. It's a harsh reality that Black people walk around with.

'It's only when I started to travel, you realise that reality, though. People have different views of who you are. When you are in a different country you see the news. And it's different. And you will understand the context.'

Usain is thirty-four years old. And that could have been me talking at the same age. I travelled. I saw it. I heard it. And then I came home again. And did I talk about it with my parents? Not really. We didn't dwell on the things that happened when I was away. I wanted to concentrate on my sport and career. Get on with building a life. And for Usain, the same is true. When you are the fastest man the world has ever seen, life tends to get pretty busy and your mind is occupied. When I got back to Jamaica after a cricket tour or a stint playing county cricket in England, the last thing I wanted to do was rake over all the racist incidents during a chat with my parents. And, boy, was there a lot of that stuff.

On my first tour to Australia as a West Indies player in 1975 I was abused from the crowd in Perth, Western Australia. 'Go back to the trees!' That sort of thing would be headline news now, although as I type this, I have to say that I've just read a story about India players getting abuse from the crowd in a Test match in Sydney. Back then, I just shrugged and thought, *Glad I don't live in this country.* But 2020 and it's still going on? Pathetic.

When we were travelling around Australia I distinctly remember being in an elevator with my team-mates and, on the way down from our floor to the lobby, the lift stopped on a floor below ours. The doors opened to reveal a middle-aged white guy who was awaiting the lift to go down as well, but when he saw four or five big Black guys, he stepped back. Fine. Maybe he was intimidated, we were a tall bunch. But as the doors shut, he shouted a racist slur. And do you know what we all did? We laughed. We thought it was funny that there were people as stupid as that in a country like Australia. In the Caribbean, where we all came from, we didn't encounter such behaviour.

My next overseas tour was in 1976 to England. I was there again in 1980. There the abuse came mainly in the form of letters delivered to the dressing room. Most were seeking autographs, but there were quite a few letters that were uncomplimentary to put it mildly. They went in the bin. I can't remember the precise words but I'm sure all the old favourites were in them. 'You Black this, you Black that, go back to your own country.'

On the field of play I never had an opposition player say anything untoward. But I do remember a moment in a game when I was 'guesting' in a reserve match for a professional team before I started playing county cricket, when I was made aware of the colour of my skin. We had just taken a wicket and were talking in a huddle about what the next move would be and one of my team-mates said something along the lines of 'get the Black so-and-so on to bowl'. Anyone who watched the West Indies team in my era will know that whenever a wicket fell, the entire team gathered together, whether to celebrate or just chat among ourselves until the next batsman appeared. Even those fielding right on the boundary edge made the trek in but that was peculiar to us, not many other teams did it and especially not county teams. This player obviously didn't realise that I had made my way in from my fielding position. It stung.

And I've come across racism in pretty much every corner of the globe that I've travelled to down the years. That includes when I was playing as well as when I wasn't. It's taken on almost a different form, too, because I am often accompanied by my wife, Laurie-Ann, who is white. She is from Antigua but has Portuguese heritage. We've walked into a hotel in South Africa and, while I'm being attended to, someone else behind the desk will approach her and ask if she needs help to check in. She's standing right beside me but of course, in their mind, there is no way she could be with me.

When on holiday in Nassau we've turned up at a restaurant with a booking and the maitre d' will look at her, not me, and enquire about our reservation. At the end of the meal the waiter hands her the bill. Obviously, she came to Nassau and picked up this Black guy on the beach. The guys attending on us are Black. The brainwashing and unconscious bias work both ways. We laugh about that one. But if we weren't laughing, we'd be crying. And there are loads more stories like those. The situations I have recounted are the ones that stick in the memory for one reason or another. And they each have the same impact. They strip away your humanity, they take away your feelings of self-worth. You feel as though you don't belong and, I suppose, on a very basic level, that you are not wanted or liked. I think all human beings can relate to that. Like me, loathe me or be indifferent – that's cool. Just don't form a negative opinion about me because of the colour of my skin. It's irrelevant.

'I just want to keep preaching love,' Usain says. 'And hope that we can see something change.'

Maybe he's right.

I want to tell one story about a man from Jamaica who was

one of the kindest men I have ever met. He was someone who preached love and understanding. And, one day, he'd had enough. This was in 1940s Jamaica, when there was a small white tourist enclave where Black people couldn't go. Didn't want to go anyway.

His name was Evon Blake. He used to take me, his son Paul and my brother, Ralph Junior, on outings every now and again. He even took us on train rides, and I remember one very memorable trip to Port Antonio where we went for a fancy lunch at one of the big hotels. 'Don't drink while having your meal,' he taught us. 'And only tomato juice after.' Man, I hated that thing. He owned a very successful magazine and was a hugely respected journalist and businessman.

Anyway, one day he went down to the whites-only Myrtle Bank Hotel. He got his swimming costume on and he jumped in the swimming pool. All the white people jumped out.

'Mr Blake, you have to get out,' the panicked manager said.

'No!' shouted Evon. 'Call the prime minister! Call God!'

Evon, one of the more financially independent Black men in Jamaica, had his own pool at home. But his accountant could swim at Myrtle Bank because he was white. Evon could not. He decided to change that.

Now, this happened in 1948 when racism against Black people was rife in Jamaica because of colonisation. The rumour at the time was that he was arrested and they drained the pool, cleaned it and then filled it back up. No white person would get in again until they'd done that because they thought he was somehow dirty. And I did not even find out myself until I was doing research for this book that the last part of the story was in fact just rumour. He was never arrested, the pool was never drained.

By the way, his daughter, Barbara Blake-Hannah, would become the first Black television reporter in England when she started working for the current affairs show *Today* in 1968. Until viewers complained they didn't want to see a Black face and she was sacked.

I tell that story for two reasons. First, because Evon's actions helped to bring to an end whites-only tourist and expat spots in Jamaica. And, second, when I left Jamaica on my travels and started having my own experiences of white supremacy, I did not think about what Evon, a close family friend, had done. I had, oddly, forgotten it. Or chosen to forget it. He had highlighted a problem. But it was one that did not interest me. He had highlighted a way to make change. But it was a change that I didn't think was required. It didn't make me stop and think: now, why did Evon do that? What did he know that I did not? Later on, when I saw and heard racism, I didn't recall his actions. I didn't say to myself, 'Evon made a stand, I could do the same.' Why was that?

CHAPTER 3

Black Lives Matter, Too

With Naomi Osaka

I was selfish. I could have spoken up, could have stood up when I saw and heard racism. Should have. I know that. But I did nothing, kept my mouth shut, turned the other cheek and walked away.

When I was abused from the crowd in Australia, I should have pointed out the offender. And said my piece in the media. It would have raised awareness, created a conversation and, sure, caused a storm. In today's world, the victim of that abuse would have the courage and the conviction to do that.

And, as part of a cricket team of mainly Black men who toured the world and had to put up with racial slurs on the field of play from the crowd and in the towns and cities to which we travelled, I know that we should have been a little bit more vociferous. And said something. Anything. And I'm not talking about getting angry and being rebellious, just going through the right channels.

It would be easy to argue that I said nothing or the team did nothing because back then, in the 1970s and 1980s, it would have made no difference. Any sort of complaint might have been dismissed as whining. 'Just get on and play the game, it's only words.' It was an era when, frankly, casual racism was rife. It was tolerated, laughed about, in the newspapers, on television programmes. Sticks and stones and all that. And for someone to say that it shouldn't have been, to make a hue and cry? You would have probably been attacked from all sides. There was no such thing as advice from the cricket board or management to deal with it, either.

But that wasn't the reason. The reason I said nothing was because I was totally selfish. When I came across racism, I thought to myself, 'These people are sick … I'll be going home soon and I won't have to deal with it.' That goes for when I was touring the world as a player. And when I was a commentator. I didn't have to live that life, that threat of daily abuse which would make you feel like half a human being. But what about the people who did? I felt it wasn't my problem. *I'll be on a plane soon.* As I said, selfish.

At times that guilt, or burden, has weighed on my shoulders. And I have sometimes wondered why I didn't say something. After all, I have had a 'name', or 'profile', which means people are interested in what I have to say.

Maybe it was because, deep down, there is some conditioning, or brainwashing, that, as a Black person, I am supposed to toe the line. As you go through these pages I hope you will understand why it is possible to feel like that, even on a subconscious level.

Maybe it was because I felt that speaking for a few minutes on camera, doing the odd interview on radio or for a newspaper, was enough. I was never one to seek attention and even now my sister Marjorie tells me I'm too 'minimal', except when I'm doing my job, that is. And it was like being transported back in time to my younger self. Could I just say, again, 'This is not my life, I don't have to live it' and disappear home again?

Maybe it was because I knew there would be a backlash. After all, I am not the first person of colour to have spoken up and I won't be the last to suffer abuse after doing so (and I fully expect people to have issues with me more than ever before, now that I have decided to put pen to paper). If you have the temerity to speak up about injustice as a person of colour, you put a target on your back. Look at what happened to Colin Kaepernick. A US Congressman actually said he and others like him who kneel should be grateful that America has given them the opportunity to earn a lot of money playing in the NFL. Maybe I missed something but was Kaepernick drafted from another country or is he American?

I mention Colin not because I am in any way trying to compare myself to him. He is a hero. It was Colin who was responsible for the 'taking a knee' movement. For raising awareness that Black Lives Matter. He was a quarterback for the San Francisco 49ers in America's National Football League. And a darn good one. He was the sixth quarterback taken in the draft in 2011 and to this day the only one drafted above him with anything to show for it is Andy Dalton, who went to the Cincinnati Bengals. Throughout the 2016 season, Colin took a knee during the American national anthem – it is the custom to play it before the start of every game – to highlight racial inequality and police brutality in America.

He paid a personal price. He has not played since the end

of that season, when his contract was up and no team had the guts to sign him. There is no doubt that his career was ended just because he said 'enough'. Donald Trump said NFL owners should fire players who took a knee. What happened to Colin is an extreme example, perhaps. But would you blame anybody for keeping quiet after that? Probably not. It is, however, exactly what the people who believe they are superior want us to do. I see that now. To keep us quiet. *Be grateful, look what we're allowing you to do.*

Without that sacrifice from Colin, the conversation about inequality and the dehumanisation of Black people would not have reached new ears. Black Lives Matter? Taking a knee? Everybody knows those phrases. And everybody has an opinion, right or wrong. They are conversation starters. Not all like what they hear.

So let's get this one out the way early on. Black Lives Matter. When I sign up to those three words I am saying that Black lives have mattered less for hundreds and hundreds of years. And it's time something was done about it. And over the course of this book I intend to show exactly why something has to be done about the persistent dehumanisation of Black people. I'm not saying that Black people matter more than white people. Or any other race of people. And it is frustrating that people against the movement use language to try to discredit it. If we just put the word 'too' on the end they would soon keep quiet.

'Oh,' some people say, '*all* lives matter.' If only that were true. It is so patently obvious that all lives don't matter because it is Black people who risk death when leaving their front door in America, Black people who are followed by shop security, Black people who are abused on a daily basis and Black people who are judged just because of the colour of their skin, before they have even spoken or acted to show who they really are. That's hard to come to terms with if you're white. And not open-minded.

And we all know what that is called, right? White Privilege. This is a very difficult concept for some people to understand. It gets their back up. 'I'm not privileged,' they might say. 'I am on benefits, can barely put food on the table.' Privilege is a word that is not meant to describe affluence in terms of monetary value or lifestyle. It's not about how much you do or don't earn, the size of the house you live in or the number of cars you drive. The privilege is . . . not having to put up with everyday racism.

That privilege is about the absence of aggravation, challenge or obstruction in someone's life. If you are white, for example, and you stand in a residential street for a couple of minutes, it's highly unlikely someone's going to call the police because they think you're going to steal a car. If you're a white barrister you're not going to be mistaken for the accused. In September 2020, Black barrister Alexandra Wilson was mistaken for the defendant three times on the same day in London. If you're trying to hail a cab, the driver's not going to drive straight by you. It's the Usain Bolt watch story, too. White privilege is driving down the road in a stolen vehicle but, because you're white, nobody stops you, the cops don't give you a second look unless there is a specific alert for that stolen vehicle. But a Black man driving down the road in a car that the police think is above his means? He is stopped. But people will keep on telling you, 'I don't get anything because of the colour of my skin, nobody has ever given me anything.' They don't recognise the privilege that they already have before they're actually physically given something.

To repeat: no one is saying white privilege ignores the fact that white people have hard lives. But what I'm saying is that those difficulties in your life have not happened because of the colour of your skin. For Black people, or people of colour, that, sadly, isn't true a lot of the time.

The finest example of white privilege I have ever seen was when Donald Trump's supporters stormed the Capitol in Washington in January 2021. The vast majority were white – in fact, I don't recall seeing a Black rioter – and they were able to wander in and through and up and round the corridors of power with the police looking on. Some were shown out of the building with a 'please' and 'thank you' and 'let me get the door for you'. Police officers were removing barriers, guiding them through at some points and there were pictures of officers taking selfies with them. Again, I am not saying all officers were complicit because the television shots showed there was pushback by an outnumbered force and, tragically, five people died. There were scenes of terrible violence. Eugene Goodman, a Black police officer at the Capitol, was a hero for guiding senators to safety. But why were Eugene and his colleagues outnumbered? Because the powers that be were worried about 'the optics' of having the National Guard on the streets. They weren't worried about the optics during the BLM protests in the summer of the previous year. If a similar number of Black people had tried to storm a government building, there would have been a massacre.

Let's compare how Trump treated around 10,000 peaceful Black Lives Matter protestors in June 2020 in Washington. They were more than a block away from the Capitol and yet were met with the full force of Washington police, US Park police and 5,000 National Guard soldiers. Helicopters circled above their heads. Tear gas, batons and horses were used to disperse them so that Trump could be photographed in front of a church holding a Bible.

Taylor Enterline, a 21-year-old Black student, was arrested during protests in Washington. She was held in jail on a $1 million bail. Riley June Williams, a 22-year-old white Trump supporter, was arrested for helping to steal Nancy Pelosi's computer during the Capitol insurrection. She had planned to sell it to Russia. She was released to her mother. There are two justice systems at work here.

James Baldwin, the American novelist, playwright and activist, put it, as you would expect, far better than I could when he said this:

When a white man in the world says, give me liberty or give me death, the white world applauds. When a Black man says the same thing he's judged a criminal. And everything possible is done to make an example of this bad nigger so there won't be any more like him.

This also seems a good time to deal with those folk now who say that taking a knee is 'virtue signalling'. Because people in America who believe that may have been inclined to join in with that coup attempt. And I think I can make that point because of what happened to Colin Kaepernick. He was labelled much worse than a 'virtue signaller'. He was called a traitor. Which is strange as I seem to recall watching the news footage and seeing a rioter beat a prostrate policeman with the handle of an American flag. And another pulled down an American flag to replace it with a Trump flag. Traitor? Then there was the Confederate flag being paraded through the hallowed halls of the building.

After what happened to Colin, do you think people are taking the knee in a fake way to enhance their own image or character? Because that's what virtue signalling is. If you never work again, or lose your career, how has that enhanced that person? You can't pay the bills with character.

When someone does something in front of the eyes of the world to promote equality, he or she is trying to help and to make a change. It's calling something out. Jesse Owens. Was he a virtue signaller when he went to Germany in 1936, blitzed the master race on the track and pissed off Adolf Hitler? Should he have apologised for that? He used his platform without uttering a word. It could, however, be argued that just doing it once or for a very short time is virtue signalling. That's why it was so pathetic that the England cricket team took the knee for just one series – those summer 2020 contests against West Indies – and then stopped. They became the first professional team anywhere in the world to stop doing it.

People will also say, 'Sport and politics shouldn't mix.' But we can talk about sport's involvement in helping to end apartheid in South Africa. Or Tommie Smith and John Carlos raising their fists in Mexico. Muhammad Ali's powerful and selfless activism against the Vietnam War and for racial justice. And we'll add Colin Kaepernick. After Colin took the knee, the protest spread through American football and into basketball.

Sport is life. It is striving, sacrifice, success, failure, pain and joy. That's why it resonates with people and that's why it is so loved. Its power is its equality. Sport is not supposed to discriminate. First is first, second is second and so on. That power has to be used to influence politics. If that's what equality for Black people is. Is it political? Or is it just about being a decent human being, showing empathy for your fellow man rather than pinning a rosette to your chest and deciding whether you're for equality or not because of its colour?

It would be wonderful if what Jesse Owens did was enough. But it wasn't. Those who have taken it further have seen the need to take it further. Risks and sacrifices by high-profile Black people have continued to be made.

One of those people is tennis player Naomi Osaka. Naomi has won two US Open and two Australian Open titles. Born to a Haitian father and a Japanese mother, she has lived in the US since she was three. She plays under the Japanese flag. Her fearless personality, charm and ability have made her one of the most famous sports stars in the world. Most articles you read about her start with 'the highest-paid sportswoman in the world'. How about that? It's a sentence that makes you think: yeah, we are getting somewhere with this thing.

But when I say 'tennis player', I should also say activist. Because Naomi doesn't want to be labelled or restricted by her occupation. When she started winning matches and tournaments, she realised she had a voice. She had some power. And she thought, *If I wasn't a tennis player, what would I do to change the world?* So she was ready when there was another 'call to action' moment.

In August 2020, Naomi said she would be boycotting a semi-final match in the Western & Southern Open in New York City after Jacob Blake, a Black man, had been shot seven times in the back by a police officer in Wisconsin. This was just three months after the murder of George Floyd. Blake was shot in front of his three children. He survived but was left paralysed from the waist down. And yet he was still shackled to his hospital bed. For the record, no charges were brought against the cop who pumped bullets into his body. The tournament organisers agreed to postpone the competition out of respect for Naomi's stance. When it resumed, so did she.

In a statement, Naomi said: 'Before I am an athlete, I am a Black woman. And as a Black woman I feel as though there are much more important matters at hand that need immediate attention, rather than watching me play tennis. I don't expect anything drastic to happen with me not playing, but if I can get a conversation started in a majority-white sport I consider that a step in the right direction. Watching the continued genocide of Black people at the hands of the police is honestly making me sick to my stomach. I'm exhausted of having a new hashtag pop up every few days and I'm extremely tired of having this same conversation over and over again. When will it ever be enough?'

Fortunately for me and this book, Naomi wanted to have that conversation again. She agreed to have a chat with me about the issues that Black people face in America and why she would continue to take a stand. We got in touch after she had won her second US Open at the age of twenty-two. I am full of admiration for her stance because I know that I couldn't – and didn't – have the wherewithal or the courage to do the same when I was that age. For her, though, it was easy to put her head above the parapet. Her attitude was 'let the haters hate'.

'When I got involved with spreading the BLM message, did I consider there could be a backlash? From fans? Sponsors? I've been asked that question a lot and I can honestly say it was never a consideration or something that entered my head.'

And there has been backlash, of course. A young Black woman speaking her mind and showing strength? Whoa. She was told to 'stick to sports' on social media, for example. After George Floyd was killed, Naomi was moved to fly to Minneapolis to join the protest marches. It was the first time she had ever been to a march. When she posted a picture on Instagram, there was predictable criticism. 'You'll loot everything, right, because that's the answer. And don't give me some speech on why looting is good or why everyone is rioting . . . Martin Luther King would be disappointed in you people.' By the way, if you're Black or a person of colour, that phrase 'you people' will always raise an eyebrow and force a double-take. We know what they mean. We see them. And, incidentally, I totally agree that looting isn't a part of pro-testing, but I hope everyone will also agree that murder isn't a part of arresting.

Naomi wasn't always destined to be an activist. She was quiet, kept herself to herself. Even on the tennis court. Her dad used to pay her a quarter every time she shouted, 'Come on!' when playing a match because he felt she needed to get energised and self-motivated. And not be afraid to show it.

And, of course, she is not literally tired of having these con-versations about equality. She's having them all over. She was on the front cover of *Vogue*. She wrote an article for *Esquire* magazine. She never ducks a question. And I'm grateful she didn't duck mine. Believe me, there are plenty of sports per-sonalities with her profile you can't even get close to.

'I'm vocal because I believe in the movement and want to try to use my platform to facilitate change. Being silent is never the answer. Everyone should have a voice in the matter and use it.

'What I'm searching for is equality. For Black people to have the same chances and opportunities as everyone else. But before we can even get that far, we need to fix systemic racism within institutions that are supposed to protect us, like the police. This is a huge problem in the USA that dates back years and years.

'How we change those systems is a question that I don't have a precise answer for; but I feel my role is to use my platform to shine a light on what's happening, so that those in positions of leadership can start working on solutions.'

Mercy, this is coming from someone just twenty-two years old at the time!

I don't think anyone has the answer and I admire the youthful curiosity – impatience even – that Naomi has about there being something to be found or searched for. There are clues to that in her personality – during lockdown she wanted to learn the guitar but she couldn't get the hang of the chords quickly enough so moved on. And in 2014 she hinted in that article for *Esquire* at her sadness that change wasn't coming fast enough.

'I remember watching the outrage at Michael Brown's case in 2014, and nothing has really changed since,' she wrote. 'Black people have been fighting this oppression alone for so many years and progress has been fleeting at best. Being "not racist" is not enough. We have to be anti-racist.'

No one actually knows why Brown was shot. We only know that on 9 August 2014 in St Louis a policeman called

Darren Wilson was driving in his duty car and came across Brown and a friend walking down the street. Minutes later Brown was dead, suffering at least seven gunshot wounds. His body lay in the street for four hours before it was removed. Wilson was not charged with any crime.

And this is what gets you as a person of colour. It might not be the sheer number of murders. It might simply be the circumstances of one – just one – that makes you think, *Could have been me.* George Floyd's killing made such an impact, of course, because it was filmed. We watched him die. And a hell of a lot of people had that thought. For Naomi, the first death that affected her deeply was that of 17-year-old Trayvon Martin, killed in Sanford, Florida, in February 2012.

Trayvon had been walking home after buying food from a shop. George Zimmerman, a neighbourhood watch member, saw him and called the police because he looked suspicious. Now what is suspicious about a kid walking on the way home while eating? Was it the fact that he was wearing a hoodie? What if it had been a white 17-year-old? What occurred next wouldn't have happened, may I suggest, if he had been a white boy. Zimmerman challenged Trayvon. There was an altercation. And Zimmerman fatally shot him. Was Zimmerman quickly arrested? Nope. It took six weeks. And that after a national campaign by Trayvon's parents. I wonder how long it would have taken had a Black guy shot someone in 'self-defence'? Zimmerman was acquitted at trial.

'I vividly remember when Trayvon Martin was shot and thinking, *Wow, that could easily have been me,*' Naomi says. 'That was a landmark moment in my life and really opened my eyes.' She was fourteen at the time and only living about three hours' drive away. 'To see the same things happening over and over still, is sad. Things have to change.'

But it keeps happening, Naomi.

'How do we prevent this movement becoming just another hashtag, something that only pricks the consciousness when there is outrage – however fleeting – on a social media platform? And how do we keep this relevant because we don't want it only being important again when another tragedy happens? It's tough. I don't think Black people can do it alone and we need allies. I think what has set the movement apart this time from previously is that more people from various backgrounds have been out there marching. And not just "liberal" and "progressive" ones; I've seen all different types of people take to the street. We need to keep shining the light as a global community. I even saw marches in Japan, which was super encouraging.'

As someone who is, shall we say, a little older, and has seen a lot more abuse than Naomi, I could easily say there is no hope, but I have to agree with her sentiments regarding progress. I also noticed the demographics of those marching for BLM during the summer of 2020. If you keep on highlighting it, at some point there'll be a reaction and something will happen. And I think people are beginning to take notice. We will keep on getting incidents and we need people to keep on saying, 'No, it's got to stop.' It's just a matter of it taking longer than it should. But if you say nothing, or you do nothing, nothing happens. If you keep on making reference to it and you keep on doing something and saying something about it, eventually, action is taken. Taking a knee: it's not difficult. It's not time-consuming. But it keeps the conversation going.

Naomi is doing it herself. During her 2020 US Open win,

played behind closed doors because of the coronavirus pandemic, she came up with a brilliant, powerful and emotional way of raising awareness about the police brutality against Black people in America.

In each round of the tournament she wore a different face mask bearing the name of a victim: Breonna Taylor, Elijah McClain, Ahmaud Arbery, Trayvon Martin, George Floyd, Philando Castile and Tamir Rice. All the way to the final. Sybrina Fulton, Trayvon's mother, and Marcus Arbery, Ahmaud's father, sent Naomi video messages of support and thanks. These, naturally, gained huge traction on social media so the message was passed on to a greater number of people. 'I'm forever grateful to the parents of Trayvon and Ahmaud for that,' Naomi says. 'It moved me to tears.'

But Naomi's protest was not without awkward moments. In an early round of the tournament one post-match interviewer asked her, seemingly excited, about whose name she might wear on her face mask in the next match. I found that uncomfortable, so I can just imagine Naomi feeling the same and it seemed strange to miss the point. Strange but, to be honest, not surprising. These were dead people. Naomi then seemed to bristle when asked by another reporter, Tom Rinaldi, 'What message were you trying to send?' She shot back: 'Well, what was the message you got, is more the question. I feel like the point was to make people start talking.'

I asked Naomi whether she felt that people actually *got* it?

'You're right, there were some awkward moments and some reporters obviously got it more than others,' she says. 'Putting the question back on Tom was instinctive but I think it was important – that was the whole point. On the whole, though, ESPN actually did a good job with their coverage, continuing to find new angles to the story each day – and therefore spreading the message.'

If that sounds like an answer with diplomacy in mind, Naomi does not shy away when it comes to the question about racism as a political or humanitarian issue. 'My message has always been humanitarian,' she says. 'We are talking about equality. But to achieve those goals I suppose requires politicians on some level – but ultimately it's the people who give them the power.'

The organisation Black Lives Matter has positioned itself as a political movement, notably calling for the police in America to be defunded. Naomi supports this but is at pains to say that, like BLM, this doesn't mean they are eradicated altogether.

This brings me to an important point about BLM and the conversation about race in general. The people who want the status quo to remain, those who feel threatened by Black people having equality, perhaps because they think they will have less of everything (money, freedom, opportunity), and the people who believe they are superior will look for any loose thread to pick at so they can try to unravel it.

An example of just the sort of attitude you often get from people when you talk about equality is this. A friend of mine – an ex-friend, actually, because I no longer seek his counsel – said to me after I had made my Sky speech: 'Why do you want to punish white people?' Wow. I don't. Black people don't. We just want to be treated the same way. And it's very interesting, isn't it, that the idea of Black people being on the same level as white people gives rise to a feeling that somebody is being punished, or dealt a bad hand. One of the best placards I saw during the BLM protests addressed that very same point quite appropriately in my opinion. It read: 'It is not a pie. Equality for us doesn't mean less for you.'

Fear and loathing are the root cause of it all. And when you understand the history of racism (and we will deal with that) you will get a good idea of why I use those two emotive words. To break it down simply: there is a fear about Black people precisely because white people are terrified that we will do what they did to us if we are given half the chance. We will touch on that throughout this book.

This is the reason people look for that thread to pull on. I think with the case of BLM they have seized upon the defunding of police, saying, 'They want to get rid of the police! They want anarchy.' No. That's not what is being said, and by the way many groups, not connected with race, have been talking about a restructuring of the finances of police forces all over the world. They say this: why don't we spend a chunk of the money for the police on other services like housing, community health, employment or education? Because, guess what, if you divert the money that way, social deprivation can be reduced and therefore crime goes down so you don't need as many police.

'Some of the funding – like payment plans to cops who have been convicted of crimes – should be reallocated to neglected community areas,' Naomi says. 'We need a holistic approach to our communities and to keeping each other safe.' And that last word there is key: safe. At the moment, in America, Black people are being threatened by the people supposed to be keeping them safe.

That is what is so frustrating about the criticism of the BLM movement. It is a deliberate ploy to spread misinformation (or focus on use of language – *all* lives matter) in an effort to discredit it. In America they called the people who kneeled 'traitors'. In the UK they called the people who kneeled Marxists. There was an occasion in the winter of 2020 when a football team's players kneeled before a match at Millwall, a club in south London with a notoriously racist fanbase, to widespread booing and abuse from the fans. And the BLM haters tried to make out that it was because those 'supporters' were anti-Marxist. Ask most football fans about Karl Marx and a lot would say: who does he play for?

As for me, I couldn't care less about the political aspirations of BLM, communist, Marxist or whatever. All I am interested in is the three words that mean everything. Black. Lives. Matter.

'Why do you think there are even detractors against the movement?' Naomi asks. 'It seems so reasonable to me that all we want is equality. I can't think of any rationale. A lack of education and empathy maybe?' That's an interesting last comment from Naomi.

So, okay, let us start with some education and learn about the poisonous, harmful, life-altering impact of every-day racism.

CHAPTER 4

Living It

With Hope Powell

I was lucky. When I was travelling the world as a cricketer or commentator, if I saw, heard or felt that threatening atmosphere of racism I always knew I would soon be on a plane back to a place where I could feel the freedom of not being judged by the colour of my skin. I didn't have to live with it. I learned about racism instead through reading books written by other people and listening to stories told by other people. Some people live it and every day I thank the Lord that I was saved that experience. Everybody else learns about it. Or, rather, should learn.

I am still learning and again I thank the Lord that opportunity has come in my mature years. Those who know about my more impetuous playing days (I was reprimanded for kicking over the stumps in a fury in a Test match in New Zealand) know what I'm talking about.

May 12, 1976, was a day I will never forget. I was

twenty-two years old and I was in the first twelve months of my career as an international sportsman. So young, in fact, that the idea of being a full-time cricketer was not even a consideration. I remember it not for sporting achievement or even the realisation that I had 'what it takes' (I wasn't even selected to play in the match), but because it was a critical stage in my journey to understanding what racism was and how it manifested itself.

The West Indies were playing a friendly match against Surrey at The Oval in south London. This was my first tour to England and I had played only nine times for our nation of islands. It was a warm-up match, designed for us to find fitness and rhythm. We were just tuning up for the big contests to come against England which didn't start until early June, almost a month later. In short, the result didn't matter to us. But it mattered to a hell of a lot of other people. And I was about to find out why.

On the last day Surrey set us a target of 239 to win in about three hours. Clive Lloyd, our captain, told us that we were not to attempt to win the game. He wanted our players to get used to playing in English conditions. The objective was for any batsman who got to the crease to just spend some time getting acclimatised. Nobody raised an eyebrow because Clive was the boss and we knew what our main aim was on the tour. Clive was always planning ahead and he is to this day revered and respected for being one of the finest leaders on a cricket field.

There were a large number of West Indians in the ground ready to cheer and whistle us on to victory. And when we started our innings, they were as loud and partisan as usual. Until they realised we were not trying to win the game. The whole mood in the stand to the left of the pavilion changed dramatically. They had come up, mainly from Brixton where so many West Indians lived in London, to celebrate a West Indies win. So they booed. And they heckled. And as the 'contest' wore on they became more and more agitated.

I couldn't work out why they were so furious and why they just didn't pack up and leave since they were so unhappy with our approach. But they stayed right until the end of the match – and beyond, as we found out much later when we headed for the team bus. As per usual, at the end of the game we hung around in the dressing room having the usual chat and a drink or two with some of the opposition members. That was the norm those days and, with some of the West Indies squad regular participants in the English domestic scene, there were many from both teams quite familiar with each other. I don't remember exactly what time we all started going downstairs to get on our team bus but it was fairly dark, even with the long evenings just about starting to set in for the English summer. Lo and behold, as the first members of the team emerged from the pavilion, the heckling and booing started again.

I was bemused. *What is wrong with these people?* I thought. I turned to Gordon Greenidge, who had only just graduated to senior player status and was someone who had played in England for years, and asked him what was going on. His answer was like an alarm going off. 'You wouldn't understand, Mikey. These guys [they were all men awaiting our appearance] want us to win every game we play in this country.' Gordon explained, though not in huge detail, what West Indians living in this country were going through at the time. They were being racially abused. They were being made to feel inferior. They felt like second-class citizens. But if we *won*, they felt like somebody. They could hold their heads high as they walked the streets, or went into their workplaces because they were from the same place as these guys who excelled on the cricket field. They felt that they were equal. That if their brethren could win on the field of play and be respected, they would gain respect someday too.

I was totally naive about the people I was supposed to be representing. And I had no idea about what their life was like. This was not the England I had been told about back home in Jamaica. It was not the way the 'Mother Country' was supposed to be. Or the way it was viewed. My mother, having spent a year in England in 1949 as part of her training to become a teacher, always spoke highly of London. Miss Joyce Couria, a great friend of the family who I became very close to, spent three years doing nursing at about the same time. She never had a bad word to say either, at least not in my company. I won't go as far as to say they thought the streets were paved with gold, but England was considered a place of fair play, opportunity and a welcoming British handshake. This was what we had been told at school. This was what families and friends believed. It wasn't a place full of hate. After all, the British had been desperate for West Indians to come after the end of the Second World War. Everybody in the Caribbean knew that.

The country was broke and labour was in short supply. Between 1945 and 1946 the working population in the UK fell by 1.38 million. People were leaving the country for places like Australia, New Zealand and Canada. They invited us, they courted us to come over to the 'Mother Country'. We answered the call and took work in factories, construction; helped run public transport, staff the NHS. They needed us. So we came. The *Empire Windrush* arrived at Tilbury docks in 1948, carrying 492 West Indians eager to start a new life.

They were the first of many. British Library articles show that between 1948 and 1952 some 1,000–2,000 people entered Britain each year, rising to up to 40,000 by 1956. This was the year Transport for London was recruiting directly from Jamaica. A Conservative minister called Enoch Powell implored West Indians to come.

One of those who came was a lady called Linever Francis. She arrived in England on 25 November 1963, married and raised two children, a son and daughter. The daughter was called Hope, a brilliant piece of foresight when it comes to choosing a baby's name if you ask me. Hope Powell continues to provide hope for the future.

She was the first ever Black coach of an English national sporting team when she took on the role of England women's football manager in 1998. Now she is the coach of Brighton and Hove Albion Women. She has thrived despite racism being rife in England's national sport. She has inspired people of all ages, races and backgrounds. And she is the perfect riposte to that venomous, racist jibe, 'Why don't you go back where you came from?'

Why? Because Hope is the living example of resilience and fight. She is the living example of what Black people bring to a country. And she is a living, breathing history lesson. The ignorant – deliberate or otherwise – don't want to be told that Hope's mum came to England because the government were begging for help. It is the plot twist their fable of supremacy cannot stomach. All the West Indians emigrated because they were told that they were needed, that they would have jobs and they would be welcomed.

This is why I wanted to speak with her. To understand what she was going through, how she rose above it, how others can do the same and, most importantly, to educate about why people from the West Indies came to Great Britain and the good they have done. Hope's story is the story of living with racism and overcoming.

Twelve years younger than me, she grew up on an estate in Greenwich in south London. It's not far from The Oval. And I'm conscious that when I was in England for the first time in 1976, she was aged just ten, becoming streetwise, just as I was, to racism. That I was so much older says a lot about our different experiences growing up.

'I have this vivid, grim memory of being a child,' she told me. 'This old white woman shouted to me as I was walking past her, "Why don't you go back to where you came from?" I didn't understand what she was talking about. After all, I was born in England. I do now. I could turn around and say, "You sent for my parents." This country was built on immigrants. And then you want people to go back? What are they talking about? Why don't they know this?'

It is a rhetorical question. Hope knows why people don't know. I know. It is because they were never told why people from the West Indies came. Not by the government. Or by the media. Or by the education system. 'Windrush' is a word you will not find in the history curriculum.

On that first tour of England I didn't read about what was really happening to the West Indians who had migrated. No historical accounts had yet been written. The internet did not exist. But nor did I seek out reading matter. I now know that newspapers at the time, like *The Sun* and the *Daily Telegraph*, were stoking the discontent. As a young man I started to learn more from meeting people and my understanding of what it was like to try to eke out a living in those times grew every time I went back to England to play cricket. Now, of course, I know more because there is a wealth of information available.

It might be easy to think that the 'Mother Country' was having an awakening of its own. Had the deep dislike and distrust of people of colour, forged hundreds of years ago, awoken from its slumber? There had, in fact, been a report produced in 1955 called 'The Colour Problem'. You can guess from its title that resentment and racism had surged as soon as the *Windrush* docked. I guess hate never takes a nap.

The report said that two thirds of Britain's population held 'a low opinion of Black people or disapproved of them'. More than a third would have no contact with people of colour, whether that be refusing to work with them or to allow them in their homes. The same ratio wanted them sent back.

Like so many people of colour, Hope and her family bore the brunt of it. When we talk, she is sitting in her office at home, tracksuit top zipped to her neck. 'You just missed my mum,' she says. 'She was here five minutes ago. Now, she has some stories about what it was like back then, what she had to put up with.'

Hope goes on to explain what it was like and I notice her voice starts to break as her memory is jogged, suggesting that maybe she hasn't been asked that often.

'My mum and brother were in a park and there was another child there, a white kid. My brother was touching him, reaching out as babies do, because babies are attracted to each other. And then the mother of the white child hit my brother to get him away from her child. And that was it, my mum lost it . . . had to be dragged away because she wasn't having it.'

Our matches against England that summer of '76 were played against a backdrop of racial tensions. Tony Greig, the England captain, had said he intended to make us 'grovel'. I wince at the word. Tony, as I realised once I got to know him much later when we worked as co-commentators, was not a racist. But he was ignorant of the slave era connotations of the word. Particularly spoken by a white South African who was only playing for England because the country of his birth was banned from international sport due to apartheid. It was incredibly insensitive. I may only have been twenty-two, wet behind the ears to the ways of the world and just beginning to understand racism, but I knew what he said was wrong. He was suggesting we lacked courage or fight. And, because of it, each member of that West Indies team had motivation to ram his senseless words back down his throat. We beat England 3-0. West Indies fans in the big cities turned out in their droves to cheer us on. And we knew that we were able to give them some sort of respite.

It had only been eight years earlier that Enoch Powell, who clearly had a change of heart about the good that immigration brought, had given his 'Rivers of Blood' speech. A sort of 'playbook on how to be a racist' and one that has been regurgitated and reused by populist politicians ever since. All the lazy, hateful lies were in there that we are so familiar with because of the Trump administration and the UK government's handling of Brexit. 'They're taking our jobs', 'they're going to take over', 'whites will be made to suffer', 'they won't integrate', 'there's going to be violence'. And, perhaps most vehemently of all, that Black people should be 'sent back to where they came from'. The National Front had been particularly vociferous about this. The children of Black people, who had been born in the UK, should be denied citizenship, too.

Powell was sacked by Edward Heath, the Conservative leader, for the speech. He said, 'I dismissed Mr Powell because I believed his speech was inflammatory and liable to damage race relations. I am determined to do everything I can to prevent racial problems developing into civil strife ... I don't believe the great majority of the British people share Mr Powell's way of putting his views in his speech.' What was telling, though, was when Powell was actually speaking (at a meeting of Conservatives in Birmingham) there was almost no anger or disagreement with what he said.

Heath was right about its divisive nature, though. The racists were emboldened by an MP saying what they had been too afraid to. And Black people, like Hope and her family, felt under threat. Cue Donald Trump in America over the past few years, and it seems nothing has changed. Just a different country.

'I do remember, and I'm sorry to be rude, but there was dog shit thrown on our doorstep, sometimes put through the letterbox,' Hope says. 'We endured that quite often, as well as the verbal abuse or the looks when you went out.'

I had heard stories like that before. But what was startling to me was how much support there was for Enoch Powell. I didn't realise it until I started researching in preparation for talking to Hope.

The polling company Gallup found that 74 per cent agreed with what Powell had said in his speech and 69 per cent said Heath was wrong to sack him. Before his speech Powell was favoured to replace Heath as Conservative leader by 1 per cent; after it this rocketed to 24 per cent, and a massive 83 per cent felt immigration should be restricted.

Governments could not ignore such numbers. There began moves to officially make people of colour second-class citizens (as if they didn't feel like that already) with new immigration laws. The 1971 Immigration Act pandered to Powell, the National Front and their supporters by birthing the 'grandfather clause'. If you had a grandfather who was British you could come in, no problem. If you didn't, tough luck. It effectively meant that immigration was eased for white people and descendants who had left the UK to migrate to parts of the old empire (Australia, New Zealand, Canada) but people from the new empire, say, the West Indies, Pakistan or Kenya, faced harassment and deportation.

The British Nationality Act followed in 1981. This was a piece of legislation that the *Sunday Times* said would define 'who belongs to Britain'. The words 'race' or 'ethnicity' don't appear in the bill but it was cleverly designed to exclude Black and Asian populations from the Commonwealth while, again, making things easier for white nationals born in the empire.

This act led to deportations with a brutal, racist police force doing the dirty work. Hence the death of Joy Gardner. Surely you all remember Joy Gardner? One of the women murdered by police for no reason? Of course you don't. Joy Gardner's name and what happened to her has been erased. At least that's what the authorities tried to do. No camera phones back then.

Joy, a 40-year-old Jamaican, was arrested for deportation in 1993. The police used force to restrain her, tied her arms to her side with a body belt, braced her ankles and gagged her with 13 feet of adhesive tape around her head. Thirteen. Feet. That's twice as tall as me. She died. Three officers faced manslaughter charges but all were acquitted. The media indulged in a character assassination to aid the cover-up. This is why you don't know Joy's name. Had there been someone there with a smartphone that day, you would have done.

Alas, Joy wasn't the first. Or the last. The 1980s was a particularly brutal decade. The police had a unit called the Special Patrol Group, which would cruise around London looking for Black people to harass. Or maybe arrest under the 1824 Vagrancy Act, which allowed police to arrest anyone they suspected was about to commit a crime. Strangely, a lot of Black people found themselves in cuffs for just standing about. Later on in this book, you will see where that tactic stems from. The same was used just after the abolition of slavery.

This police brutality was a major cause of the 1981 Brixton riots. The 1985 Brixton riots were sparked by the shooting by police of Cherry Groce during one of these searches. Again, people don't know her name. Cherry was unarmed and had been shot 'by mistake'. Her 11-year-old son recalls how his mother was gasping for breath, saying, 'I can't breathe.' Sound familiar? She was left paralysed for life. The police officer who shot her was acquitted. It took the Metropolitan Police twenty-nine years to apologise. Funny that. Apologising for something the officer got acquitted for?

The Broadwater Farm riots followed a few weeks after Cherry's shooting. But in between Cynthia Jarrett had died while police searched her home. She had a heart attack and family members claimed they saw police officers push her to the ground.

England was ablaze in the eighties. Riots in Toxteth in Liverpool, Handsworth in Birmingham, Chapeltown in Leeds, St Paul's in Bristol and Moss Side, Manchester, were not all to do with race. Poverty and class were also significant contributors. I wonder when Powell made his speech, and he warned of the violence and civil war that would follow, whether this was what he had in mind? I suspect not. He didn't envisage Black people being discriminated against and killed and brutalised by the state and the police respectively. He thought it would be the Blacks rising up, trying to take over. Instead, Black people just wanted to be treated as human beings.

The West Indies toured England in 1980 and 1984. Each time we returned the atmosphere between Black and white in the towns and cities seemed to be worse. And the treatment of our fellow West Indians was getting worse because they told us about it.

Hope was still living it. And, all these years later, I wanted to know how the hell her mother brought up a young family in such a dangerous and hateful environment. In 1985 Hope was nineteen. Had her mother told her what was happening and why as she grew from a girl to a young woman?

'She did,' Hope says. 'But I'm not sure that I understood it completely. And I guess, growing up, I think I was aware of the differences. I think I tried to, and still do, live in hope that people just accept it.'

I asked Hope whether, because of the colour of her skin and what was happening in the country at that time, her mother told her she would have to work twice as hard and be so much better than others? Some call it the rule of two. To get anywhere you have to work twice as hard. To get anywhere you have to keep your head down and not make a fuss.

'She aligned it with and wrapped it around education. "Education is the way forward," she would say. "Education is the way out," she would say. Even today, she'd still say education is a way to achieve, to become better, to elevate.'

That resonated with me. My mother was the same, as a teacher and a headmistress. She used to say, 'Get yourself a piece of paper behind your name, Mikey.' That is why at the start of this section I said I didn't think professional cricket was a realistic career. My mom meant a certificate, a diploma, a degree, or whatever qualification I could muster. And I have always thought – and saw and heard with my own eyes and ears – that West Indian families and West Indian parents always push that. Education coupled with the way you presented yourself. You had to be smart in both senses of the word. For me, it was a way of life. For Hope, though, education and looking the part was a survival mechanism.

'I'm so thankful that she really drummed that into me and my brother and the way we present ourselves. We used to go shopping, and we had to look like a million dollars, and present yourself in a way that nobody, and these are my words, that *nobody* can look at you and say, "You look like a scruff." Because they would. They would take that opportunity to say, "You're not clean" or, "You can't speak properly" or, "You're not educated." And I think that was her way of protecting us from what was really going on.'

It comes as something of a surprise that when Hope started playing football, racism had a day off (small mercy, huh?). There were, of course, a couple of incidents that stick in Hope's memory. But it was not the every-week occurrence that one might have thought, especially as she played for Millwall during her career.

'When I played for England in Croatia, I pulled my hamstring,' she says. 'And I remember it as clear as day; the dressing-room area was down some stairs underground. As I was walking off, and it sticks in my mind because it was a young boy, and he did the Hitler salute. I just thought, *This is really sad*. I couldn't have been more than twenty-five. And he was a small boy, no more than twelve. Immediately I thought, *His parents taught him that*. Where else?

'As for experiences in England, a player called me a Black "whatever". My Black team-mate went for the girl that said it. My brother, who was watching, got involved. And it didn't stop there; it went on after the game. As a manager for England, I can honestly say, on the sideline, I haven't experienced it, thank God. I think I've been lucky. And I think maybe the reason it didn't happen is because I guess I was a success in sports and people like to align themselves with success. So "she's all right" – if I was doing really badly, there's a possibility there might have been more. But I think because I did well, people want to associate themselves with things that are positive and going well.'

Hope played sixty-six times for England as a midfielder, scoring thirty-five goals. Her first game for England came when she was just sixteen and she played in the 1995 Women's World Cup. Three years later she was made manager of the national team, leading them to the World Cup quarter-finals in 2007 and 2011 and European Championship final in 2009. She also restructured the coaching of the women's game from Under-15 to Under-23 level, and she was the first woman to achieve the highest coaching qualification possible.

Some people might read those achievements and think, *Well, how can racism exist if she was able to do that?* And even more might say it when they consider the Football Association is one of the most old-fashioned British institutions to survive. It is not an exaggeration to say that back when Hope got the top job it was run by establishment white geriatrics, who would sit around in their blazers and old school ties, puffing on cigars and drinking brandies. As I type this, the FA chairman, Greg Clarke, has been forced to resign for using the term 'coloured' and claiming that 'different career interests' meant British South Asians choose jobs in information technology over sport. He was speaking to a government committee about racist abuse of players on social media. It makes you wonder how Hope got the job. Well, she was thinking the same.

'Was it a "ticking a box" exercise? Female, tick. Black person, tick. What was it? And I asked the question, and I said, "Is this a token gesture?" Even today, how many Black coaches are there in the men's game? At the highest level, it's 6 per cent [five head coaches from ninety-two professional clubs]. So, fifteen years ago, it was probably even less. Not even 1 per cent. So I did question it. I didn't feel I wasn't good enough. I was very suspicious, rightly or wrongly. So I did challenge it. I questioned why, they gave me a reason and I accepted it. I spoke to my friends, a really good Black friend in particular, who also played with me internationally. And she just told me, "You have got to take this job, you have to take it."

'And one thing I was absolutely clear on in my own mind was: "I cannot fail." Not for women, nor for Black people. They were my drivers. "I don't care if I have to work like a dog, I will make sure this works." And I knew people would say: "See, told you she couldn't do it." "Look, we gave a

Black person a chance, we gave a female a chance and they couldn't do it." That was in my head constantly. And that is the case still today. I still look at that, and go, *I have to do this.* For me, it's really important that there's visibility for the next generation. And, look, if I've done it, bloody hell, anybody can if they work hard.'

Hope has come a long way. Has Britain? Well, progress has been made but perhaps not as much as I thought. The UK government's own figures show issues remain. People of colour have twice the unemployment rate of their white peers, they are twice as likely to live in social housing. And, guess what, they are more likely to be stopped by the police and searched. An Oxford University study (the European Social Survey), inspired by that data, found that 18 per cent of the British public thought some races or ethnic groups were less intelligent, and a staggering 44 per cent thought some groups were more hard-working than others. Depressing. Keep those numbers in mind the next time someone tells you this is just an American problem.

So, as a trailblazer, it is important that Hope – and others like her – continue to be, as she says, 'visible'. It is so important that white, Black, everyone *sees* her in a position of authority in an industry and is made to think twice about how the world is changing and how it can continue to change. There is still an awful lot of work to do across the spectrum of society. And she says that football needs to do so much more. The sport, back in the 1980s, was often the way in which racism was 'visible', if you like. And for some it still is. John Barnes, born in Jamaica and star for England, used to have bananas thrown at him on the pitch. A decade later, Les Ferdinand, who played as a striker for the national team, told a story about how white supporters wouldn't celebrate if a Black player scored a goal.

'The amount of Black footballers in the men's game doesn't translate or transition into management, or positions of authority or decision-makers, and even less so in the women's game,' Hope says. 'I know since Black Lives Matter there's been a real opportunity to enforce and advocate change. And a lot of people are really pushing the FA. I'm on some panels, I chair a panel for women and Black coaches to try to enforce change through the FA, and have had some very, very heated discussions around that. And I'm hoping that, like everybody, given current events and what's happened, that this is an opportunity, and hope that things will change for Black people who have the ability to do jobs within football. Certainly, there's discrimination there.

'It was not overt but the fact that I was female and Black was a definite issue. I still believe this to this day, if I was white, I would never have been fired. I'm not saying I would always have done that job. But I would have been offered something else, technical director or something, I categori- cally believe that. And I was seen as a troublemaker, because I asked questions. I was relentless at it. And had I not been, I don't think the game would have moved as it did. But it would have moved a lot quicker had they supported the things I was saying earlier. I know I did a lot for the game but I could have done so much more.'

This is really important. Even at the top of her game, Hope experienced that racism. She experienced it when she was a small child. When she was growing up. When she was playing for England. This is the crystal-clear dehumanisation of Black people in the modern world. They are made to feel worthless, made to feel as though somehow it is their fault. 'You stay down there, you know your place and don't get any ideas.' That is what the message is.

This is the life of Black people. This is normal. Why should she have had to put up with any of it? I have heard or read hundreds of stories like it and every time I count my blessings that it didn't happen to me and impinge on what I wanted to achieve. As I said, I was fortunate. And I want to make it clear that I am not reproducing Hope's thoughts and feelings here just so they can be dismissed as a list of complaints or gripes. They are here to make people think carefully about what each of those incidents must feel like. Try it. Please try really hard. Put yourself in her shoes in those situations she has described for just a second and tell me there isn't a problem.

Hope is tough. Good for her. And it's lucky she is like that. I wouldn't have blamed her if, when she suffered racist abuse for the first time in her life, or on that football pitch, she had said, 'No, I don't need this.' In a sporting context, how many others have suffered something like she did that made them walk away? How many dreams were dashed and ambitions ruined? Extend it to any industry or walk of life you like. The person who didn't get the promotion, the job they wanted, the university place. It doesn't matter. It is all the same.

The vast majority of the time it is not about having a policeman's knee on your neck. That is crude, brutal vio-lence. The everyday racism that most people suffer is therefore more subtle. Hope has described it as a 'drip, drip' effect, deliberately designed to wash away confidence (Ebony Rainford-Brent said the same on Sky). And there's no real comeback to that. If you stay silent, nothing changes. If you push back, you are a troublemaker.

Being 'other' and not fitting in will be feelings recognised by a lot of people of colour in white-dominated environments. It makes me think back to the story about my mom's family rejecting her because, in their eyes, she had married someone who was too dark. It's the idea of trying to blend in, to be as white as possible, so that you can be treated with equality.

Luckily, Hope pulled herself up by her bootstraps. But my guess is that when she did that, the powers that be didn't like it so much. Their noses were put out of joint and they were looking for any excuse to get rid of her. That's a problem going forward. It's one thing Black people being given responsibility, it's another to let them actually do the job. Perhaps I'm too cynical now about it all but, with an organisation like the English Football Association, it sounded like Hope was being told, 'Know your place, this is your level and what's been assigned to you since 1400.' No change.

'I have to be careful what I say, Mikey, but as a Black person when you have an opinion, or you disagree with something, some people don't like it. If I was white, and male, it would have been okay.'

But let's be clear, this is not solely a football issue. It is just one context. This is not really a book about sport, either. It's a book about society. Football reflects society in the same way that cricket does. Just like every sport. Just like every other industry. The experiences Hope has had would have been repeated all over the world day in and day out on the factory floor, in the office block, in the board room, on the shop floor, in the dressing room. It would have been repeated on public transport, in restaurants, bars. Or just walking down the street.

You see, George Floyd died because a cop put a knee on his neck. It was a senseless, tragic murder. But, as I said earlier, that is the extreme end of the spectrum. And, of course, we notice that and it gets the attention it deserves. But there are small deaths. Every single day. Slowly, quietly, subtly, Black people are having the life and breath squeezed out of them. At some stage in their life, most Black people have metaphorically felt that knee on their neck. Like Hope did by being abused on the street or having dog faeces put through her door, victimised by people who had the power to control her career. Dehumanisation comes in many different forms, some obvious, some not. To start to prevent this dehumanisation, to get that knee off our neck, people have to understand why it exists in the first place. How it came to be like this and why. And when you understand that, you can also understand the huge, important struggle that humanity has on its hands.

WHY WE KNEEL

CHAPTER 5

Dehumanisation

When I was growing up my father was what you might call the strong, silent type. He spoke to be listened to, not just to be heard. And I remember one day going to work with him – he was a master builder who would run construction sites – and he was the same there, too. But if something needed saying on the job, if something wasn't right or someone had stepped out of line, boy, did you hear him. I have grown up to be very much like my father. You step on me, I have something to say. Otherwise I can keep my counsel.

I have similar traits to my father because of what is known as learned behaviour. And you do too because of the relationship with your parents. That learning process begins as soon as a baby is born. One of the first developmental stages for infants is mimicking the faces cooing back at them in the cot. And, throughout those early developmental years, human beings are copying what they see from their parents or the significant people in their lives. We copy everything – speech intonation, facial expressions, the way we sit or stand or walk, eat our food. We react to situations in the same way, raising our voice in the same manner, throwing our arms in the air or showing delight. Our personality traits, ideologies and knowledge are borrowed, passed down from generation to generation.

Give or take, we become our parents. I have a friend who is terrified of becoming his father. He has exactly the same facial expression when he is about to lose his temper. And, much to his dismay, his 6-year-old daughter does the same. Learned behaviour keeps those psychotherapists in business. Hell, when I was running away from racism for so long that was learned behaviour, too. My family liked to pretend that there had been no fallout when my mom married my dad. Didn't talk about it. Kept it a secret.

For the family set-up, read society. One reflects the other. And learned behaviour is one term. It could also be called indoctrination or brainwashing. It has been handed down from governments to populace, historians to scholars, teachers to pupils, parent to child. Like a nasty habit, for hundreds of years. When people are told something over and over again, when they see it and when they hear it, it becomes as natural as the passing of the seasons. 'That's the way it's always been.' Like a tradition or a recipe. 'Well, we always do it like that.'

And it affects all races. As I've said, my mother's family didn't want her marrying my father because his skin was 'too dark'. Once you understand and accept the idea and 'knowledge' that Black people are inferior, then you can begin to see how the dehumanisation of Black people has thrived for centuries.

Two psychologists conducted a powerful study in 1939 and 1940 to show the impact of that feeling. Kenneth and Mamie Clark, a husband and wife, showed two dolls – one white and one black – to African-American children at a segregated school in Washington, DC. They were asked which was nicest, which would you like to play with. There was an overwhelming preference for the white doll in the study. Some Black children ran out crying when they saw the black doll. This experiment was actually used to help end school segregation laws in the US in the 1950s.

Many people think that slavery was the start of dehumanisation. But it wasn't. It was a symptom. You don't just wake up one morning and think: 'Let's try to enslave an entire race.' The idea that Black people were lesser beings needed to be planted and it needed to grow. It did not happen overnight.

In fact, there was a time when the pasty-faced Europeans were thought to be inferior to Black people, according to PhD historian Joe Hopkinson. This was a belief held in the medieval period and grounded on the difference in climates. Europe, cold and wet, as opposed to warm and dry Africa, produced the 'slow-witted and unathletic'. African people were thought to be keen and vital. Obviously, this stereotype did not last.

What was important was difference. Human beings are naturally inclined to think that anyone or anything that is different, or other, is inferior. This was the jumping-off point for racist ideology. 'Black otherness' was demonised in religious imagery and literature, particularly after the invention of the printing press in Europe. This coincided with the 'discovery' of the New World and later gave rise to the pseudo-science of 'racial hierarchy'. This justified and strengthened the slave trade. Or, to put it another way, race and racism allowed Europeans to distribute power to different human groups. They chose to bestow power on their own and take from those who did not look like them.

The indoctrination, the brainwashing and the learned behaviour was happening before the slave trade. During and after, however, it would gather pace, proliferate, become so unstoppable – use any term you like – that it became ingrained in society and culture. The slave trade was a symptom, but it was such a potent disease that it would mutate and grow into the illness that we see today.

It wasn't just Black people who suffered, of course. In medieval times, Jews and Muslims were persecuted and treated as 'unhuman'. And it is inarguable that both today continue to suffer dehumanisation. In the 1275 'Statute of the Jewry' in England, Jews were segregated from Christians, and there was a mass expulsion of the Jewish population in 1290. In Europe in the medieval era, Muslims were not considered human. The Crusades – the supposed 'Holy Wars' which attempted to rid Europe of Islamic influence – followed. Historians will point to these Crusades as a foundation for colonialism.

Religion has much to do with planting the seed that white was good and Christian but Black was bad and evil. Africans would be portrayed in medieval art as the killers of John the Baptist and torturers of Jesus Christ. Religion is always a, shall we say, tricky topic to broach so I don't want to get too bogged down in it aside to say that the Church has quite a bit to answer for when it comes to brainwashing.

Jesus Christ, to this day, is depicted with blue eyes and blond hair. Really? Tell me who in that part of the world in that era in history had blue eyes and blond hair? Jesus was a brown-skinned Middle Eastern Jewish man. It might sound shocking to you but that's okay, you've not been told any differently. Who hasn't gone into a church or art gallery and seen the depiction of Jesus as white? Very few of us. In television and film, Jesus is also white. In *The Passion of the Christ*, probably the biggest ever Hollywood biblical drama, Jesus was played by a white man. The film was made in 2004. And don't get me started on the fondness of casting agents to pick a Black man to play Judas.

There is a long history of white Europeans creating and distributing pictures of Jesus in their image. Back it goes – and probably further – to the Renaissance era. When colonisation occurred, white Jesus went on his travels to reinforce the stereotypes – Europeans at the top of the tree and those with darker shades of skin lower down.

While we're on the subject of creating someone in your own image, don't forget that God was supposed to have done that with his son. He was created in his image, right? I am not a highly religious person, one to start preaching about religion or quoting the Bible, but its pages are pretty clear. If Jesus was a person of colour, so was God. That is probably too much of a stretch for some to imagine or even contemplate but I'll tell you one thing, the Big Man (or Woman!) in the sky sure as hell wasn't – and isn't – white.

Why does it even matter how Jesus was portrayed? you might ask. Well, in Africa and India Jesus has also been shown to look like the indigenous population. And this makes it easier for those populations to identify with Christianity. Spreading the word of God and all that. But, on the flip side, does a white Jesus create another disconnect between white people and people of colour, the former being less likely to feel empathy for the latter? It shouldn't be much of a leap. Jesus as a brown-skinned person suffering violence, oppression and discrimination?

These are not just my views. A Stanford University study from 2020 found that when people imagine God as white, they are more likely to consider white males for jobs than Black females. It is surely the most obvious and least surprising study ever conducted. If a white man rules the heavens, then why wouldn't you believe that white men rule on earth? A Google search on the word 'God' showed that 72 per cent of the images returned were of white men. Six per cent were of Morgan Freeman, who played God in the film *Bruce Almighty*. The only winner there, I think, is Mr Freeman.

The Stanford study also asked 176 Christian children to draw a picture of God. They had all the available colours to draw with. And, of course, they drew a God who could be identified as white. This is the brainwashing on a large scale that has been taking place since at least the fifteenth century.

That timeframe is important because, at the same time as the printing press was being invented by white Europeans, they were also 'discovering' the Americas. So you have a situation where Europeans are meeting indigenous people, or people of colour. They are interacting across the world. The Europeans are able to send back what is essentially propaganda about these new people. The idea of white supremacy begins to spread and it is why we have that example of children depicting God as white hundreds of years later.

The Spanish and Portuguese were the first colonisers. Spain took captives from Africa to the Americas as early as

1503. Fifteen years later they were shipping them directly from Africa to America. Most came from Benin, Nigeria and Cameroon. The Portuguese captured Black people from Africa and took them back to Europe – as much as 10 per cent of the population of Lisbon, the capital, was believed to be of African descent by the early sixteenth century. With this expansion by these two countries, and the growth of the publishing world, myths and falsehoods flew around the entire continent of Europe.

It would eventually go beyond telling stories or false imagery, though. Hugely significant was the rise of the pseudo-scientist, who presented ludicrous theories as fact about the white European's supremacy in mind, body and spirit. It was racial hierarchy in order to justify colonisers' expansion and the money-making machine that was the transatlantic slave trade. Let's take a look at some examples.

First up we have Carolus Linnaeus, a botanist, physician and zoologist from Sweden. In 1735 he defined the concept of race, categorising humans: *Americanus*, *Asiaticus*, *Africanus* and *Europeaus*. Each race was given characteristics.

'Yellow' Asians were melancholic, greedy, inflexible and governed by superstition; red Americans were hot-tempered, stubborn, free and governed by tradition; and the Black Africans were 'of Black complexion, phlegmatic temperament and relaxed fibre ... Of crafty, indolent, and careless disposition and are governed in their actions by caprice.' White Europeans? Well, knock me down with a feather, they were just perfection. They were 'of fair complexion, sanguine temperament, and brawny form ... of gentle manners, acute in judgment, of quick invention, and governed by fixed laws and their mother'. Behold the master race.

'So what?' you might say, 'this was 1735! We've moved on!' Have we? Can you honestly say that those descriptions are not still used today? And why wouldn't they be? Linnaeus's nonsense was being used to support ethnic cleansing in 1930s Europe, let alone its past use to enforce slavery in the colonies.

Next, we have Petrus Camper, a Dutch professor of anatomy from the eighteenth century, who produced works claiming that the ancient Greeks were human perfection. He did this by using Greek statues to rank the beauty of human faces. Laughable, of course, but taken seriously and repeated all around Europe.

Then there's Johann Friedrich Blumenbach, the German scientist who invented the term 'Caucasian' to describe the species of man found along Europe's eastern border in 1795. He claimed it was the 'original' race and therefore the most 'beautiful'. For balance, Blumenbach also insisted that there was nothing inferior about Black people.

Finally, there's Samuel George Morton, an American anthropologist. In the mid-1800s he was the guy who reckoned intelligence was linked to brain size. After measuring a vast number of skulls from around the world, he concluded that whites have larger skulls than other races and were therefore 'superior'.

All of this is gibberish, of course. But it was science then. And you can't argue with science, right? With such supposedly intelligent and learned men espousing such theories, and the masses taking them as fact, we had the legitimisation of racism. Instead of racism being something that had been invented by man to justify its worst side, it had suddenly become rooted in scientific theory.

Renowned philosophers had their say too. Immanuel

Kant said in 1781: 'The white race possesses all incentives and talents in itself . . . The race of Negroes can be educated, but only as slaves . . . The [indigenous] Americans cannot be educated, they care about nothing and are lazy.'

The enlightened historian and philosopher François–Marie Arouet, otherwise known as Voltaire? Not so much. The Frenchman believed that all creatures should be graded and that Black people were at the bottom, just above monkeys. He wrote that Africans were 'animals' with a 'flat Black nose with little or no intelligence!' He also invested personally in slave-trading companies, like the French East India Company.

Celebrated Scottish philosopher David Hume wrote that Blacks were 'naturally inferior to the whites'. He also advised his patron, Lord Hertford, to invest in slave-trading companies. These views were taken seriously then. Kant-Hume-Voltaire reads like an all-star cast of the world's great thinkers.

The influencers of the day were lining up to say, 'It's okay to treat Blacks badly.' Thomas Jefferson, third president of the United States, was another. He may well have written in the Declaration of Independence that 'all men are equal', but it's been said that his desire for emancipation weakened when he realised the damage to his own wealth. He also demanded all Black people be sent back to Africa or the West Indies because he didn't think Americans and Blacks could live together.

Jefferson was rich off the back of his slaves, owning more than 600 during his lifetime. Boys aged ten to sixteen were whipped to work in his nail factory. He said that slaves smelled bad and were lazy. He also fathered six children with a teenage slave, Sally Hemings. He must have held his nose when he was copulating.

Religious ideology was in play, too. The Africans were heathens and a bit of slavery would give them some much-needed rigour and discipline to prepare them for European 'civilisation'.

By the end of the nineteenth century, with Europeans dominating the world, it would stand to reason that the people from those countries who were powerful believed absolutely, that they were superior in every sense. Just because of the colour of their skin. Those who were not white were sub-human. They had no rights, no spirit, no physical or emotional feeling, no hopes, no dreams. They were cargo.

Without this dehumanisation, slavery could not have started, survived and prospered. It is estimated that more than 11 million Africans were forcibly transported – stolen from their homes and families – to the Americas over four centuries. Fewer than 9.6 million would survive the passage across the Atlantic in ships not fit for cattle, let alone humans. Africans were kept below deck, crammed in with barely an inch between them. The number of Africans enslaved by the Arab world would be more than nine million in a trade from AD 650 to the nineteenth century. In total up to 25 million Africans were taken, but some historians, notably from Africa, estimate the figure to be double that.

The horrors of slavery are clear for all of us to see now. But when they were actually happening in real time at the zenith of the trade, there were few prepared to protest.

Consider the story of the slave ship *Zong*, which departed Africa in September 1781 with 470 slaves on board – more than it could actually hold, by the way, but many captains overloaded their human cargo to maximise profits.

When the *Zong* got stuck mid-Atlantic in a part of the sea called the 'doldrums', where little or no wind could leave ships stranded, the crew and slaves began to die of illness. The captain, a Luke Collingwood, thought the answer was to 'jettison' the slaves to their deaths so the ship's owners could make an insurance claim. He threw 132 slaves overboard. Cue outrage at this mass murder? Not really.

Criminal charges against the company, Collingwood and the crew were thrown out. A flabbergasted Justice John Lee, Britain's solicitor general, said: 'What is this claim that human people have been thrown overboard? This is a case of chattels or goods. Blacks are goods and property; it is madness to accuse these well-serving honourable men of murder. The case is the same as if wood had been thrown overboard.' The insurance company paid out.

If slaves were 'lucky' enough to survive the journey across the Atlantic, nothing improved. They would be greeted by men like Edward Long, a British-Jamaican slave owner, who justified his money-making plantation on the grounds that Black people were not only inferior but not human. 'An orangutan husband would not disgrace a negro woman,' he wrote. This was not an attempt at humour.

Such views meant that barbaric conditions for slaves on Caribbean plantations were not given a second thought. If a slave was not sold at auction they were often just left to die. The cheapest slaves were bought with the sole intention of working them to death. Families were separated. Usually they were branded with their master's initials. Malnourishment was so common that women's menstrual cycles stopped. Slaves that displayed 'difficult' behaviour were sent to 'seasoning camps' where half of them would die.

The working hours were from dawn until dusk. At harvest time it meant eighteen hours in the fields. Beatings, murder and rape were all everyday occurrences. Other punishments included having iron hooks hung around their necks with iron chains added to them. Olaudah Equiano, a former slave who published his own life story in 1789, wrote: 'I have seen a negro beaten till some of his bones were broken for even letting a pot boil over.'

In the American south, Black people's status as inhuman was enshrined in law. For example, no Black woman could be raped by a white person because they were considered to be promiscuous. Masters would use sexual violence as a weapon to remind women of their enslavement.

In Virginia it was written into the statute books that it was not a crime to kill a slave. This was known as the Casual Killing Act, a law required because of the sheer number of slaves dying as a result of, shall we say, the 'overenthusiasm' of owners meting out punishments for minor offences. There was also a spate of killings of Black children by white women. This was how the law book read in 1669, as reproduced in the 1975 work *American Slavery, American Freedom* by Edmund Morgan:

> If any slave resist his master (or other by his master's order correcting him) and by the extremity of the correction should chance to die, that his death shall not be accompted felony.

And if a slave should run away? Virginia law sorted that problem out three years later. The 'act for the apprehension and suppression of runaways, Negroes and slaves' stated:

If any Negroe, mulatto, Indian slave, or servant for life, runaway and shall be pursued by the warrant or hue and cry, it shall and may be lawful for any person who shall endeavour to take them, upon the resistance of such Negroe, mulatto, Indian slave, or servant for life, to kill or wound him or them so resisting ... And if it happen that such Negroe, mulatto, Indian slave, or servant for life doe dye of any wound in such their resistance received the master or owner of such shall receive satisfaction from the public.

Why were such laws required? Well, it wasn't just to compound slaves' status as sub-human. There also needed to be some sort of protection if, Lord forbid, any of these people felt some guilt for what they had done. They would be able to say, 'I was just trying to teach them a lesson ... the law says that's okay.' And the key phrase protecting whites beating Blacks to death in the first instance is 'should chance to die'. So you are also covered if you beat them to death by accident. How hard is it to beat someone to death by accident, do you think?

In an era where one race was considered not human, it was inevitable they would be used for medical experiments. James Marion Sims, a gynaecologist, operated on Black slaves without anaesthetic – or any form of pain relief – because, he said, they felt less pain than white people. He was also reported to have ideas (perfectly normal for the time) about developmental differences between Africans and white people, including that African 'skulls grew too quickly around their brain', making them less intelligent.

Sims operated on at least ten women, one of them up to

thirty times. There was no question of these women providing consent. They had no rights, so they suffered. And they suffered for profit. Sims would open a practice and offer the technique he perfected on white women – with anaesthetic and for a fee.

Unfortunately, Sims also experimented on enslaved babies who suffered with neo-natal tetanus. This was a disease that he liked to blame on Black people for being stupid and work-shy.

'Whenever there is poverty, and filth, and laziness, or where the intellectual capacity is cramped, the moral and social feelings blunted, there it will be oftener found,' he wrote. 'Wealth, a cultivated intellect, a refined mind, an affectionate heart, are comparatively exempt from the ravages of this unmercifully fatal malady. But expose this class to the same physical causes, and they become equal sufferers with the first.'

In an attempt to find a remedy, Sims would use a shoemaker's awl to prise open the baby's skull and move bones apart. While the baby was alive. This had a 100 per cent fatality rate. Not that it was his fault. He blamed the deaths on 'the sloth and ignorance of their mothers and the Black midwives who attended them'.

Sims is remembered as the father of modern gynaecology. And, indeed, lionised. There were six statues of him dotted around America. One of them could be found in Central Park, New York City, before protestors demanded its removal in 2018. Yes, 2018 for those who keep talking about 'a long time ago'.

Another nineteenth-century American physician, Samuel A. Cartwright, 'discovered' that slaves suffered from a significant mental disorder which he called 'drapetomania'. This was an uncontrollable urge to escape from slavery. So slaves who wanted their freedom were labelled mentally ill. The cure was to make running a physical impossibility. So doctors prescribed the removal of the big toe on each foot. Cartwright's medicine was 'whip the devil out of them'.

I make no apologies for the, no doubt, uncomfortable nature of this section. I did say there would be some parts of this book that would be a disturbing read. To fix the present and future, we have to confront the past.

Maybe you knew some of this already, maybe you didn't. I suspect it is the latter because the true nature of slavery is largely glossed over to save the feelings of the perpetrators.

I don't think history should be ignored just because it makes folks feel uncomfortable. Indeed, it is far, far easier not to deal with it. And, by and large, that is exactly what has happened. People turned the other cheek. They pretended it wasn't happening, that what was happening didn't matter or the people to whom it was happening did not matter. When women were crying out in agony because of what Sims was doing to them, did he not think, *Huh, I thought they didn't feel pain?* That's called cognitive dissonance.

Cognitive dissonance has allowed the dehumanisation of Black people to go unchecked. It created slavery. It created the colonial conquest of Africa by the European powers. It created the economic gulf between the West and Africa today. It caused the murder of George Floyd and thousands of others, the abuse and discrimination that Black people suffer every single day.

People say that Black people should 'get over slavery' because it was a long time ago. But its impact has touched every single one of us. And that is learned behaviour. Black people still suffer the mental scars of that era. It has been passed down through generations that they are worth less, that they are bottom of the pile and should just be grateful that they now have their freedom. It is a post-traumatic stress disorder. Internationally renowned researcher and educator Dr Joy DeGruy, whose brilliant talks you can find on YouTube (or you can buy her books) and encompass much of what we've discussed here, has termed it 'post-traumatic slave disorder'.

White people are suffering from it, too. How else do you explain the disease of white supremacy that still exists? Donald Trump in the White House, for goodness sake? Black people in America financially unable to improve their lot in life because they can't get a bank loan because of the colour of their skin? Slavery was a horrific, brutal and chilling part of the dehumanisation. But it was just the opening act. We are watching it unfold still.

Slavery by a different name

On 1 January 1863, US President Abraham Lincoln made it official that 'slaves within any State, or designated part of a State ... in rebellion ... shall be then, thenceforward, and forever free'. The Americans were a little late to the party – the British freed more than 800,000 enslaved Africans in the Caribbean and other colonies twenty-nine years earlier.

So, all over then. Done and dusted. Nothing to worry about. The trade in Black people was over and slavery was finished. Black people could, finally, live a life of freedom and be afforded the same opportunities as their former masters. If only it were that simple.

At a stroke of a pen, a politician can amend a constitution or tweak a bill to receive assent. But laws do not change attitudes. And the hatred and dehumanisation of Black people in America and the colonies was so deep-seated that the notion that emancipation in America, or abolishment by Britain, would suddenly and dramatically improve the lives of Black people proved unsurprisingly false. After all, the American constitution, in black and white, declared that any person who was not free (it did not use the term 'slaves') was only three-fifths human. All the pseudo-science, racist philosophy and hatred of otherness that we have discussed can be seen in that entry.

It can also be seen in the way that the slave trade came to an end. In short, the traders had to be paid off with vast sums of money to stop their human trafficking, rape, murder and abuse. This was called reparations. For the misery they inflicted they were paid compensation. That's right. The slave owners were paid. Not the slaves. The British bill, in today's money, was £300 billion. The French demanded 90 million gold francs (£14.7 or €17 billion today) in 1825 from Haiti, which had won a bitter war for independence from its masters. This was ten times the country's annual revenue and was only paid off in 1947. Haiti has still not recovered from bearing that burden and probably never will. David Michael Rudder, the Trinidadian calypsonian, refers to this in one of his songs, 'Haiti I'm Sorry'. (Every now and again I will draw reference to some of our great musicians of the Caribbean whose music many listen to but don't really hear.)

Britain's bill was not paid off until 2015. That basically means, all people paying taxes in the UK were helping to pay off the former slave owners who were being compensated for their 'loss'. How ironic it is, then, that descendants of the slaves, now working in Britain, were still helping to pay the descendants of their former masters through their taxes paid to the government. Think about that.

In America compensation was rejected by slave owners in the South as the nation became bitterly divided. The factions who argued against slavery and for it would clash in the bloody Civil War, with the abolitionist North versus the 'slavery is a positive good' South.

America was divided. Thomas Jefferson was at least half right when he said that slaves should be returned to where they came from because white and Black couldn't live together. But only because Black people feared they could never truly be free and would continue to be oppressed and victimised. When they were asked what they wanted post-slavery many said they wanted to live separately from white people. Freedom meant being left alone by the white man in their own enclaves.

And they were absolutely right. America was divided post-slavery and it is divided now. The entrenched attitudes remain because they have been continually reinforced. From the Jim Crow era of segregation in the South, to domestic government policy and the encouragement of racism in institutions like banking, housing, education and the police force to keep the Black man down.

America's story post-slavery is hugely important. As the saying goes, 'If America sneezes, the world catches a cold.' As the dominant global power, America's persistent failure to tackle systemic racism has informed the world's view of Black people and, you might say, encouraged racism.

But I want to go back to that post-slave era in America. To dwell on it. Attitudes did not change overnight. A slave didn't go to bed on Monday and wake up a free man on Tuesday with all the trappings of a white man. It was impossible. Slavery continued, just in a different form.

This was, of course, because the American economy relied on this free labour. Although the African slave trade – the continued trafficking of Black people from the continent – had been banned in the US in 1808, domestically people were still traded. And the enslaved population would nearly triple in the next fifty years, so that by 1860 there were almost 4 million slaves. Half of them were surviving in the South. And after the Civil War the South was flat broke.

So the Black man couldn't simply walk out of the plantation on that Tuesday morning to a new life. No way. The 'former' slave owners in the South and the lawmakers needed to come up with a new way to subjugate.

Laws were introduced to make it illegal for a former slave to be without work. And how would a slave, often illiterate (because it was illegal to teach a slave how to read and write) and with skills only suited to slave work, get a job? If a Black man was found on the street he could be arrested and beaten. So they stayed on the plantations.

Those who stayed, called sharecroppers, had to earn their freedom, and those who didn't suffered a worse fate, which we will get to later.

Sharecropping was when the masters gave the slaves the tools and the seeds to work the land and plant the crops. These were given in the form of a grant. Harvest a certain amount and your grant – or debt – is paid. Of course, the slave owners made sure the terms of this deal were grossly unfair to the slave and his or her family. Rarely was the debt ever paid.

There were other laws, too, which were called 'Pig Laws'. An example was that if somebody stole a pig worth $1, they would go to jail for five years. Strangely, a lot of Black people were convicted of such crimes and barely any whites. Black people were also arrested for looking at a white woman, vagrancy and loitering, with up to twelve years in prison the punishment. And, as you can imagine, with the 'freed slaves' unable to get jobs as they couldn't read or write, there was a lot of 'loitering'. Sound familiar? England in the 1980s comes to mind. So basically, if you didn't stay on the plantation, you were almost certain to end up in jail. The Black prison population swelled disproportionately in relation to the numbers of white criminals (nothing has changed on that score).

So, what to do with all these Black prisoners? thought the powers that be in the South. Put them to work. It's almost as if they had planned to convict Blacks on made-up crimes so they could get free labour again. It was called 'convict leasing'. From county courthouses and jails, men were leased to local plantations, factories and railroads. And it was so successful that, by 1894, three quarters of the state revenue of Alabama came from convict leasing.

Convict leasing was not much different to slavery. Businessmen bought convict leases and the prisoner would only be free again once that fee had been paid off through work. But when prisoners were working to pay off those debts the paperwork that showed how much they owed was often 'lost', meaning they were never freed. Prisoners were often separated from their families and conditions were as bad – if not worse – in prison, with illness, malnutrition and torture rife.

'Peonage' was another barbaric ruse to continue slavery in the South. The 13th Amendment of the US constitution said that slavery was illegal. But there was a loophole which read: 'except as a punishment for crime'. The old slave owners would pay to prevent a Black man from going to jail for one of the many concocted crimes. And that man would then work, for free, until the debt was paid off.

It wasn't until 1928 that Alabama became the last state to ban convict leasing. Unfortunately, in its place came the chain gang. Same forced, free labour but instead of for individuals, it was for the state, or community. Chain gangs might build roads or repair them and, once again, it was the masters who benefited: better transport access meant it was easier to get their crops to market. This time it's the American, Sam Cooke, who sang about the men working so hard trying to get back to their women in his song, 'Chain Gang'. Peonage was still taking place in pockets of the South in the early 1940s.

So much, then, for the end of slavery. And so much for the end of a Black people being dehumanised. That is important because history books will record emancipation on the date above and people might think, *Phew! Glad that's over . . . long time ago, why are Black people still going on about it?* We are still going on about it because the truth is never taught. And we're still going on about it because it has not darn well stopped. Blacks were dehumanised before slavery. They were dehumanised during slavery. They were dehumanised after slavery.

There was never even a flicker of hope for the

African–American to start to have a feeling of self-worth or for the brainwashing and indoctrination to stop. It was repeated but with different names or terms used. That desire to dominate, punish, exploit and dehumanise the Black man could not just be turned off like a tap. Black people cannot forget about the past until society forgets about the past, and there is evidence of society still having those hang-ups. Cue the Amy Cooper story in Central Park, New York, in May 2020. I will get back to that. But what happened, also, to that desire to inflict pain, to murder, to rape? This was when lynching began. After the proclamation of emancipation.

The lynchings

Between 1877 and 1950, there were at least 4,384 lynchings by white people of people of colour in America. Most of them were in the South but they occurred all over the country. Why did these occur? We know why, of course. Because Black people were not human. But with 'freedom', that otherness threatened white people's way of life, their power. They didn't want Black people taking their money, their jobs, their women. The 'contamination' of the white race was a not insignificant factor for their ire. But it is something of a myth that lynchings happened because Black people had been accused of raping white women, touching them, looking at them the wrong way, murders or assaults. Research by the Equal Justice Initiative (EJI), a non-profit organisation set up to end mass imprisonment and excessive punishment in the US, says that only a quarter involved an alleged sex 'crime' and less than a third were due to claims of violence.

Most often people were lynched because their crime was to be Black, like Jack Turner, who was organising Black voters in Alabama in 1882. Lynched. Bud Spears complained about the lynching of a Black man in Mississippi in 1888. Lynched. Robert E. Lee, who heartbreakingly changed his name to that of the Confederate general thinking it would spare him, knocked on the door of a white woman in South Carolina in 1904. Lynched.

Going to watch a lynching was a day out, like a family outing to a cricket or soccer match. Moms, dads and children. Thousands would turn up. Seventeen-year-old Henry Smith was tortured and burned on a 10-foot-high stage in Texas in 1893 with 10,000 spectating. Almost 20,000 watched Will Brown burned alive in Omaha in 1919. Photos were taken with white folk standing in front of the bodies smiling, laughing, pointing. Postcards of the event were sold. Like the lynching of Laura Nelson and her teenage son, LW, in Oklahoma, 1911. Both were 'kidnapped' from the county jail by a white mob, who raped Ms Nelson and then hung them both from a bridge over a river, deliberately close to the Black part of town as a warning message. Postcards of the hanging, with the mob standing proudly on the bridge, could be bought in novelty stores.

What is noticeable when reading about such stories is the consistent complicity of the police. The white mob did not need to force their way into courthouses or jails to 'kidnap' their victim. They were rarely met with any resistance whatsoever. They just walked in and dragged them off to be murdered. Is it at all surprising, in the context of learned behaviour and ideology passing down from generation to generation, that in America the cops are hated so much by Black people?

Rarer still than any objection by police or law enforcement was any conviction for the lynchings. Case after case is concluded with 'no charges were brought against the murderers'. That was because the police were as racist as the mob itself, and also due to the peculiar condition of all the hundreds and thousands of white people who had been involved, or attended the spectacle, to suddenly be struck down with a bout of amnesia. No one ever saw anything.

Sometimes law enforcement actively encouraged the violence. This is how the EJI recorded one of the more notorious incidents of racial terror:

On May 31, 1921, Dick Rowland, a Black 19-year-old shoe shiner, was jailed in the Tulsa County Courthouse after a white woman reported he assaulted her. The charges were dropped, but police kept him in the courthouse to protect him from a growing white mob that sought to lynch him. Members of the Black community also stationed themselves in the courthouse to protect Mr Rowland from a potential lynching.

Thousands of white people joined the mob. Reports show that local authorities provided firearms and ammunition to the white rioters, who began to shoot at the men protecting Mr Rowland, forcing them to retreat to Greenwood, a Black neighbourhood anchored by a thriving Black business district. The white mob, including city-appointed deputies, followed and terrorized Greenwood, shooting indiscriminately at any Black person they saw and burning homes and buildings. Numerous survivors reported that planes from a nearby airfield dropped fire-bombs on Greenwood. The Oklahoma National Guard was dispatched the next day to suppress the violence, but they treated the attack as a 'Negro uprising' and arrested hundreds of Black survivors. No members of the white mob, local government, or national guard were prosecuted or punished.

Over 10,000 Black people were displaced from their community. Several hundred Black people were likely killed, but there is no reliable account of the casualties because public officials did not keep a record of Black people who had been hospitalized, wounded, or killed.

This was known as the Tulsa Massacre. At least thirty-six Black people died and the Black community was destroyed. This incident and the thousands of others researched by the EJI were, plain and simple, terrorism. The attacks were designed to enforce white supremacy and normalise the dehumanisation of Blacks. No excuse was in fact needed for the violence. And that's the way the mob wanted it, to ter-rorise African-Americans into thinking that if they stepped foot out of the door, a misplaced word here, or accidental bumping of shoulders in a shop there, it could happen to them. Speaking disrespectfully, refusing to step off the pave-ment when a white person approached, using bad language, using an improper title for a white person, suing a white man, arguing with a white man, bumping into a white woman and insulting a white person were all enough to get a Black person killed.

The lynch mobs were emboldened and backed by racist

leaders, politicians and authorities of the day, of course. US President Woodrow Wilson had refused to support an anti-lynching bill despite at least a lynching a week in the southern states. He had also screened at the White House the 1915 film *The Birth of a Nation*, which glorified the Ku Klux Klan for 'protecting' white women from the 'sexual aggression' of Black men. Wilson said the film was like 'writing history with lightning and its perceptions were all so terribly true'.

In the American South the Jim Crow era of segregation was in full swing. If slavery was a second act in the story of dehumanisation, the seeds of 'otherness' being the first, this was the third. Jim Crow was not a person. He was a stage character played by a white man in blackface in minstrel shows. The character, who was dressed in rags, would sing and dance and was portrayed as lazy, stupid and worthless. Jim Crow was used as an insult. Hence its use in the laws that ensured Blacks were third-class citizens. The Jim Crow laws era spanned from the 'abolishment' of slavery until the signing of the Civil Rights Act in 1964. Most historians recognise that it was slavery by another name. Folks, I was born in 1954. It's not that long ago.

The laws differed state by state. Segregated schools, transport facilities and restaurants are the most well-known. But in many states Black people were denied the opportunity to own property, to own a business, and were prevented from freedom of movement. They were also often denied the right to vote by 'literacy tests'. These took the form of questions like, 'how many bubbles in a bar of soap?', 'how many windows in city hall?' and 'how many seeds in a watermelon?' Although laws like that were supposed to have been illegal, according to the post-Civil War Reconstruction Amendments to the constitution, the reality was that the US government had little appetite to challenge the South. Hardly surprising when you had racist presidents like Wilson in the White House. And it was easy for the southern states to do as they wished. They had murderous groups like the Ku Klux Klan and the lynch mobs to terrify any dissenters and impose laws that were designed to deny Black people their rights and ensure the status quo remained – Blacks at the bottom.

Thank goodness, then, for the Civil Rights Act, signed by President Lyndon B. Johnson, who called it 'the nigger act'. The Jim Crow laws were smashed. Segregation on the grounds of race, religion or national origin was banned and employment discrimination was made illegal. Martin Luther King called it 'the second emancipation'. Literacy tests were banned in the Voting Rights Act of 1965, and the Fair Housing Act of 1968 banned discrimination in the sale, rental and financing of property. So, what has an African-American got to complain about today?

The virus

Old habits die hard. History repeats. And why wouldn't they and why wouldn't it? I have tried to show that racism in America (and America is being named here because in my opinion it seems a bit more acute there. Many other countries could be substituted, including Britain) is entrenched learned behaviour, passed on from generation to generation. And if that wasn't the case, I wouldn't be writing this book because George Floyd and the many others would not have been murdered. The police brutality and discrimination, so evident in the southern states during the Jim Crow era, is still with us. American leaders and politicians, post-Civil Rights Act and to this very day (Trump, anyone?), continued and continue to embolden and rationalise racists and racism.

It is tempting to say that the racism and hatred are not as overt as the lynch mob days. And of course that is true. But then I think about George Floyd, his murder caught on camera. There are many others but, to get an idea, remember Naomi Osaka in the US Open wearing the names of murdered Black people on her face masks. Seven masks for her seven games. If there had been more games scheduled, she would not have run out of names to use. And then I think about the murders that were not caught on camera by bystanders. How many more do we not know about?

Examples of police brutality are plot lines in the third act, if you will. The story is far from over. Black people in America generally remain economically and educationally inferior. Their lives matter less. A point unequivocally proven when a virus showed up and locked down much of the world. Viruses don't discriminate, we were told. Yes they do. It was people of colour, who are poorer, less healthy, less valued and kept at the bottom of the pile, who bore the brunt.

Maybe we could call the racism covert. But it's only covert if you refuse to look. From the first two acts of dehumanisation and the deep-seated impact of centuries of brainwashing was born a system: institutional racism was designed to retain the racial hierarchy and make Black lives harder. It isn't about segregation or lynching any more. And, of course, that's a huge positive, but are we supposed to be grateful for that, say, 'Thank you, sir' and suck up the rest?

David T. Wellman, the author of *Portraits of White Racism*, a

1977 book which argued that racism was a strategy to defend social advantage, described the system like this:

> Culturally sanctioned beliefs which, regardless of intentions involved, defend the advantages whites have because of the subordinated position of racial minorities.

It is a vicious cycle which stops and obstructs people of colour getting the opportunities to better themselves. America is that wheel but it is happening all over the world, too. Housing, education, the criminal justice system, employment and the media are the establishments, or sectors, that keep the system spinning and they are all linked to keeping Black people at first base.

Let's break this down. If you are Black and living in America you are more likely to be living in sheltered, or cheap, housing. This means that taxes in your area are lower. Since taxes are used for social services, this means that educational provision in your area is poorer. This obviously leads to lower standards of education, and when kids do badly at school because they are denied resources? The criminal justice system comes calling. This is where the media gets involved, fond of portraying Black people as dangerous or feckless.

The media is powerful and influential in how they report and cover stories. I remember seeing in 2020 in one British newspaper, just two pages apart, a Black kid who kicked a policewoman termed 'a thug' but a white kid who killed a Black 14-year-old was a 'teen'. During the Hurricane Katrina disaster in New Orleans in 2005, I saw a picture in a newspaper of Black people wading through water with belongings held above their heads; the headline read: 'Looters'. A similar picture of white folks wading through water with stuff held above their heads had the caption: 'families saving their belongings'.

So this negativity influences judges handing Black people longer sentences. Which again leads to one-parent families, low employment opportunities, poverty, impoverished communities and ... housing disparity. We're back where we started. And that's not a list of complaints. These are statistical facts in America today.

A study by Brandeis University found that the average white family owns 700 per cent more wealth than the average Black family. Now, is that because Black people are lazy, stupid, more likely to commit a crime or any of the other slavery-era, before, during or after, tropes that were so enthusiastically encouraged? No. Of course not. It's because of that vicious cycle.

Why can't Black people get better housing? That's because from 1934 to 1968 the Federal Housing Authority would not give mortgages to people of colour. Neighbourhoods would be rated according to how suitable the people living in them were to receive a loan, big or small. Predominantly Black neighbourhoods were marked red and assigned the lowest ranking. Just for a second, cast your mind back to the pseudo-scientific theories of how the human race was ranked. You see, there is nothing new under the sun.

The same ranking system was used by the banks to deny loans to prospective Black homeowners and Black businesses. This was called redlining. African-Americans were also blocked from buying property in white areas because the banks said this would devalue white property, despite all evidence to the contrary. At the same time the government was subsidising builders to build homes, the requirement for getting the investment being that they could not be sold to Black people. It is estimated that Black families have lost out on at least $212,000 in personal wealth over the past forty years because their home was redlined. Such practices, like redlining, were supposed to have been made illegal in 1968. But the debate rages about whether it is still going on. What the governments were doing was segregating whites and Blacks through housing law.

And, as you would expect, the effects are still being felt. Without access to those loans, Black communities have suffered. Homes could not be improved, businesses could not grow or expand. Children could not go to college to further their education so that they could help themselves and their families going forward. The result is ghettos. Black people kept in their place, segregated from whites. Or, to use the term from earlier, a housing disparity which leads to low taxes, poor education ... and round and round we go. Let me just pause again here and address those who may still be saying, 'That's in the past.'

In September 2020, a biracial family in Florida decided they needed a valuation on their home because they wanted to remortgage. Their first valuation was for $330,000. They figured that was a bit low considering what other homes in the neighbourhood were being valued at. The wife, who is Black, thought to herself that racism was at play, and I can just hear the usual cry from the non-believers: 'Playing the race card!' or, 'She has a chip on her shoulder!' Anyway, the couple decided to remove all signs of anyone Black being associated with the house. They removed wedding pictures, photographs of their son, pictures of Barack Obama, pictures of

Black family members. In fact, all the photographs that were not just of her white husband and his family were removed. They removed books from the shelves by Black authors like Toni Morrison and Zora Neale Hurston.

Another valuation was sought and this time around the wife was not in the house when the surveyor arrived, neither was her son. They made sure of that. Lo and behold, this time the valuation was for $465,000, a full $135,000 more than when there was evidence of 'Blackness' in the house. The date of this story again? September 2020, not September 1920. And, as I said on television, these types of stories can be found quite easily on the internet by doing a simple search; they are not figments of the imagination.

Anyway, let's continue. An unfortunate consequence of those low taxes in poorer communities we were talking about is that they guarantee a lower standard of education. That's because 45 per cent of the education budget comes from local taxes. If the taxes are low, the school has less money. Less money for teachers, specialised tuition, class sizes are bigger. What can follow poor education? An introduction to the criminal justice system.

That criminal justice system, which has earned America the dubious crown of the largest prison population in the world and the highest imprisonment rate per capita, is biased against Black people. The number of Black convictions for the same crime is higher than white people. Black people account for 40 per cent of the US prison population but only 13 per cent of the country's population is Black. Surely history isn't repeating itself from when Black people were imprisoned in huge numbers post 'abolition'? I'm afraid so.

And we know that the cops who do the arresting are

historically racist. Examples abound (as we have already discussed) and entire books have been written about it, notably one by a former policeman, Norm Stamper, who worked in the Seattle and San Diego forces. It's called *Breaking Rank*, and exposes the everyday racism that dehumanises, like the language used on radio calls. Officers would use the call sign 'NHI', which stood for 'No Human Involved', when radioing in a Black death. Or, 'It's just an 11-13 nigger.' The code 11-13 was actually supposed to refer to an injured animal.

It continues. In January 2021 a police chief and patrol man in Georgia were forced to resign for making racist comments on their body cameras. They used the n-word and the police chief, a Gene Allmond, had this disgusting, ignorant take on slavery: 'For the most part it seems to me like they furnished them a house to live in, they furnished them clothes to put on their back, they furnished them food to put on their table and all they had to do was fucking work. And now we give them all those things and they don't have to fucking work.'

The UK is the same. Who can forget the tragic murder of Stephen Lawrence in south-east London in 1993? Stabbed to death at the age of eighteen while waiting for a bus, his killers went free because the Metropolitan Police were institutionally racist. Only after an inquiry (the Macpherson Report) years later, which found that investigations into the murder were 'marred by a combination of professional incompetence, institutional racism and a failure of leadership', did the family receive some justice. And I say 'some' because only two men were eventually convicted.

Did that report change anything in policing and justice? Well, a 2017 government report found that the colour of your skin is the most important factor in how you are treated by the justice system. It proved that if you put a white man and Black man in a courtroom on the same charge with similar evidence, the Black man was more likely to be denied bail, convicted and sent to prison. And when he was there, he was more likely to reoffend and more likely to die in custody. The UK's Sentencing Council found in 2021 that ethnic minorities have up to a 50 per cent greater chance of skin colour being a factor in sentencing. Unsurprisingly, the number of prisoners of colour has gone up – from 25 per cent in 2006 to 41 per cent today. Lots of reports happening but no real action, eh?

The US prison population went through the roof after President Richard Nixon launched a 'war on drugs' in 1971. Nixon's domestic policy chief, John Ehrlichman, said Black people and so-called 'hippies', who were protesting the Vietnam War, were deliberately targeted. 'We knew we couldn't make it illegal to be either against the war or Black,' he said. 'But by getting the public to associate the hippies with marijuana and Blacks with heroin ... and then criminalizing both heavily we could disrupt those communities.'

By the way, whites and Blacks use drugs in similar numbers in America but guess which group is more likely to receive prison sentences for drug-related crimes? Well, 13 per cent of drug users are Black but 36 per cent of arrests for drug-related offences are people of colour and 46 per cent are convicted. One out of three Black males in the US will currently go to prison at some point in their lives. Remember convict leasing? You don't need to because it is still happening.

If cleared by a doctor, an inmate is put to work, often earning as little as two cents an hour. There are convict-leasing partnerships with mining and agriculture companies. Some prisons make military weapons, others sew underwear for Victoria's Secret, or man call centres.

When people of colour are released from prison they will, on average, earn 21 per cent less than white people if they are lucky enough to get a job. And so the cycle begins again. As you would expect, the awareness of this cycle, this system, this institutional racism differs depending on the colour of your skin. More than half of Black people think racism is built into the laws, structures and foundations of American life compared to 30 per cent of white people.

Stepping away from domestic America for a moment, on the world stage the US was trying to keep the African man down. The 1974 Kissinger Report openly stated that US foreign policy was to slow population growth in Africa, specifically Nigeria, Ethiopia and Egypt, because it would lead to political, economic and military power. And that just wouldn't do, would it? So the US employed several measures to keep the worldwide status quo with America at the top and Africa at the bottom. They influenced birth-control programmes and threatened curtailing food supplies to states that did not comply. Those other states included India, Bangladesh, Pakistan, Indonesia, Thailand, the Philippines, Turkey, Mexico, Brazil and Colombia. I wonder what the common denominator between these peoples was?

In another echo of the past, the pseudo-scientists, or race scientists, made a comeback and, once again, Black people were experimented on. Between 1932 and 1972, 399 Black sharecroppers from Tuskegee, Alabama, who were suffering from syphilis, were offered treatment by the US Public Health Service. Initially, this study was to last six months. As the dates confirm, it lasted forty years. They received no treatment and instead were monitored for the purpose of studying the disease. When penicillin became available in 1945 as a treatment, the men were denied the antibiotic by researchers who lied about their conditions, preferring to continue to observe the effects of the illness. By the end of the study, only seventy-four were still alive – 100 were dead of related complications, forty of their wives had been infected and nineteen children had been born with congenital syphilis. No one was charged.

An entire book, *Medical Apartheid* by Harriet Washington, has been written about medical experiments on Black people. And people remember. The Tuskegee Experiment has been blamed for African-American scepticism about Covid-19 vaccines. *The Guardian* reported in February 2021 that only 5.4 per cent of vaccination recipients in the US were Black. The same month in the UK, figures were released that showed Black people and those of mixed heritage aged 70–79 were 31 per cent less likely to get the jab than white people in the same age bracket. Politicians keep on saying, 'The Black community doesn't trust the vaccine.' Perhaps more appropriately they should be saying, 'We have a history of abusing Black people, thus we violated their trust.'

Ah. Covid. How tragic that the illness has proven to be just another example of history repeating. The exposed, vulnerable, exhausted, maltreated, broken and malnourished slaves hundreds of years ago were more prone to disease. And in 2020 it was Black and ethnic minorities, the exposed and the vulnerable, who suffered most.

It is no coincidence that those groups, who have been kept at the bottom of the pile by institutional racism, are the ones who have suffered most. The American Public Media

Research Lab found that Covid-19 had killed one out of every 1,000 African-Americans at the time of writing, a truly shocking statistic. Data through to July 2020 showed that Black people aged 35–44 were dying at nine times the rate of white people the same age. Also, Blacks were three times more likely to be infected in the first place. That vicious cycle would prove to be lethal.

And, worst of all, they had died in greater numbers because they were trying to escape that cycle. Research has shown that young Black men were particularly vulnerable to Covid because of stress. The stress of two jobs, trying to work twice as hard (the rule of two, which Hope Powell spoke about), to provide for their families and to raise themselves up. Low-paid jobs in sectors like transport, the food industry and healthcare, which were often not protected by government bailouts, under-resourced neighbourhoods, poor diet caused by low incomes and the chronic underlying health issues which so often went hand in hand, meant Covid ravaged the community.

This wasn't just in the US. People of colour were disproportionately affected the world over because they are disproportionately worse off in life. In the UK, those of an African background had the highest chance of death, with a rate 2.7 times higher than that of white males; while for females the highest rate was among those of Black Caribbean ethnic background, at almost twice that of white females. The US healthcare system is, of course, infamously unequal, and because Black people are towards the bottom of the pile, they suffer poorer medical care. In the UK there is a health gap which means people of colour have more long-term illness.

Governments then have the gall to turn round and say, 'We

need more research to find out why this is.' Give me a break. It has happened because of the racist system they have upheld. And now Covid will start that vicious cycle all over again for so many families of colour, all over the world. Because they will, more than likely, be last in line to get the economic help they will so desperately need because of job losses.

Forgive me, but sometimes it's hard not to think that very little has changed.

CHAPTER 6

Show of Strength

With Ibtihaj Muhammad

There are people who have the power to force change. Naomi Osaka is one. Ibtihaj Muhammad is another. African-American. Muslim. A woman. Those are some pretty big hurdles to clear right there. Early on in her life she decided she was not going to apologise for who she was. She wanted to defy the system that put up barriers, obstructing the hopes and dreams of so many like her. And then smash them down. She did it. Even though she experienced shocking moments of discrimination and hate. 'Those spurred me on,' she tells me. 'To keep focused on the mission.'

Ibtihaj Muhammad is thirty-five. She won a bronze medal for America in the 2016 Olympics in Rio in women's fencing. She is the first ever US Olympian to compete wearing the hijab. She was a three-time All-American in fencing at Duke University. She mentors 200 kids at a foundation in New York City.

She has also found time to work with Special Olympics as global ambassador, helping to raise awareness about inclusion for people with disabilities. After her Rio success she was named in *Time* magazine's 100 Most Influential People. In February of the same year, she was invited to a private meeting with President Barack Obama alongside other famous Muslim Americans at the Islamic Society in Baltimore. He looked for her in the audience. 'Where's my Olympian?' he said. 'Stand up,' urging her to acknowledge the applause.

That sure is something. But America is not only a country where you can be picked out by the president; it's a country where you can be walking down the street and be accused of being a terrorist. That happened to Ibtihaj when walking through Times Square. A man – she managed to take a photo and put it on social media – followed her for several blocks and started shouting abuse at her. No one did anything.

Ibtihaj had started off our call by telling me she'd been for a drive-through Covid test – 'it was negative' – and the staff there asked her to pronounce her name.

'The guy's response was, "Wow, that's so difficult." He didn't even realise how damaging a comment like that is,' she says. 'It may seem simple, but taking the time to pronounce names correctly conveys inclusion and respect.'

This gives a clue as to why Ibtihaj is important. It's because she beat the system. Despite the roadblocks, she achieved and continues to do so. And that's why I wanted to talk to her. Growing up in Jamaica, being Black but protected from racism, is one thing. And what Hope Powell suffered was another in London. But (I'm not awarding points here) Ibtihaj was in it from the word go.

She grew up in New Jersey in a town called Maplewood.

Her dad is a retired police detective, her mum a teacher. She went to Duke University and graduated in 2007 with a double major in International Relations and African-American Studies, and a minor in Arabic. She was an outlier before she waved that sabre for her country. How did she do it? Well, she had parents who railed against the system.

'I was blessed with a mom who is an educator,' she says. 'She was always challenging us. And she held our teachers accountable; there was no getting one over on my mom's kids, you know, but not everybody has a parent, or parents, like mine. And I always wonder what happens to those kids who have working parents or who are maybe being raised by grandparents or an aunt or an uncle, and maybe they don't have the time to put in or they don't know that maybe their teacher, or someone whose care you've placed your child in, does not have your child's best interests at heart.'

Ibtihaj started to realise that her pathway from childhood to adulthood was littered with problems. From the town she grew up in, to how her school split children up in classes based on their colour.

'There were things that were happening in my town – and I like to think of Maplewood as progressive – that were the norm growing up. And now as an adult, I see even how systemic oppression was prevalent in my township. In middle school, high-school kids made fun of you for being from "the Black side of Maplewood". And back then I wasn't really aware of the township being separated literally along lines of colour. But it was. Because of *redlining*.

'As a young person, I had no idea that this was happening, not only in my town, but all over the United States. Where

I grew up homes were only being sold to African-Americans on one side of town. Recently the school district was found guilty of allowing racial segregation of schools and class-rooms, by grouping students based on perceived abilities, essentially systemically discriminating against Black students. I knew something wasn't right when I was a kid – often only one or two or three African-Americans in my classes – but this case didn't reach the Supreme Court and [wasn't] ruled unlawful until 2020. How is that possible?'

That's a tough realisation to come to as a child. That your colour of skin is something people can use against you. When she was younger and her parents warned her that life might become difficult as she made her way in the world, she remembers saying to them, 'Nah, white people aren't like that.' It is the very picture of the innocence of youth. Fast-forward a few years and Ibtihaj is wiser. But she is not negative. She speaks at a thousand words a minute, with her enthusiasm and positivity crackling over the Zoom call. Even in bleak times she manages to turn it on its head.

'I feel really moved by what has happened this year with the protests for Black lives,' she says. 'Because it's not just people of colour who are having that realisation that systemic racism seeps into every part of our daily lives. There are people who are like, "Wow, I had no idea this was happening." That's here in the US, and I know that's happening in Europe, too. Even though these are difficult conversations to have, this is our reality as Black people. It hurts, but at the same time, it's a welcome respite from this lifelong marathon that we've been running since we were born. We're given half as much and expected to thrive and to live, but not given the same access, the same opportunity or the same chances. And that's why that whole idea of the American dream and pulling yourself up by your bootstraps, it's a false promise.'

Bootstraps? From where I'm standing, I'm not even sure if they give you the boots in America.

'Right, because you can work really hard and not have the same opportunity because of colour.'

Even in sport, where all are supposed to be equal until the starting pistol is fired, Ibtihaj found that there was discrimination. She would have to be doing twice as much training or practice to be talent-spotted or get the same amount of credit as an athlete who was not of colour. She could have given up, weighed down by the 'baggage' of what she looked like, particularly when the environment in the US fencing team had, on her account, turned toxic. Ibtihaj uses the term 'psychological warfare' and was made to feel like a 'pariah'. Her coach allegedly accused her of being lazy and faking injury. Lazy, huh? There again, it stems from the old 'scientific evidence' produced by the quacks all those years ago. But we are told we should 'move on, it's a long time ago'.

Ibtihaj tells me she endured years of racist behaviour from staff and some team-mates. Her name was omitted from official team sheets, she was excluded from team emails and not invited to team dinners. She apparently told USA Fencing about her treatment. Nothing was done.

'I was the only woman of colour on the US women's team in its history, but when I think about my team-mates, they just kind of had the opportunity to go out and compete, they're not bringing anything with them. I had to show up and be exceptional. In order to be accepted. You have to kill it every single time and be damn near perfect, just to get a seat at the table. And they don't have that pressure. They just get to be like, "okay", and lose sometimes and not be fierce, not be ferocious. There was pushback for me, always.'

But it's important to make the point with Ibtihaj that it is not just about the colour of her skin. It's the fact that she is a proud Muslim and that she wears a hijab. America's ill-treatment of Black people is long-standing, so she suffers it from one side. America's ill-treatment of Muslims is, perhaps, a relatively new thing since 9/11, so she cops it from the other side, too. Ibtihaj's mom remembers being screamed at in the street in the aftermath of the terrorist attacks and feeling worried about the safety of her family. Twenty years later, Ibtihaj is accosted in the street, eyed with suspicion at airports when travelling to compete in national qualifying and, at a conference in Texas, ordered to remove her hijab. When explaining she couldn't, the security guard said, 'You're in Texas now.' It is difficult to imagine what her life is like in that context of almost continual harassment. And when I ask her, it is hard to hear because she uses the word 'fear'.

'I always feel like, you don't want to show any of those people that you're afraid of them. Even though there is real fear, I have to show that I am *not* afraid. And I feel like that every day when it comes to wearing the hijab, because people always have these misconceptions about Muslim women, about us being docile and oppressed and not having a voice, and feeling like they can cut you in line at Starbucks or be rude to you at the airport or whatever it is.

'I feel like I'm always trying to show people a different image of Muslim women, one that's strong and totally challenges their misconceptions that they have, but also, at the same time, showing a different image of Islam in general, one that contradicts the really dark terror-driven storyline that people have about Muslims. The kind you see perpetuated in the media and Hollywood and on the news. I always feel like, I can do that with a smile. I can do that by just engaging with people. But I can also do that by being strong. And that's something that I feel like I carry with me all the time. You always feel like you're on edge. Because you're like, "Why are you trying to mistreat me right now?" Is it because I'm Black? Is it because I'm Muslim? But, honestly, I don't really care. I'm going to show you just how strong Muslim women and how strong Black women can be.'

It must be exhausting. I don't disagree with Ibtihaj. How could anyone? There is nothing wrong with showing strength or showing that you are not afraid. It is what millions of Black parents are trying to tell their kids. Or, rather, not to confuse a 'show of strength' with being arrogant or disrespectful, particularly when it comes to the cops. But, of course, it is what the supremacists want. They want fear.

'Yeah, I'm not saying that with rose-coloured glasses on. Get rid of them. When you look at the conversations that Black parents are having with their very young Black boys, especially after Tamir Rice was killed, it was, "Whatever you do, do not put your hood on", "Whatever you do, when you get pulled over, put your hands on the steering wheel, yes sir, no sir, yes ma'am." And the kids will say, "Why?" because that's just what kids say. But the question really is, "Why?" And what can we do to change it?

'The answer is education.' Her words, said without a prompt from me. Maybe her mother and my mother being teachers has us thinking similarly. Ibtihaj took it upon herself to learn about Black history and the history of America because, as the years ticked by from childhood to adulthood and the discrimination got worse, a switch was flicked. She realised this was happening because there was no education in America about Black history. 'As a young person, I don't ever remember thinking, *Wow, our education system sucks.* This is something I realised as an adult.'

Black history is not taught in America. Unless you think it started with slavery. And it sure doesn't go into the kind of detail that I have gone into. Ibtihaj recognises that there is a huge knowledge gap, a chasm. And that is the true point of difference between people of colour and white Americans. People of colour are taught only one thing – that they were former slaves. This reinforces that white superiority. The second issue is as important. People of colour are lied to about their history because for decades governments have been worried about what might happen if they knew the truth. And white people don't want to know the truth because of shame, embarrassment and, frankly, they like their position at the top of the chain.

'I think that the US owes it to the Black community to teach Black history, because the way I see it, Black history is American history, right? This country was built on the backs of enslaved people. And to ignore that is to ignore our history, and its totality. How do you not teach about the ways in which people were stolen from their land? Literally treated as a commodity?

'I'm a child of African-Americans, but I think [ignoring of history] is a major part of why my parents converted to Islam in the 1970s. And if you look at Black history in this country, you see a great deal of African-Americans leaving Christianity and converting to Islam. It was like an effort to kind of shed a faith that was passed on to them by their oppressor, when you think of who was brought from the west coast of Africa to the Americas. A lot of the Africans were Muslim. So these great lengths that slave owners went to, to separate families, to shed you of your culture ... slaves were beaten for speaking their native tongue or trying to practise their faith, and they used the Bible as justification for enslaving these people. It was like, "Look here, even God says that you're inferior to us."'

She's right. In Genesis 9:20–21, Noah demands a curse on Canaan, the son of Ham.

'Cursed be Canaan! The lowest of slaves will he be to his brothers.' Noah then blesses Shem and Japheth, declaring, 'Blessed be the Lord of Shem! May Canaan be the slave of Shem. May God extend the territory of Japheth ... and may Canaan be his slave.'

This text was used to argue that the slavery or subjugation of the Black races was, in fact, God's word. Pastors and writers argued that the word 'Ham' really means 'Black' or 'burned', and refers to Black people, and God commanded that the descendants of Ham become slaves to Japheth, who, they argued, represents white people.

'My parents wanted to kind of offset what our school and what our public education wasn't giving us. So learning about our history as Black people in this country was really important to my parents – even when I think about picture books that I read, as a kid, it was a lot of Jackie Robinson, Althea Gibson, of course, Muhammad Ali and Ella Fitzgerald, and people like that. But African-American studies was something that I kind of owed to my ancestors, to understand their plight and their fight and their resilience. I truly believe that we exist today, and continue to exist, because we're resilient. And even just being unapologetic about being Black in this moment is an act of resistance.'

And it's not just Black history. History repeats even though it is forgotten. Donald Trump's Muslim travel ban was born from the Muslim backlash post-9/11. And it could be argued that was learned behaviour from Japanese internment, when the US government rounded up people of Japanese descent after the Pearl Harbor bombings in 1941 and put them in isolation camps in California, Washington and Oregon. It affected almost 120,000 people. And they were all American citizens. The government had considered rounding up Italian and German families, too. Until they realised this was unpopular. Why? Because they looked like them. This is not taught in American schools, either.

Ibtihaj has travelled to Nigeria and Ghana to visit the different ports and castles where slaves were kept in dungeons for months before being shipped to the Americas. She wanted to learn more about the atrocities that were committed against Black people, to understand where African–Americans come from, and why those things happened. You don't need to be Black to be interested in that, because it is everybody's history. She has also been to Rwanda to learn about the brutal civil war there. She tells me the first thing you have to do when getting off the plane, by mandate of the government, is to visit the memorial so you understand better the country you are in.

'And then I think about the US,' she says. 'And it's like they don't want to talk about anything, what they did to the Native Americans, what they did to the Japanese, what they did to African-Americans, what they do today, to the people at the border [with Mexico]. The South Americans who are coming up across the border now. We don't even want to talk about the horrific things that are happening. So how can we say, "Okay, we'll never make that mistake again", when we won't even acknowledge that we did it in the first place?'

The answer is to teach it.

CHAPTER 7

History Lesson

'History is written by the victors' is one of those sayings that can divide a room down the middle. Those who reckon that history can be interpreted and is based on studious fact-finding with a fine-tooth comb on one side, and on the other those who say the winners have the power to shape the past, present and future through the spoils of victory. The answer might be found in the fact that no historian is quite sure who the original quote can be attributed to. The Nazi Hermann Göring at the Nuremberg trials or Winston Churchill, who liked to joke that he intended to 'write history myself'. History is complicated, confusing, harrowing and hurtful. Perhaps that is why over the years there has been a drive to make it simple and easy to understand. We want our history to be basic. To be clear. Complications and confusions give rise to complicating and confusing emotions. People want their history in black and white.

But history is two things. It is what actually happened. And it is what you are told happened. Only if you have the time and inclination for the former do you realise that the latter has sold you down the river. At school we are told what is easy and convenient. There are not enough hours in the school day to unpick every who, what, why and when of the past. So we have to be selective. And that brings me back to our starting point. History may or may not be written by the victors, but it sure as hell is taught by them.

Given the oppression, dehumanisation and brutality suffered by Black people throughout the ages, who do we think decides what is taught? Is it the oppressed or the oppressor? The 'master' or the 'slave'? The abuser or the victim? It is those who have the opportunity to lead politically and culturally, who have the power to decide the storylines and timelines of the history textbook that kids flick through, the statues you see in towns and city centres, the films you watch. Those who have the ability to push to the front narrow, self-interested personal opinions about why the world works as it does and why it should continue to work in that way.

I think history has been taught in my lifetime, and the many, many preceding years, from the perspective of people who want to retain the status quo, the hierarchy, if you will. And guess what? Those making those calls have not been Black. With so few Black people in those positions of political and cultural influence down the years, it is perfectly understandable that the history we have been told is from a narrow political and cultural perspective. In short, we've been taught a white history. One that isn't too complicated, confusing, harrowing and hurtful. One that continues to oppress and dehumanise Black people.

I am slightly embarrassed to say that when I was a kid in

school in Jamaica fifty years or so ago, I hated history. All those dates and facts were not for me. Maths was my thing. But I was turned off by the subject matter in history as much as anything. If you cast your mind back to your schooldays for a second and consider this question: what were you taught about Black history?

If you are honest, you might say you were taught 'all' about the slave trade. To most folks – and the folks who decide what goes in the textbooks – that is where Black history starts. Africans taken to the Caribbean and America on ships, hard labour, treated appallingly, emancipation. Phew! Thank goodness that unpleasantness is over. Now we can move on to Britain's Industrial Revolution and the civil rights movement. But we are going to pause here. Let's think for a moment about the impact for Black people of what was taught about slavery. I can tell you about my own experience, for a start.

I was taught about slavery at school, and maybe this is what turned me off the subject in the first place, in a way that made me feel I was a lesser person. And by that I mean I felt that somebody, somewhere, was saying to me, 'Hey, this is where you came from, so don't get ideas above your station.' My ancestors were brought over in chains from West Africa. So I should be grateful that my race had 'progressed' and those days were gone. There was very little focus on the ills and brutality of the slave trade. And if anything there was a romanticisation of it. That may be surprising to hear because this was Jamaica, but don't forget we were a colonial island back in those days so it was the British who decided what was taught and how, and you can't blame them for that. Anyone else would have done the same. The British role in the slave trade was not taught to me at school. Nor to my sister, Rheima, who is twelve years older, or Marjorie, my other sister, who is ten years older. But this is where I have a problem with the majority of our leaders after independence. Jamaica got independence in 1962 and most other islands achieved theirs not long after that. Have the teachings changed to reflect our experiences in the Caribbean? Have they changed to reflect the 'new knowledge' of what really took place in our history? Is it wrong to have a more balanced curriculum, teaching both sides of the coin instead of what was convenient for the colonisers? I know it may take time to make adjustments, but I left high school more than a decade after independence and the same lessons were being taught and have continued to be taught for many decades since. Usain Bolt, as we have heard, had to teach himself too, and he came three decades after me.

The story of Kunta Kinte in *Roots* is a case in point when it comes to the romanticising of the slave trade. You might have sat through the TV miniseries at school. A godsend for teachers who perhaps felt uncomfortable dealing with the harsh realities and consequences. They just put the video on. It is one of the most viewed series ever in American history. There's nothing particularly wrong, or inaccurate, with the television series, which was adapted from the bestselling novel by the esteemed author Alex Haley, one of the most famous African-American writers of all time, and is based on his own family history. But it is a story that is more acceptable, shall we say, because its adaptation from the book seems to reinforce the ideas (eventually) of opportunity, the American dream and that 'everything was all right in the end, see?' My problem is, that is what most people's knowledge, or lesson, on slavery or Black history amounts to. It was a palatable version for the masses.

Another palatable version for the masses was how the British Empire is taught. A plucky nation of islanders took to the seas to bring civilisation, infrastructure and riches to poor, basic and illiterate folks all over the globe who didn't know any better. Who were fortunate to wake up every morning with the Union flag fluttering above and being led by a people who were the most ingenious and modern force ever, growing an economic system from country to country to benefit all and sundry. They built the railways in India (but don't dig too deep to enquire exactly why — it may have had something to do with transporting the bounty to the coast for shipping to far-off lands). They abolished slavery.

Then there is Christopher Columbus, who is revered in history lessons. The title with which he is remembered gives a clue – Explorer. Wow. Just the word conjures images of bravery, battling against the elements, the unpredictable nature of the cruel sea, on a mission to the unknown, eh? He spread the word of God, too. Heroic stuff, we were taught. There he was, forging paths to undiscovered lands so that trade routes could be established and all could prosper. Endangered his own life to prove that the earth was round — that was another one.

The truth — which has rarely been taught — is uncomfortable. I want to try to redress the balance somewhat. We have been taught acceptable, idealised versions of elements of Black history. And then vast swathes of it were left out. Mr Columbus is a good starting point, I think, largely because whenever I hear his name I am reminded of a song . . .

I and I old I know
I and I old I say
I and I reconsider
I and I see upfully that
Christopher Columbus is a damn blasted liar
Christopher Columbus is a damn blasted liar
Yes Jah

He's saying that, he is the first one
Who discover Jamaica
I and I say that,
What about the Arawak Indians and the few Black man
Who were around here, before him
The Indians couldn't hang on no longer
Here comes first Black man and woman and children,
In a Jam Down Land ya
A whole heap of mix up and mix up
A whole heap a ben up, ben up,
We have fi straighten out,
Christopher Columbus is a damn blasted liar
Christopher Columbus is a damn blasted liar
Yes Jah

It's by a Jamaican reggae singer called Winston Rodney, stage name Burning Spear. Rodney was a contemporary of Bob Marley and, like the great man, proof that you don't have to be a politician to be able to have a say over what is taught. This was an example of someone with the skills and ability to teach through music, to lead through culture.

Winston was an educator. He brought the ideas of Pan-Africanism – Black people coming together to show solidarity after enslavement and colonisation – and self-determination to the ears of millions through his records. Anyone hearing that song in the 1980s might have been moved to go and do their own research. Many people would have learned that Christopher Columbus was not the man the textbooks said he was. But unfortunately, just like the music of Bob Marley, too many listened and danced without actually hearing.

Columbus might be better remembered as a murderous mercenary. His goal was to find new land for the Spanish to rule over, and be rewarded with 10 per cent of the profits and governorship. In the 1490s he actually set out for Asia, only to end up in the Americas. He first arrived in the Bahamas, where the Arawaks lived. And yet the history books tell us that Columbus 'discovered' the New World? How can something be discovered if people are already living there? The answer lies in arrogance and self-belief of supremacy.

These were the observations he made in his diary at the time:

> They do not bear arms, and do not know them, for I showed them a sword, they took it by the edge and cut themselves out of ignorance. They have no iron. Their spears are made of cane. They would make fine servants. With fifty men we could subjugate them all and make them do whatever we want.

Columbus exploited this 'ignorance' and inflicted a reign of brutality – raping, pillaging and murdering. The Arawaks were set to work to find gold to send back to the king and queen of Spain. He promised them 'as much gold as they need and as many slaves as they ask'. Anyone who disobeyed was killed or had their hands chopped off. Upon landing in Cuba, the Dominican Republic and Haiti, the violent spree continued. We know this because his journals were translated by a Catholic priest called Bartolomé de las Casas. In his book, *History of the Indies*, he wrote: 'There were 60,000 people living on this island [Hispaniola], including the Indians; so that from 1494 to 1508, over 3,000,000 people had perished from war, slavery, and the mines. Who in future generations will believe this?'

Who indeed. Columbus should be remembered as one of the founding fathers of the slave trade. And his crimes should be remembered as state-sponsored genocide. Instead, American children have been taught he discovered their country – he never set foot there and millions were already there anyway – and he was rewarded with Columbus Day, the holiday that celebrates America's 'discovery'. And let's not forget my little island, Jamaica. He 'discovered' my birthplace in 1494. This is history written to ensure the status quo as the Europeans being superior to other races. How does it happen and why does it happen?

Is it as simple as embarrassment or shame? Is it, and apologies for the crude term, a public relations stunt? Perhaps the truth of how Columbus achieved what he did would have been so unedifying that there would have been some mass hand-wringing in Europe and crisis of conscience, although I doubt it. It proves that once you tell a lie it just gets bigger and bigger until it is out of control.

Whitewash

This brings us nicely to the British Empire and the way its purpose and consequences have been taught in schools. It's not so much a lie as a deliberate indoctrination of British people against the horrors of what was committed in their name. If people were truly educated as to what the empire was, what it did to people, then how could a civilised Western nation produce a YouGov survey in 2016 which found that more than four in ten Britons view the British Empire 'as a good thing and colonialism as something to be proud of'. Only one in five Britons thought the empire was regrettable.

The initial reaction to that latter statistic might be: 'what cruel people'. But they don't know the truth. They were not properly taught. What the empire actually entailed has been largely ignored in British schools. And to be clear, I'm talking about the human suffering it caused. Yes, it appears on the curriculum but if it's really being taught properly, how do you explain that statistic above? Maybe the answer is in the sort of attitude that meant in 2014 the national curriculum in England was changed, removing a focus on racial and ethnic diversity. Also, a study of exam data in 2020 showed that only one in ten secondary school pupils studied the empire. There is widespread ignorance that colonial rule, imperial rule, call it what you want, is this: invade another country, take away the indigenous population's freedom, steal their resources, exploit their labour. Some experts in the field say that the British have 'forgotten'. I'm not sure the wider population were ever conscious of what was happening in far-flung lands, let alone aware of the atrocities that were taking place.

Is the true, horrific partitioning of India ever properly taught? Britain carved up India and Pakistan in 1947 along religious lines, resulting in more than a million people dying in sectarian violence. Or how about the famine in Bengal four years earlier? Winston Churchill diverted food to British soldiers while 4 million starved to death. In total, 29 million Indians died of starvation during British rule. Most people, and rightly so, remember Churchill as a great wartime leader. But he really was writing his own history when he blamed the deaths on Indians for overbreeding. 'I hate the Indians,' he said. 'They are a beastly people with a beastly religion.'

The Boer War? Fought over diamonds and gold in land that the Boers felt was theirs. The British imprisoned more than 100,000 in concentration camps and up to 30,000 died. And what about the Amritsar massacre in India? In April 1919 a crowd protesting against British rule were fired upon. In ten minutes, 1,100 were injured and between 400 and 1,000 protestors were killed. It would have been more but for the British running out of bullets.

And what about the Berlin Conference? Have teachers really been able to adequately describe the misery? Britain and other European powers had been colonising Africa since the 1870s. They were hungry for the continent's resources to fire their industrial economies. It was known as 'the scramble for Africa'. France, Germany, Belgium and the Brits would colonise countries so they could take what they needed. In 1885 this colonisation was rubber-stamped by the Berlin Conference. In exchange for making all this thievery look fair and justified, the promise was made to end the overland slave trade. The *Lagos Observer* reported, 'The world had, perhaps, never witnessed a robbery on so large a scale.'

The European powers carved up the continent with a ruler here, a pencil there, a rubber there. You have this bit, we'll have that. The goal was to avoid military conflict with each other. They had no issue with using force on the ground against the indigenous people, however. This crude dividing up of a continent, with no respect or even knowledge of the areas they were bagging for themselves, is something Africa continues to suffer from to this day.

The most infamous, and horrifying, result of the conference was the emergence of the Congo Free State. This was a personal playground for Leopold II of Belgium. Unfortunately, his idea of fun was to kill up to 10 million Africans through war, starvation and disease.

Why, in my view, is none of this properly taught? Perhaps because the lives of these people did not matter. The British considered them inferior, either because of the colour of their skin, or because of their religion or culture. The British believed they were superior, which was why they invaded in the first place. Maybe it is also not taught today because of overwhelming guilt. Sorry is the hardest word to say, for sure, but a collective outpouring of 'we were wrong' is nigh-on impossible. The human psyche is hardwired to rarely admit fault, however big or small the crime.

The British curriculum asks teachers to cover topics that educate students about Britain's place in the world. Surely, they would be better off knowing that place in the world, and how the country is viewed by others, including the former colonies, if they are told the truth? It is not my place to say the British Empire was good or bad. But surely both sides of that particular coin need to be taught so people know where they came from and how their country came to be. In primary school, the words 'slave' and 'colony' are absent from the curriculum. Africa has one namecheck.

And, of course, it is difficult to hear about the bad things. And the bloody things. But, by and large, the things the British Empire did that are likely to make people feel uncomfortable and guilty are ignored. There is a huge chunk of history left out between what happened to Charles I and the start of the First World War. It's about two centuries' worth. The eighteenth and nineteenth centuries shaped the Britain we know – and love, by the way, as I don't want anyone to get the idea that I'm some sort of hater – and its role in the world. So teach it. And if you do that, you have an enlightened, educated society. One that understands the importance of 'bloody foreigners' to the nation's fabric, the impact of Black people and the importance of allies and people working together for common goals.

The most significant whitewashing of history by Britain is its role in the slave trade, it seems to me. The Atlantic slave trade is only taught in schools in the UK so they can get to the bit where it can be explained that, in fact, they shouldn't feel too guilty because they were big players in its abolition.

This is Black history 101. The slave trade existed, here's a picture of some sharecroppers with their tools, it was unpleasant. And then the bulk of the learning is the British portrayed as the cavalry coming over the hill. There is a nice meme that does the rounds on social media which sums this up well. On one side is a picture of a cuddly dog with the caption 'The Brits in British history books', and on the other a snarling dog with the words 'The Brits in every other history book'.

It is true that Britain played a significant role in ending

slavery. They finally did so in 1834, twenty-nine years before America. But forty-two years after Denmark. William Wilberforce, the MP who was the leader of the abolitionist movement, took twenty years to convince parliament that slavery should be illegal. In that time more than 750,000 Africans were transported by British slave ships. Wilberforce is a name that is taught in Britain's schools. He was the guy who wielded the stick. But not much is known about the carrot of reparations. As we know, this was the scandalous 'compensation' scheme which rewarded slave owners and demanded slaves work for another four years to earn their freedom. In 1834, Britain spent 40 per cent of its budget (taxpayers' money) on compensating slave traders.

And this is a big reason why the powers-that-be want it forgotten. It creates awareness, which leads to anger, which leads to protest for justice. But isn't anger greater when you find out that you have been lied to? Isn't it easier to forgive when you have received an apology? The British government has never apologised for its role in the slave trade. And it never will. That's because of instead of saying things like 'We regret it', which is the official line, they were to hold their hands up and say 'Sorry', they would leave themselves open to legal challenges from the ancestors of the real victims and that would cost them a whole load more money. So it is swept under the carpet. It is my belief that they think that if they started teaching this stuff – deeply, with feeling and the horrible truth – they'd have to start paying for it. So not much is likely to change.

Few people are told that Britain received around 200 years of free labour. And that Britain's economy was built and modernised off the backs and toil and agony of enslaved people

which, at the last count, came in at more than 15 million individuals. Port cities like Glasgow, Bristol and Liverpool were
rich in the eighteenth century because of slavery. In 1700,
Glasgow's population was around 12,000, and this quadrupled
in 100 years. Glasgow was the port that received the majority
of the tobacco from the colonies. Liverpool grew wealthy
from plantation cotton and Bristol's riches were largely down
to slave-produced sugar. And there was London, of course,
which was the busiest slave port in the world.

Canals and railways were built as a result of the investment
of profits from the slave trade and taxes were kept low because
of the wealth generated, stimulating further investment. This,
in turn, played a role in the Industrial Revolution. Modern
Britain was built on slavery. Streets are named after slave
owners, statues put up. Money was given to iconic institutions
like the British Museum, Royal Academy or Tate art gallery.
The Bank of England, railway companies, insurance companies and the Royal Mail all benefited from enforced labour.
It is an uncomfortable truth. And some will say undeniable.
But so far they are doing a good job of denying it.

Likewise the carnage that was left behind. The Caribbean
is poor and playing catch-up on educating its people. Post-
colonialism, 60 per cent of the islands' Black population were
illiterate. Disease and poor health were rife because for hundreds of years people were brought up on a sugar-based diet.
That was what was produced so that's what they were fed. We
are still feeling the effects of that today, with the Caribbean
having one of the highest rates in the world for heart problems, while Barbados and Jamaica are listed as 'amputation
capitals of the world' because of the rate of diabetes. Shouldn't
there be true reparations for that damage?

This selective history has damaging consequences that you can't really show with statistics and percentages. How does it make a Black British person feel when they do their own research about what really happened? They might feel that their country has deliberately lied or hidden things from them, doesn't value their contribution or culture, doesn't see them as truly part of the fabric of the nation and, worst of all, has fed the racist abuse and discrimination that has marred their lives. It's enough to give someone a chip on the shoulder. To suffer a personal crisis.

When people start researching these periods in the past, some might end up wishing they hadn't. A person of colour might feel cut adrift, unable to trust, respect or recognise the society that they wanted to be accepted by. But how could one ever be accepted by a society that refuses to educate its people with honesty and truth about why that society behaves as it does?

A fair and equal society would teach a fair and equal history. But we know society is neither of those things. So a fair and equal history of Black people is not taught. It is not because Black history started when they put the first set of chains on a Black person and transported them from one continent to another. That is the history that has been chosen. And I'm talking all over the world now. So what else could be taught? There is plenty to choose from. History that could not just empower Black people but say to them: there is more to us than this. Only teaching slavery as Black history, it seems to me, compounds those ancient, ground-in feelings of low self-worth. Even just a small tweak to the curricula would raise us up. We need to rise and that *we* is universal. Black and white would benefit from the full teaching.

I am not a history scholar by any stretch, but even from the amount of research I have done, I know how beneficial it can be to read 'good news' about Black history. And there are so many positive stories, not just the often ignored fact that everybody's family tree has roots in Africa, the cradle of civilisation, and that the continent gave rise to the first great empires. I have picked out three moments in time that could be added to syllabuses. I bet they will surprise you . . .

Pre-Columbus African explorers

A good starting point, given the apparent obsession with reminding Black folks of their subjugation, might be to skip back a few years and question the lie of 'discovery'. There is a wealth of evidence that African explorers were in America hundreds of years before Columbus.

African presence in the 'New World' has been dated as far back as prehistoric 40,000–6,000 BC. The Nubian-Kemmiu (from modern-day Egypt) arrived in the Americas around 1200 BC, while the Mandinka from West Africa arrived about AD 1307.

There is nothing sensational about this, save for the fact that, as part of the concealment of African history, it has rarely been taught. Leo Wiener, a Harvard linguist, was one of the first to challenge the status quo with a three-volume book called *Africa and the Discovery of America*, pointing out that Columbus himself is the chief witness. Wiener says that in his *Journal of the Second Voyage*, Columbus wrote that Native Americans had traded in gold-tipped metal spears with black-skinned people. These spears were inspected and found to be identical in terms of their ratio to gold, silver and copper alloys found in West Africa. Black 'settlements' were also reported by European explorers post-Columbus in Florida, Venezuela and St Vincent.

Historians, linguists, botanists, anthropologists and archaeologists have all since conducted research to show that there were Africans in America pre-Columbus. Portraits of Africans in clay and stone have been found in South and Central America pre-dating Columbus, and vast statues of African heads were discovered in the heartland of the Olmecs, the first civilisation in Mexico. Bananas, yams, tobacco, cotton and peanuts – all indigenous to Africa – were found in Central America. How else did they get there?

Septimius Severus

Julius Caesar is the name most people recall when they hear about the Roman Empire. He came, he saw, he conquered. But not many know about Septimius, the African emperor from 193 to 211. Yes, you read that right. There was a Black Roman emperor. He was also one of the most important, responsible for making the empire the largest it had ever been, at more than 5 million square kilometres. He was born in Libya, Africa, and died in York, England.

Severus was hailed as the emperor who brought a century of peace to Britannia, repelling and defeating the Gauls and Saxons, and giving the country semi-autonomous rule. He rebuilt and restored Hadrian's Wall.

He also had a hand in the most famous example of Black Romans in Britain. A military garrison had been set up by Severus at Burgh by Sands, near Hadrian's Wall, with the African auxiliary unit Numerus Maurorum Aurelianorum stationed there. It's often cited as the first Black community in Britain.

The City of London, known as the Square Mile, was defined by Septimius because he ordered its walls to be built. In Rome he reformed the law and was hailed as an emperor for the people because of his generous spirit and the lavish games that he staged. The aristocracy hated him.

You can see his bust in the hall of the British Museum. But you won't know he was Black because it is in alabaster stone. In the era of empire it would have been painted the right colour to denote the colour of his skin.

The Moors

Black people used to rule the world. They were called 'the Moors'. Moor was a synonym for African. William Shakespeare used it to describe Black people, likewise his contemporary Christopher Marlowe. But the word has also been used in the context of describing the reign of Muslims in Spain and Europeans of African descent from 711 to 1492.

In 711 a group of North African 'Moors' captured Al-Andalus, which is known today as Spain and Portugal, sparking historic change in Europe. The Moors' advances in mathematics, astronomy, art and agriculture helped propel Europe out of the Dark Ages and into the Renaissance.

Education in Spain would become a basic right at a time in Christian Europe when only 1 per cent of the population was able to read and write. The Moors had seventeen universities in Spain – in Almería, Córdoba, Granada, Jaén, Málaga, Seville and Toledo – compared to only two in the whole of Europe. In the tenth and eleventh centuries, public libraries in Europe did not exist, while Spain could number more than seventy, including one in Córdoba that housed hundreds of thousands of manuscripts. Universities in Paris and Oxford were established after visits by scholars to Spain.

The Moors represent just one African civilisation. There are scores that pre-date European civilisations. Why are we not taught about the trade routes to Asia from West Africa? Or the amazing architectural works of Great Zimbabwe?

How do we teach?

So that is the 'what' sorted out. But just as important are the how and by whom. To truly level the playing field in life, children of colour have to be taught in the same way and treated the same way. And, as herculean a task as changing the curriculum seems, it is probably nothing compared to changing minds. Deep, inherent bias exists, as we know, and the damage that has been done is, sadly, irreparable for many people of colour. None more so than the organised racism in the British school system in the 1960s and 1970s.

Often while researching this book and talking about it, I have found myself saying, 'Well, nothing surprises me.' But this did. The West Indies child in 1970s Britain was termed 'educationally subnormal'. It's a shocking statement and one that you may think is hyperbole, but it is true. And it was all done in the name of racism. Black children were considered 'problematic'. So huge swathes of them were taken out of the normal school structure and placed in special schools called ESN schools. The ESN stood for educationally subnormal. Previously they had been called MSN schools. Mentally subnormal.

And why were they deemed so? For the simple reason that they were different. For some reason it came as a surprise to the authorities that, after encouraging West Indian economic migration after the end of the Second World War, the children of those coming to the country to work might find it difficult to adjust to a completely alien way of life, particularly as some had been separated from their parents for several years. Often parents would send for their children only when they were settled with work and a home. And when kids are displaced, troubled and anxious they tend not to do so well in class. The response of schools, one would have hoped, would have been to recognise this and help them fit in. But no. Schools didn't want them, with many accused of institutional racism, arguing: 'If the Black kids do well here, more Black kids will come ... and we don't want that.' So local authorities dumped them in ESNs. By 1970, in 'normal' London schools, 17 per cent of pupils were from ethnic minorities. In ESN schools it was 34 per cent.

What was an ESN school like? Well, if you were in one you were almost certainly damned to a life of low-income jobs. Children barely received an education from teachers who couldn't care less. Steve McQueen, the revered filmmaker of *12 Years a Slave*, went to an ESN school in London when he was a kid, struggling with dyslexia and feeling like an outsider. He said: 'Even though we were from different backgrounds and races ... we all knew we were being fucked over. There was no help ... you were left to your own devices ... there was no interest.'

The man who exposed the endemic levels of racism in British education was Grenadian writer, and later politician, Bernard Coard. Coard was a teacher in ESN schools. He had gone to England in 1966 to do a master's degree at Sussex University. After completing it he began a PhD in development economics. He ran evening clubs for children from seven schools for the 'educationally subnormal', and then taught full-time at two other ESN schools. What he saw at those schools shocked him. He discovered 'that the system was using the ESN schools as a convenient dumping ground for Black children who were anything but "educationally subnormal"'.

Outraged, Coard decided to write a book to expose the scandal. In his pitch to publishers, he promised to reveal the racist policies and practices of the education system, the racism in the curriculum itself (nothing has changed, eh?), how teaching expectations were minimal and how destructive the situation was. No publisher would touch it. So the Black community raised funds and two Black publishing houses took on the book, printing 10,000 copies. All were sold. It was called *How the West Indian Child Is Made Educationally Subnormal in the British School System: The Scandal of the Black Child in Schools in Britain*. What happened next was extraordinary. Coard was called a liar, he was threatened, followed and spied upon. And this was done by the government.

Coard wrote of the reaction: '[Education] spokespersons denied everything. They said on radio and TV that the book was "a pack of lies". Within days, based on the feedback they were getting, they amended their position to: "There is some truth in it, but most of it consists of lies." By the third week of sustained publicity, they said "most of it contains some truth, but there are many untruths too".

'The other aspect was Big Brother-like,' he said. 'My phone was tapped by the first night of publication. My wife and I were sometimes followed by security personnel. Finally, our 11-year-old nephew, who was spending his holidays with us, was harassed by police in our presence (deliberately so). My nephew was even threatened with a trumped-up charge, with the sergeant in charge all the time looking pointedly into my eyes, seeking to gauge my reaction and clearly trying to send me a message: if you think you are a tough guy, we can always pick on your 11-year-old nephew to whip you into line.'

But the Black community, white teachers, student teachers, university students, trade union leaders and, crucially, the media wouldn't let the story drop. After six months, education authorities finally admitted Coard's book was 100 per cent accurate. Strangely, the abuse, phone-tapping and threats all stopped. ESN schools were eventually closed down.

If you were a Black child at school in Britain in the sixties and seventies and you succeeded, you did so in spite of the system. Coard's book urged Black communities to set up their own 'supplementary schools', which operated on weekends. More than 150 of these schools were set up. Some of them taught the real Black history. Steve McQueen went to one in Hammersmith and another in Acton.

He learned that 'there is a problem and the problem isn't you' and was rescued from a pathway that would have seen him leave education altogether at thirteen. 'You are marked, you are dead, that's your future,' he said. He discovered a love of art and learning.

All's well that ends well? Not quite. There are consequences to actions. And the consequences of those days were grave and continue to be. As Coard wrote only recently, those ESN children are the grandparents and parents of today's kids.

'Large numbers of [Black children] are being suspended

and excluded from schools, or placed in "special units" or streams. For many reasons true then as now, Black boys were affected far more than Black girls. The lesson to be learned for today's problems in the school system is that they were "hatched" decades ago, in the previous two generations. When society fails one generation of children, it lays the foundations for similar, even worse failures in the generations to follow. We human beings "inherit" not only through our genes, but often also from our social circumstances.

'Those in charge of the education system have chosen not to seriously address and solve the problems. Instead, they have shifted around the problem; even sought to hide it from view. Yes, they (eventually) closed down the ESN schools. But they found other ways to shunt Black children with educational difficulties (emotional, cultural, medical, and so on) into a corner and essentially ignore their needs – and potential – rather than put the resources needed into addressing them.'

Those other ways are what are termed alternative provision (AP) and pupil referral units (PRUs). ESN but with a different name, say critics. These 'schools' are for children who have been excluded from school, have behavioural problems that a school can't (or doesn't want to) handle or have complex needs or illnesses. Black Caribbean children are to be found in PRUs at four times the expected rate.

A Black child retaining his or her position in a proper school does not solve the problem, however. Even if they complete the course, as it were, barriers are still being put up to stop them progressing the way others might. In 2000, Ofsted, which inspects schools in Britain, commissioned a report to examine links between race and educational achievement.

It found that, although there had been a dramatic rise in exam pass rates in the 1990s, children of colour were not part of that uptick. They were left trailing behind their white peers. Across the country African-Caribbean, Pakistani and Bangladeshi pupils were markedly less likely to manage pass grades in the core subjects than their white and Indian peers. And African-Caribbean and Pakistani pupils were further behind their white peers than ten years previously.

Shockingly, one local education authority in a city showed that African-Caribbean pupils entered compulsory schooling as the highest-achieving group but left as the group least likely to pass five subjects at a C grade or above. In all six of the local education authorities that provided data on pupils based on ethnicity, the level of attainment by Black kids fell below the average as they moved through the system. And, in one of the largest local education authorities, Black children entered the system twenty points above the national average. And left twenty-one points below the national average as the lowest performers.

David Gillborn, co-author of the report, said: 'This is a shocking report which underlines the need for some form of national monitoring. Black pupils often enter schools ahead of their white peers. It is scandalous that they fall behind and end up in restricted ability groups.' As you would expect, when in a 'restricted ability group' or AP or a PRU, you are not going to receive a very high standard of education.

And who by?

It is not just about what you are taught, though. It is who you are taught by. And just like the rest of us, teachers are susceptible to the same brainwashing that I have described in this book so far. They are part of a society that promotes systemic racism, so they reflect that. Just like every walk of life does.

In my life, teachers are revered. I have four members of my family who are teachers. My mother taught for fifty-odd years and eventually became a headmistress; my eldest sister taught; my younger sister's daughter taught; my eldest daughter teaches. So it's important I make this point now: I am not singling out teachers or saying they are the problem. I just want to explain how they – and you and me and everybody else – are part of the problem. But teachers can, and probably will, go a long way to start to solve it because of their compassion and professionalism.

Sadly, the bias, stereotyping and racism people suffer starts as soon as they enter the classroom. A 2016 study found that Black students in the US are nearly four times as likely to be suspended as white students and nearly twice as likely to be expelled. Black pre-schoolers – that's an age range of two and a half to five – are 3.6 times more likely to be suspended. At the time Black girls represented 20 per cent of female preschool intake, but made up 54 per cent of pre-school child suspensions. The study was conducted by the US Education Department, canvassing more than 50 million students, and was called 'disturbing' and a 'systemic failure'.

We don't even have equality in the classroom at that young age, so it is hard not to throw your hands up and say: 'What chance do Black folks have in life?' The answer is, very little, particularly in America. That's partly because they have something which is, depressingly, called 'the school to prison pipeline'. You have to consider for a moment the fact that the problem has got so big, there is even a buzz phrase for it. And it starts with these school suspensions. This is how the New York Civil Liberties Union describes it:

The School to Prison Pipeline operates directly and indirectly. Schools directly send students into the pipeline through zero-tolerance policies that involve the police in minor incidents and often lead to arrests, juvenile detention referrals, and even criminal charges and incarceration. Schools indirectly push students towards the criminal justice system by excluding them from school through suspension, expulsion, discouragement and high-stakes testing requirements.

So, because of this bias and these resulting suspensions you have pre-school kids, on their very first day, prone to being fed into a system which can see them end up in jail. You've got to plug the pipe. How do you do that?

Not long after that study the Yale Child Study Center, a department at the Yale University School of Medicine which conducts research and supports children and families, thought it a good idea to work out why these suspensions were happening. The answer is not surprising: the bias that is created by the system is reinforcing the system. And in most cases teachers aren't even aware they are doing it. It's unconscious. And these biases are present in white *and* Black teachers.

The research showed 135 teachers a video of a classroom with a white boy and girl and a Black boy and girl (all actors).

They were being asked to detect 'challenging behaviour' or 'behaviour before it becomes problematic'. There was no challenging behaviour in the videos. And yet 42 per cent of the teachers identified the Black boy as challenging.

At the same time, the teachers' eye movements were being tracked. This technology found that teachers 'show a tendency to more closely observe Black students, and especially boys, when challenging behaviours are expected'.

The second part of the study asked teachers to read a description about poor student behaviour and then decide what action they should take: suspension, expulsion or none. Some of the teachers were told the children were called typically Black names, DeShawn or Latoya. Others were told the behaviour descriptions were by kids called Jake or Emily.

Results showed that white teachers went easier on children they thought were Black while Black teachers were harsher. The *Washington Post* reported:

> Researchers said that the racial differences in their response are consistent with the theory that white teachers see Black pre-schoolers as more likely to misbehave, so they don't see a Black child's misbehaviour as severe. Some teachers received background information about the child's difficult family life, to test whether such additional information might spur a more empathetic response. The empathy kicked in only when the teacher and the child shared the same race.

Teachers expect problems from Black kids. And at a heart-breakingly young age, too. The results prove how deeply rooted racial biases are. Don't take my word for it. Walter

Gilliam, who led the research, said: 'Implicit biases do not begin with Black men and police. They begin with Black pre-schoolers and their teachers, if not earlier. Implicit bias is like the wind: You can't see it, but you can sure see its effects.'

Thankfully there is good news. Teachers don't want to be racist, unconsciously or otherwise. They believe they are there to help kids grow and learn. They are there because they really love their job and they love kids. I know all those teachers in my family would say this. No teacher is in it for the glory or the money. So only one of those 135 teachers wanted their data withdrawn from the study. I wouldn't want to speculate as to why but the other 134 were embarrassed by the findings and are already making a difference and, as I said, helping to start to solve the problem. It would be great if these studies and their results were highlighted more so that people could learn from the experiment and realise the existence of this unconscious bias. If you're not aware of it, you can't fix it.

In Britain, this same bias exists. In 2010 a study found that Black schoolchildren were being systematically marked down. Low expectations from teachers damage their prospects because their unconscious bias is telling them 'these kids aren't smart'. The study found that when you took the teacher out of the equation and conducted an external assessment, the children performed better.

The study was done by the University of Bristol. One of its co-authors was Simon Burgess, a professor of economics. He said that the issue was particularly pronounced in schools where there are fewer Black children. 'What is worrying is that if students do not feel that a teacher appreciates them or understands them, then they are not going to try so hard,' added Burgess.

One teacher trying to tackle that is Jeff Harriott. Jeff is originally from Australia and is now a head of school in Manchester. He sent me an email after he saw my speech on Sky Sports. He was spot-on with what he wrote to me about teaching and education:

> Make sure we are part of the solution and not reinforcing the problem. I guess it's a bit like trying to open a locked door and no one will give you the keys. We can bang and bang but ultimately we have two choices: we can walk away, it's too hard, continue our ignorance, continue to restrict what's on the other side, or we knock the thing over and open up new possibilities. Our curriculum is an ever-evolving piece and what you have said this week is ensuring that we are even clearer on what we need to do. Your voice, your comments, you will have an everlasting impact on our school.

And I guess Jeff's words helped me to find the confidence to go ahead and write this book, just like Thierry Henry's and Ian Ward's did. I dearly hope some of these pages will be used as an educational tool. Clearly, Jeff was a guy I had to speak with. We managed to find some time for a Zoom call just before the end of the 2020 summer term, with Covid still rampant, of course, denying us the chance to meet face to face. He was in his office, looking weary after a hard day, and he was open and honest about the exact sort of bias that can have an impact on a child of colour's teaching. We talked for nearly two hours. In that time, he described in detail the multiple problems that the education system faces. Teacher attitudes, multiculturalism being used as a badge of honour by schools and nothing more, the gap of understanding between students and teachers about cultures and subcultures, and the lack of role models in popular culture and in family life. Combine that with what I have already discussed – what is being taught and what is being reinforced – and we have quite the perfect storm.

He immediately told me a story about his early days in teaching, which resonated strongly with that Yale study. He was teaching a class that had a Black boy, who we will call Philip, whose mum was from Zimbabwe. Teachers had struggled to control the class as a whole but when Jeff turned up 'all was good'. After all, he was an Aussie. And they can get on with anyone. Philip loved his accent. He would talk to him about *Neighbours*, the TV soap opera, and kangaroos. But then the relationship started to break down. It is probably best that I let Jeff tell the story because his experience is frontline, real-life stuff and can add some context to the numbers and the data from that Yale study:

I lost this boy. His behaviour and schoolwork continued to go down. And I continually blamed him for the behaviour. 'This is my classroom, this is what it should be like, you need to be like this.' I had no understanding of him, I had no understanding that his mum had come over from Zimbabwe to get away from the dangerous situation in the country. I had no understanding that his mum was also working really long hours, that his mum would hit him because she didn't know another way. So this was going on at home and then he was coming into school with me, who had no idea about that, no knowledge of Zimbabwe, no knowledge of his culture, no knowledge of any of those things that actually would allow me to teach him effectively. It was all about my worries, not about his worries.

And Philip hit me once and I lost it. I marched him down to the headteacher's office. But actually him doing that was the best thing that ever happened to me. Not straightaway because I wasn't intelligent enough at the time and I wasn't ready but since then he's made me sit back and go, 'Do you know what? I didn't do anything for Philip.' I didn't know Philip, I couldn't tell you what Philip needed. I wasn't there for him. I had no understanding of what it was like to be him. It wasn't that he wasn't responsible for his behaviour, but it was me who was responsible for the environment for him to behave in.

This is what I think happens too much in teaching, and particularly towards Black boys. Teachers don't understand what the boy is going through, and they see him as a threat. They're not developing the relationships well enough with Black boys. As a teacher, you've got to be passionate about different cultures, subcultures, understanding them, to be able to say that, 'You can be whatever you want to be in the world but these are going to be your barriers; this is who you are, and you need to understand who you are to find a way around them.' And it's a really important thing. And for me, one of the big problems is that not enough people try to walk in somebody else's shoes or understand what somebody else's feet are doing.

Jeff felt he failed that kid on a personal level. And that is a big thing to admit to a guy he had just met on Zoom. I have no doubt there are many teachers all over the world who might be able to relate to that story. And I am sure, knowing teachers as I do, that many have sought to improve. But, unfortunately, it is just one cloud in that bleak-looking sky. And it's the first on the horizon. As Jeff says, if we've got teachers who can't relate to children of colour, and have no experience or understanding of their culture or life, then as soon as that kid takes their first steps through the school gates they are heading for a fall. I asked Jeff to try to pick through the problems that the education system needs to solve. And we started with one of those buzzwords, which politicians like to throw around but don't really know what it means: multiculturalism. Jeff says that some schools do it too. They say, 'We're multicultural.' So does that mean that school has students of colour? Is it just a box ticked? Or does it mean they have students of colour and they are trying their best to understand them? For those schools, Jeff thinks it is the former.

'In schools that I have been in, that struggle, they say they are multicultural, but it's just a group of different cultures together. It doesn't mean that school understands all of the different cultures, that schools embrace all the different cultures,' he says.

'Schools will hold events for Eid, for example, and that's an easy one to talk about. You either really do it or you pay lip service to it, which is to hold a party or a festival or something like that. But if you are *really* going to do it, and the really good schools do, you have to understand what Eid means. What does it mean to those people? What does it mean to their lives? Not just, "We're going to have an Eid party, an assembly and walk away." For us, 500 kids have to be immersed in that. Developing empathy for others is key.'

Instead, Jeff asks the kids to talk among themselves about

different cultures, to explore the cultures of their friends. In his example of Eid, he will encourage his students to ask questions, debate what it means to people and try to get them to 'walk in someone else's shoes', and to make comparisons with their own lives. That's a trickier experience, for sure, than holding a party. The child, just like the adult, will remember the party or the event, not any of the reasons for who, what, where and why they were holding that party. They will connect with the good time that they had rather than the human element.

And this gets to the very heart of the issue because if we have teachers who are struggling to identify with people of colour and their culture and students too, we have a system that can create outsiders. And I don't need to tell you that the child who doesn't feel a part of something is going to have to be extremely strong-minded to do well. And, most important, they are unlikely to find a role model to help. Just as Jeff admits that he couldn't help Philip. Role models for children at school, Black, white, everyone, are fundamental to a good education.

We can also not ignore the important fact that kids don't always have great role models at home or in their families. It can spell double trouble for a teacher, just as that Yale study suggests, when they are not only trying to understand the child but also the family, their culture and their subculture. And trying to find common ground, some chemistry or a small bit of trust to help bridge the gap.

'It's a constant battle,' Jeff says. 'Some kids' cultures are this hybrid of their parents', their grandparents', but also their own. I previously taught a boy whose idol was his uncle, who was regularly in jail. And his uncle was a drug dealer but his uncle had the latest trainers, his uncle had the latest PlayStation, he had all the bling, and that kid loved it all. And a lot of that is reinforced on social media or in the movies.

'I've worked with kids who have themselves been drug dealers, or couriers, so they get given money to take a package somewhere or they get new trainers or the latest phone. I think the youngest one, not at my current school, but the youngest one I've known about in my career was seven.'

How does a teacher deal with that? It is hard for a kid to see all that fancy stuff and not be impressed. Who wouldn't be at that age? Jeff told me that a teacher coming down hard on that 'subculture', if you will, was only really succeeding in widening the gap. But nor can they be seen to condone it. So he tries to use people of colour from the public eye to try to help his students.

Luckily for Jeff, John Amaechi, a basketball player who went to the very top in the NBA, went to school just round the corner at Stockport Grammar. Amaechi, fifty, is a psychologist now and was the first former NBA player to come out. He has visited Jeff's school twice to talk to the kids. And anyone who has heard him talk about white privilege and racism on a couple of video blogs for the BBC cannot fail to be impressed and inspired. But not every school is as lucky to have someone like that on their doorstep.

'It's a real challenge to continually find and hold up people. But we've been holding John up and saying, "Be this guy." But that's just one guy. You need this base of people to hold up. We're constantly looking for awesome examples of people changing the world, constantly finding a range of role models within our curriculum to hold up and say, "You could be this." I think we've got about thirty languages in our school.

Whether it's Asian girls, Black boys, Black women, we have to be able to show those kids people to be inspired by.'

And this enforces the reason why we have to re-educate folks in our history. Why we have to reveal the great things Black people and people of colour have done in the past to show that there are role models and have been role models who should have been taught about. The Black race has been great for centuries, producing role models who've been hidden or airbrushed into oblivion to make sure the false narrative of white superiority isn't upset.

Jeff's thoughts go back to Philip, who would eventually leave for America with his mother. He doesn't know what happened to him. The system, and the people in that system that Jeff described, failed. 'I regret it,' he says. 'And the problem is, when you fail a kid as a teacher, or that kid gets a reputation because of that failing, it can have an impact on the entire school. You could equate that to a dressing room, perhaps, in sport, when a captain or coach doesn't give a misunderstood character what he or she needs. Discontent can spread and long-term damage can be done. It can be a self-fulfilling prophecy for all concerned. The teacher thinks the pupil is a problem, so the pupil becomes a problem.

'They're there in a box that says, "They're going to be troublemakers", because the teacher has decided they're going to be troublemakers. To a lesser extent, you get it with staff looking at families, if they've been in school for a long time, and they go, "Well, his brother was like this", therefore, they're like that. So they've got this preconception of what the family is going to be like, and that's the difficulty – getting past that preconception is really, really important.

'I always talk about Philip because he reminds me that

without an understanding and an empathy, you shouldn't be in a classroom; you will hate it and forget why you loved the job so much in the first place. It becomes hard to breathe. And you stop thinking about what you're trying to achieve. You start thinking about survival. I imagine it's a bit like a batsman facing you when you were bowling. The batsman goes in with the best intentions, but then they'll fall back into survival mode. And that's what I think happens in a lot of schools – then you get a fear of Black boys or any of that sort of stuff because your brain's not in the right place to think this is what they need, they need understanding, they need somebody to be there for them, that charismatic adult sort of person.'

I have huge admiration for Jeff. And I know he won't mind me describing him as someone who, in the past, had personified the problem. That's because he now personifies the solution. Be like Jeff. He admits that he was ignorant of facts and circumstances. But he proved people can adapt and learn. He used to be afraid, now he isn't. Fear is at the very core of this issue and he has overcome it. But you still have to ask that question: what are people afraid of? What is it about Black people and people of colour that for centuries has made people attack and subjugate them?

CHAPTER 8

Fear

With Michael Johnson

I know a thing or two about what it's like for people to be afraid of you. I made a career out of it. When I was a fast bowler, the batsman at the other end, a lot of the time, would have been scared. That was because he feared that he would be hit. I bowled at more than 90mph. Sometimes that fear would be greater than that of him being embarrassed or losing his wicket. He might suffer physical pain. He might not. The thought would have been at the front, or back, of his mind. It was all part of the challenge of elite cricket.

But I also now know, as a much older and wiser man, that when the West Indies team that I was part of were beating every team out of sight, we made others afraid. And not just those batting at the other end. Not just the opposition. We personified the white man's greatest fear. There I was, and there we were, showing superiority, showing dominance and a ruthless attitude to get what we wanted. It was why, among some sections of the media, we were so unpopular. They called us 'muggers' or used derogatory terms associated with violence. That fear is sometimes at the front, or back, of the mind with a lot of folks when it comes to Black people.

Fear underpins this entire story. Black people are afraid of being abused, discriminated against. In extreme cases there is a fear of physical violence from those who are supposed to protect them. They are afraid of speaking out or being labelled a troublemaker. We know that. Ibtihaj Muhammad spoke eloquently about fear. It is the central, crucial, constant force that ensures the survival of the system that we have described. One that keeps Black people at the bottom.

But the system works another way, too. It tells white people that Black people are uneducated, that we're poor, that we're aggressive, that we're low-skilled, that we don't look like them, we don't behave like them. We are other. Be afraid. For Lord forbid what would happen if we were ever to rise up, take over and exact our revenge. In the cricketing context – and I absolutely note the small measure here – the West Indies cricket team did that.

And it is something of a taboo. People don't like to talk about it, admit it or recognise its importance. So let's bottom-line it. Let's put it down in black and white, if you will. White people are generally afraid of Black people.

Well, that's my opinion anyway. Am I wrong?

'Not to me,' Michael Johnson says in his distinctive deep voice. He's sitting in front of a sideboard showing off a few trophies and the iconic gold shoes that carried him to the double Olympic gold for the US in the 200 and 400 metres in Atlanta in 1996, and the 400m world record in Seville three years later.

'You know something?' Michael says. 'My wife often says, "Why are white people so afraid all the time? They're always afraid, what are they afraid of?"'

Johnson is not a man who does anything for the sake of it. On the track he won four Olympic golds and eight World Championship golds. He is still the only man to have won both 200m and 400m events at an Olympics. He is a true sporting great and there probably aren't the words to do him justice. When he stopped competing, his opinions and voice were in high demand. And it would have been easy for him to say, 'No thanks', or even just to offer up a few platitudes now and then. But now he's a true great in his commentary role for the media, too. That is down to his presence and authority. And at the start of our call, I admit to being slightly star-struck meeting him in the past. I was in the same lift with him once at an awards dinner and I really wanted to speak with him and tell him that I was a fan. But I didn't. 'Then you robbed us both of a moment,' he laughs.

The guy has an aura. And it is even noticeable on a video call. When Michael Johnson speaks, you listen because you *know* there's a story to be recounted. So, we're going to have a go at trying to answer his wife's question. But there's a story worth recounting at this point, which I share with Michael.

It's 1990 and Louis Farrakhan, the leader of the Nation of Islam, a civil rights group which combined elements of Islam and Black nationalism, is taking questions from white Middle Americans on *The Phil Donahue Show*. Farrakhan, another guy who could grab your attention, has calmly and brilliantly described the subjugation of the Black race for hundreds of years. How everything that gave them an identity was stripped from them – names, culture, language, religion. You name it.

Then a white woman stands up and, presumably in an effort to try to explain or defend systemic racism, says this: 'What scares us, I think, is we hear *violence*.' Farrakhan has made controversial statements in the past and I don't endorse everything he has ever said. But his reply was perfect then. And it is perfect now.

> Isn't it sad that we who have been the victims of so much violence ... now whites fear violence from us. We do not have a history of killing white people. White people have a history of killing us. And what you fear, it is a deep guilt that white folks suffer. You are afraid that if we ever come to power, we will do to you and your fathers what you and your people have done to us, and I think you are judging us by the state of your own mind and that is not necessarily the mind of Black people.

A year later Rodney King was beaten at least fifty-three times with batons by four Los Angeles policemen. We know that because it was secretly recorded. All four were acquitted in court, sparking the six-day LA riots. I'm talking to Michael only a few days after white supremacists have stormed the Washington Capitol, cajoled by President Donald Trump. We've not yet even mentioned George Floyd, Breonna Taylor, Jacob Blake, Michael Brown, Tamir Rice, Trayvon Martin.

'What we saw at our Capitol building and all of that, people are starting to see now this is really jacked up. I think that there's just a tremendous amount of fear,' Michael says. 'There was an amazing video that I reposted on my social media last summer when all of the riots and protests were going on. People were crashing, smashing windows and things. And there was this one Black woman, very passionate, talking to a reporter. And she said, "Look, you guys broke the contract. You said that we were equal, you said that we have all of these rights. We have all of this justice. We haven't seen any of that – you're killing Black people. We don't have opportunities. You broke the contract. We didn't." And then she said, "So that's all we're out here doing is trying to get your attention to let you know that we're not gonna stand for it any more. And all we want is equality." And she looked directly at the camera and she goes: "And y'all are *lucky* that we don't want revenge."

'And we don't. You know, even families who have lost loved ones because white police officers killed them because they were "afraid" don't talk about revenge. That's what they will say. So it's not our fear. What does a white police officer say after he shot an unarmed Black man? "I was afraid." Or, "I felt threatened."'

Going back to what Louis Farrakhan said, it is perhaps not surprising that white people have that fear. Those who do know of the punishment and abuse that Black people have been subjected to, and those who have been brainwashed to still believe that we deserve that punishment and abuse, will no doubt reckon they are justified for thinking that way. It's not surprising at all. As I said, for some it will be at the back of their mind. For others at the front. But there is a scale of fear. The fear of orchestrated, violent revenge at one end. At the other there's physical intimidation. I'm thinking back to that incident in the lift when I was in Australia. And how the media love to portray Black people as dangerous and violent. And, let's be honest, a lot of white people might see a young Black guy on the street, strong, tall, and be fearful. They will fear being robbed or attacked. They've been conditioned to think that way.

But for Michael, the fear is something different. Sure, he recognises that physical 'threat', but he sees it in a more subtle, dangerous way that ultimately led to those rioters trying to overturn the 2020 US election. And it's more dangerous because of the way Donald Trump was prepared to say what Michael terms 'things other conservative politicians thought, and would work away in the background trying to achieve, but would never actually say'.

'I think the bigger fear from white people is that they will have to compete now,' he says. 'I think that they know that they have privilege and they don't want to lose that. People don't like change. They *do not* like change. So they don't want to lose that privilege. Look, what is privilege? Privilege means you get priority status over other people. That's what it means. Come on, Mike, you were an athlete, I'm an athlete, we get some privilege, right? It feels *good*. But at the same time, if that privilege is at the expense of someone else, then, to me, it doesn't feel so good. And in this case, *it is* at the expense of someone else.

'It's hard now, it used to be easy. Growing up as a young white man, as long as you stay out of trouble and do the right things, you're gonna succeed in life. That's not the case for young Black men. Right? That was always the case for young white men. While it's not where we want it to be, there has been a tremendous amount of progress. And that progress has made it more equal for a lot of people. And that means that a lot of young white people or young white men now have to compete and they don't like that. It doesn't feel good. So they are afraid. "Yeah, I'm gonna have to compete, too. I am no longer gonna have this privilege." I think that's part of it.

'The conservative movement is all about stopping change.

The progressive movement is all about continuing to move forward and evolve as a society and as humans and they don't want it. What does "Make America Great Again" mean? It means, "Take us back to when it was great for white people because we were on top. Take us back to when we owned the land and when we owned the Black people."'

Michael then surprises me. He tells me that the suicide rate in the US among white males is 'out of control'. And after our call I go and find the data. He is right, of course. According to the American Foundation for the Prevention of Suicide, white middle-aged males account for 70 per cent of cases.

'Is that because of progress made? When you have Black CEOs of companies, you have a Black president, you have Black people starting to actually be in positions of power, you now have a young white man going to interview for a job, and where always before it was another white man sitting across from him it may now be an Hispanic woman, or a Black woman, or Black man, or an Asian woman. So you have to compete. Previously you were *up* and the only way that's going to equal out is, you know, in order for Black people to start getting those equal opportunities, is for you to come *down*. That's what equal is. That's what equality means. Everybody's on the same page. But if one is up and one is down, in order to equal out, yeah, you're gonna have to give us something. I know that people don't want to hear that, but you gotta give it up. You got to give up the privilege.'

Michael's perspective is interesting. And it's very specific. It really does get down to the nub of the issue, if you like. The guy handing out the jobs is not necessarily white any more. But it also gives a different slant on equality. The idea that for everybody to be level, someone has to lose out? I don't believe in real terms that when you bring one up, the other has to come down. The key word, I think, is that *mentally* people believe they are being brought down. That's because they are so accustomed to having that white privilege that when they no longer have it, they think they have lost something. They are not losing anything in real, physical terms.

'Yes, because they're so used to it, some of them don't even *know*. So yeah, you're gonna have to give that up. Because you're up here, because you've been put up here, this country has been built in a way to actually put you up there on top. We *have* to acknowledge as well that America has been built and established in such a way where it is unequal, it is completely unequal. And it's tilted in favour of white people and white men. And even to a point where some don't even know it.

'When the conversation sort of rose to prominence, there were many who said, "I didn't realise I had this privilege, I don't want it, I don't feel good about this." So it's very interesting, but I think we have to be very careful about that idea of bringing someone down for someone else to come up. But at the same time, I think we do have to do it. If that's an uncomfortable situation or a conversation, you know, I think we have to have the uncomfortable situation. It is needed. The only time I want to bring someone down is when they're somewhere they should *not* be. And when you have this privilege, and you have deliberately been put in a group of human beings who are seen as on top of another group of human beings, that shouldn't be the case. And so, yes, *you* need to come down.'

The 'conversation' that Michael is referring to, of course, is the waves of Black Lives Matter protests in the wake of

George Floyd's death. It would be wrong to say that he had an 'awakening' about what racism was or its toxicity, but he felt that it was the time to speak and to react as if there had been a sort of 'our time is now' moment.

'I have always been outspoken in regard to my thoughts, my position. I rarely hold anything back,' he says. 'But I have been much more outspoken as of late. Because I think that I just finally have had enough.'

Growing up in Dallas, Texas, Michael did not really experience racism. It was a close, multicultural community bonded by the fact that 'we were all struggling'. Only when he moved out of his community did he start to notice something was up. At high school in 1986 a white friend of his called Martin Luther King Day 'that Black people's day'. Michael was taken aback. 'I just thought, *Huh, there's something not right about what she just said.*' When he went to the predominantly white Baylor University in Waco, Texas, he was left in no doubt.

'I was targeted, for sure. I fought back. It might be the n-word, or something like that, so you push back. This is what happens, people say these things, and I gotta stand up and defend myself. But is there anything that can be done to stop it? I can stop it in a moment with a fist on your lip, but that's it. But it's taken years, decades even, for me as an individual to recognise that I need to do something about this. And I need to be a part of the community. After my athletics career I started to feel like I needed to be part of the solution with regard to making change, actively making change. I can tell you that I always felt, as a Black athlete, that I had a responsibility to my Black community to represent them well, and to sort of defy the stereotypes and that sort of thing.'

But there was one incident that enraged Michael. It was the death of 25-year-old Ahmaud Arbery in Brunswick, Georgia, in February 2020. Naomi Osaka wore his name on a face mask in the US Open. Ahmaud was out for his usual daily jog on a Sunday afternoon. The sun was out. The birds were singing. It was the same jog he'd been doing for years. Neighbours would see him and say, 'There goes Ahmaud.' Unfortunately, a white father and son had taken exception to Ahmaud's run that day. They followed him in their white pick-up truck. And when he ran past them, they shot him to death with a shotgun. We know this because, again, it was all caught on camera. And yet the police were dragging their feet on the investigation until that video came to light.

It would still take countrywide protests for anyone to be arrested and charged. Michael was involved in those protests. He took part in a 2-mile run to apply pressure, raise awareness. In May, Gregory McMichael, a former police officer, and Travis McMichael were charged with murder and aggravated assault.

'I don't know why but, for some reason, that one just really hit me, touched me in a different way,' Michael says. 'And I think part of it was, I just thought there's a very good chance the men who did this are going to get away with it, and that burned me up. That just really pissed me off, like *nothing* else. And then, of course, we just had more and more incidents, like George Floyd. But I'll be honest and say, it's hard when it's just you. And I think that it's become much easier for me when we have other people speaking up about this so that you feel like they are in it with you.

'When I've looked at the Black Lives Matter movement and seen all of these young people out there, Black and white, of all different ethnicities, marching for equality, marching for social justice, nobody knows who these people are. If I've got a platform, then I owe it to myself to be supportive of them, or to them rather, and to do what I can. And I've always wanted to do that. I've always been a big advocate for sport for social change, you know, and been involved in starting organisations and working with organisations to use sport for social change around the world. But to be honest, prior to this year, I've done more of that work outside of this country than I have in my own country. Because, again, I think we just sort of get numb to it at some point.

'I think there's a conservative effort to make us numb to it in this country. We had a Black president, what more can you ask for? Right? You know, you start to get lulled into that false sense of security. And I think it was a big wake-up call for a lot of us. The Covid pandemic meant everyone's kind of at home, you have a little bit more time to focus on things, everything slows down, and to see this white police officer with his knee on George Floyd's neck, killing him, or see this privilege that Amy Cooper exercises over a Black man . . . it's just horrible.'

Ah, yes. Amy Cooper. She was the young woman who, when out walking her dog in New York City's Central Park, took exception to a Black man asking her to put a leash on her dog, as per the rules. She called the police. 'I'm taking a picture and calling the cops,' she said. 'I'm going to tell them there's an African-American man threatening my life.' The man's name was Christian Cooper (no relation). Of course, he was not being threatening in the least. And, by the way, we only know this because Christian filmed the encounter.

Fortunately, Christian was not harmed (Cooper underwent

racial-bias training). But it is an important moment because, for a start, it reinforces the idea that white people are terrified of Black people. And, second, that they have the privilege of phoning the police and using the term 'African-American' knowing that the majority of the time the police will turn up – and darn quickly, too – and believe her. And not the Black person. And that's when tragedies happen. When murder becomes part of arresting.

'There was an example just the other day, a perfect example of it,' Michael says. 'A Black man's family called 911 because they needed assistance from health and human services, because he needed psychological help. So 911 sent the police. They killed him.' Right. And they are able to get away with it because the police can play the fear card. 'Oh, we thought he had a gun.'

'Not only is there fear, fear has become weaponised. It has become a defence mechanism and also become a weapon for white people. I realise now that this stuff has just become normalised. And it shouldn't be normal!

'I think back to the discussions I've had with my son about how to behave if the police turn up. He's twenty now but the first time we spoke about it was in his early teens. He's tall, he's athletic, he was starting to be independent, go out on his own. And I think back and it's crazy! At what point did this become normal? My dad had that conversation with me, my brothers, my sisters. That's ridiculous, absolutely ridiculous.'

Of course it is. And that's Michael Johnson saying it. An American idol, legend. Someone who the majority of Americans were more than happy to revere when he was king of track and field, to bask in his reflected glory and claim him as one of their own. But here he is talking about being made to feel worth less than those people. Having to sit his kid down and tell him his life is in danger because of the colour of his skin. And it's been happening for hundreds of years. He is not alone. The author Candice Brathwaite, in her bestselling book about Black motherhood, *I Am Not Your Baby Mother*, writes about leaving London with her small son because she didn't think it was safe to raise him in that city. So even when Black people do great things, nothing changes. And often they do those great things because they think it will help to make it stop. That they will be seen as equal. Or be accepted.

CHAPTER 9

Acceptance

One of my earliest memories is from when I was six years old. I climbed into bed one December night with my mom and dad. They were listening to coverage of the 1960/61 West Indies tour of Australia. I remember snuggling up between them as they had the transistor radio tucked up in the bed-head close to their ears to make sure the volume didn't have to be so high as to disturb the rest of the household. Do I recall that because I was a cricket obsessive? Was this an early sign that I was destined to be an international cricketer? No. I remember it for reasons of love, family and warmth. It was easy for me to pretend I wanted to listen to cricket so I could tuck in between them both. I was asleep before I even knew who was batting or bowling. But that memory might begin to take on a different theme in the context of this story.

Of course, West Indies cricket teams and Jamaican sporting teams, along with track and field athletes, had enjoyed sporting equality for some years – that chance for Black people to pit themselves on an equal footing against others on the field of play or on the track. Anyway, while I was dozing I'm sure my mom and dad must have felt immense happiness about that, thinking back. We must remember, when the West Indies toured Australia in 1960/61, the country still had a whites-only immigration policy. The hope for the future my parents must have shared, particularly as the civil rights movement in America gathered pace.

So, in 1975 when I became one of those Black players competing on equal terms and starting off in the same Australia, I'm sure my parents had thoughts and feelings beyond familial pride. Not that they would have ever said so. To me. To each other. To other family members. My dad was in the stands to watch me make my Test debut against Australia in Brisbane. My mum was no doubt listening on the radio in bed.

What I and my family had in that moment was a form of equality. And I had that throughout my sporting career. As I have become older and wiser, I feel a mixture of emotions about that. I was darn lucky that in my chosen career as a fast bowler I was not discriminated against because I was Black. By and large I was accepted. There is some guilt that it was so easy for me when the vast majority of Black people couldn't have imagined such a situation. And guilt – as I have said – that it took me a while to face up to that, to realise it.

Likewise that I perhaps wasn't aware of how important it was to be visible to other Black people. To be seen. To say, 'Hey, here we are taking them on. We're as good as them at anything. Not just sport.' In fact, in recent years, since I've been going to work in South Africa, I came to realise through stories told to me by Black Africans there that they could never watch the all-conquering West Indies team of the 1980s. Apparently the apartheid regime of the time did not want Black Africans to see other Black people triumph, showing how good they themselves could be. The regime didn't want them to start getting ideas in their heads.

What we have described so far in this book amounts to what is known as systemic racism, where every aspect of life is organised to keep the Black man down and the white man on top. Scientists, governments, educators, economists and bankers are the people who make the world turn. And they make sure that it turns away from Black people. Sport is different. It hasn't always been that way – and I want to talk about that in more detail later – but I bring it up here deliberately to make a point about equality.

It is all we want. To be treated the same.

And, by God, Black people have gone to extraordinary lengths to get it. Have given their lives, even. I played cricket for a living. And, yes, I gave a bit of joy and relief to Black people. But then I went home to Jamaica again and didn't dwell on the privilege that I had and they didn't. The sacrifices that others made while I ran around a cricket field? Well, let's say one pales into insignificance.

I am talking about Black people laying down their lives in conflicts just so they could be treated the same as white people.

Maybe you just did a double-take or had to read that sentence again. I don't blame you. Black people gave their lives fighting for the Americans and the British in the belief that, once the guns and bombs and death had stopped, they would be seen in a new light. 'Hey, these guys are not so bad after all ... give 'em their rights.' But you won't have read about those stories because they are another part of history that has been ignored. Black sacrifice – to be recognised and treated with equality – has been covered up like it's a dirty secret.

175

It is a harrowing symptom of the system. The slave era fostered a deep insecurity and lack of self-respect in Black people, which was then compounded by experiences in everyday life, such that they felt they had to prove they were as good as white people by dying for the cause. Were they treated the same? Did it work? Did it hell.

The ultimate sacrifice

In America at the outbreak of the First World War, Black people couldn't vote. But they sure could die 'for their country'. But only once the armed forces realised they didn't have enough white soldiers. African-Americans were allowed to enter the armed forces in 1917 after the Selective Service Act was passed. It required men aged 21–30 to register for the draft. This, as you would expect, was used as another tool to discriminate. The Black population of the US was 11 per cent, but 13 per cent of the draft was Black. More than 2.3 million African-Americans registered to fight. The Marines refused to take any people of colour. The Navy took small numbers and gave them menial jobs. So the US Army picked up the slack.

There was even a special training camp set up to train Black officers. Many felt that this was a God-sent blessing. Here was a chance to show their white 'brothers in arms' that they were worthy of respect. It was a chance, perhaps, to heal the racial divide, to unequivocally prove that the racist stereotypes which afflicted American life were nonsense. After all, everyone was on the same side, right?

Many African-Americans were drafted into the all-Black

369th Infantry Regiment of the New York Army National Guard. They would fight and die in both world wars. They were nicknamed the Black Rattlers. There were early signs that white soldiers would be accepting of them. At a training camp in October 1917 in Spartanburg, South Carolina, two Black soldiers were racially abused by white shop owners and were refused service. Soldiers from the white 27th Division came to their aid. When there were similar incidents in other shops in Spartanburg, the 27th told businesses that if they wouldn't serve Black soldiers, they would boycott them. 'They're our buddies. And we won't buy from men who treat them unfairly.' As usual, because in no endeavour do you find all good or all bad, there were white people who didn't and wouldn't put up with the discrimination, but that was among individuals, not in the hierarchy of the US military.

It was a false dawn. White regiments refused to fight with the 369th. When deployed in France, units of the 369th were given mainly labour, service and supply jobs. They were subjected to racist abuse and treated as inferiors. Just like at home, then. With the white Americans refusing to have anything to do with them, the generals had a problem. What to do with the 369th? The solution was to make them fight alongside the French army, not the Americans. They wore American uniforms but were issued with French weapons and helmets.

The French were delighted to have them, not least because they had suffered desertions and were desperate for reinforcements, and treated them as they would any other unit in their army. Not that they came with exactly a ringing endorsement. In one of the most shameful and racist documents I have had the misfortune to read, the US Army produced a pamphlet called 'Secret Information Concerning Black

American Troops'. Written by US General John Pershing, it was stunning in its vehemence and hatred of the Black race. This is how the New York State Military Museum records the episode and, I have to say, I couldn't put some of the objections better myself.

> Pershing stated that the Black man is an 'inferior' being to the White man. The Black man lacks 'civic and professional conscience' and is a 'constant menace to the American'. It is startling that Pershing called the Black man a menace to the American, as if the Black Americans were not really Americans. And this is how the US Military regarded Black units. Pershing continued, 'We must not eat with them, must not shake hands or seek to talk or meet with them outside the requirements of military service.' The use of 'we' in Pershing's words essentially places French and Americans on the same side for being White. Pershing also added that 'we' must not commend too highly the Black American troops, especially not in front of White American troops. Pershing added that an effort must be made to prevent the local population from 'spoiling the Negroes'. Startling is his use of the word 'Negroes'. Later he adds, 'Familiarity on the part of White women with Black men is furthermore a source of profound regret to our experienced colonials, who see in it an overwhelming menace to the prestige of the White race.' Pershing seemed more concerned that his White troops not be offended, than by the outcome of the war.

Maybe if you are white you are reading that and thinking, *Wow.* As a Black man I read it and just shrug my shoulders. It is not surprising to me in the least. I just want to repeat the hatred for a moment, to let it linger. Blacks inferior intellectually. A degenerate danger to the white race. A menace to the prestige of the white race. A threat to white women (by the way, the US Army falsely accused Black soldiers of a cumulative number of rapes more than the entire army put together). And also, 'spoil'? Does he mean being treated like a normal human being is to be spoiled?

What was that I was saying about being on the same side? The irony was that during the conflict the Germans produced propaganda leaflets which they dropped on the 369th questioning why they were fighting for their oppressors and saying that 'the Germans have never harmed you'. Despite their own side spreading hate against them and not even wanting to fight with them, the 369th were unmoved and the German pamphlets only made them more determined to prove everybody wrong.

Luckily, the French were having none of it, either. Pershing hadn't done his research. The French had plenty of Black soldiers and they had performed with bravery and brilliance in fierce battles at Verdun, Aisne, Compiègne and, infamously, the Somme. They had fighters from Morocco, Senegal and Algeria. It was normal for white to fight alongside Black guys and they welcomed the 369th with open arms. This served to infuriate and terrify the white Americans further.

A memo, signed by colonel J. L. A. Linard of the American Expeditionary Force Headquarters, raised white American concerns that Black soldiers and officers working with the French were being treated with too much 'familiarity and indulgence'. They couldn't stomach the French socialising with the Black soldiers. They wanted the French to treat them the same way as they did, which was to put up 'whites only' signs in camps, impose curfews and refuse to shake their hands.

They went further. The Americans spread rumours that the 369th were incompetent. The French investigated. Their report concluded: 'the Blacks were regularly subjected to racist white officers and non-commissioned officers, and that these white officers often provided poor leadership and sent poorly equipped troops into battle, then covered up their mistakes by placing blame on their Black troops'.

The French needn't have bothered to investigate. The 369th were fearless and they soon realised that. They earned the nickname the 'Harlem Hellfighters'. The Hellfighters spent 191 days under fire in the trenches, more than any other American unit. They never lost a foot of ground. They never had a man taken prisoner. Only once did they fail in their objective, and that was down to artillery support not turning up. They fought in Champagne, Argonne, Alsace. And they suffered 1,500 casualties, the highest of any US regiment. They were the first Allied unit to reach the banks of the Rhine. I had no idea about that until I started researching their story.

The 369th had in their ranks one of the great war heroes. Private Henry Johnson was a railway station porter from Albany. One night in the Argonne forest, Johnson and Private Needham Roberts were attacked by dozens of Germans. Johnson and Roberts were almost immediately wounded. But they fought on. Johnson used grenades, his rifle and then, when the Germans made it into his trench, he used his knife and bare hands. He killed four, wounded twenty and the Germans did not break through. He suffered twenty-one wounds and needed a steel plate inserted in his foot. The French recognised his valour – he was awarded their highest military honour, the Croix de Guerre. The Americans did not. He didn't even get a disability pension. He died in poverty in 1929, aged just thirty-seven. Only after a campaign highlighting his bravery did Johnson receive a Purple Heart, America's highest military honour. It only took another seventy-two years. Johnson was one of 170 soldiers of the 369th to receive a Croix de Guerre. The regiment as a unit also earned a Croix de Guerre and many other awards.

Upon their return to New York, for a time it seemed as though the Americans would be as proud. The 369th were given a hero's welcome as they marched through the city to Harlem in February 1919. The *New York Tribune*, which estimated the crowd at 5 million, reported: 'Never have white Americans accorded so heartfelt and hearty a reception to a contingent of their Black country-men.' The *New York Times* said that, to those there, 'all the men appeared seven feet tall'.

So, were African-Americans finally accepted? They had proved they were as brave, as strong and as smart as their white counterparts after all. They had fought and died and been wounded for the same cause. This was equality, right? Of course not. Indeed, such was the fear that they might be considered as equals, the US military swung into action.

In October 1919, General Pershing, the same man who had called Black people 'a menace to the white race', led a victory parade through the streets of New York. To wild and raucous cheers more than 25,000 soldiers wearing full combat gear marched behind him. The 369th were not among that number. They were banned from taking part. Military police were banned from saluting a member of the 369th. The US also banned the French military from including the fallen of the 369th in the French war memorial. They were banned from the Paris parades, too.

Around 400,000 African-Americans fought in the First World War. There were more than 2 million from African colonies and Indo-China, and 1.5 million from British India. And 100,000 Chinese labourers fought for the Allies, too. That's 4 million non-European and non-white soldiers who participated. All of them were banned from the victory parade. The only group to be allowed was a Sikh regiment, which fought with the British. Tall, strong and physically imposing, the British felt they were worthy of representation. But no one else.

Why did the elites not want a Black or brown face to be remembered by history? It was pretty simple: they were worried about white supremacy being challenged. In Britain and the US, racism was rife. Many people believed not only that whites were superior but that different races were competing for survival. It would do untold damage if present and future generations were to be shown and told that people of colour were as good at war, at fighting, at conquering, if you will, as white people. Another theory was that, once the reality took hold in people's minds that Black had killed white, it could destabilise the world order. The ruling elite thought they would be removed in some sort of orgy of Black-on-white violence. The Brits thought the empire would fall. All if the truth got out. It sounds ridiculous, doesn't it? Well, that fear was very real and it was exposed in very small, almost irrelevant ways. Take the example of the first time a Black man hit a white man in a Hollywood film. There was a huge furore when Sidney

Poitier's character, Virgil Tibbs, a black detective, returned the compliment after being struck by the white mayor in the movie, *In the Heat of the Night*. This was 1967. Kudos to the director Norman Jewison. But he was Canadian so possibly had a different outlook.

The First World War was won by white people. That was what I was taught at school. And every image you ever saw was of white soldiers being brave and heroic. And every history book about the conflict told stories about the same. It reinforced white supremacy. Only now, through the power of the internet and campaigners, do we really know what went on.

Black troops had been similarly shabbily treated by the British. Just like African-Americans, people of colour across the empire believed it was their duty to fight, to show them they were as good, to gain acceptance. The British War Office did not want them, though, because of the fear of upsetting the hierarchy. My West Indian brethren came anyway. So many, in fact, that the British West Indies Regiment (BWIR) was formed.

Soldiers of the BWIR received lower pay than their white counterparts. None of them could ever rank higher than sergeant. They were initially given back-breaking labouring jobs, digging trenches, stocking munitions, cleaning latrines or laying telephone wires. This was frontline, unarmed work and not some easy, safe, away-from-the-action role. Their losses were high. In total more than 15,000 served. And 185 were killed in action and more than 1,000 died from illness. No doubt some of them perished through poor equipment and maltreatment because of the colour of their skin. They fought in Palestine, Jordan, France and Flanders.

Discrimination continued when the war was over. Stationed in Taranto, Italy, the regiment was expecting to celebrate like everyone else. No chance. While the white soldiers partied, the Black soldiers were put to work. They were to build and clean latrines for the white soldiers. When they found out that the white soldiers had been given a pay rise, the BWIR said enough was enough. In December 1918 they signed a petition complaining about poor pay and lack of promotions. This 'mutiny' was put down by force. One Black soldier was killed. Later, sixty of the BWIR were tried for mutiny and sent to prison. One was executed by firing squad.

All lives matter, eh? Not if you're Black. The Great War was many things to many different people. For Black people and people of colour, such was their status in life that they actually saw the senseless slaughter as something life-affirming. It was an opportunity to be the same. Sadly, it is just another tragedy to add to the long list from that terrible time.

In the end, all that was affirmed for them was that they meant less than white people. They didn't have equality. Try to imagine that for a moment. What it must have felt like for a member of the 369th, who had seen his friends blown to pieces and maimed, who had signed up in the hope of gaining respect, to be treated in that way. What did that do for his self-esteem? What did it do to his friends and family who witnessed that cruel rejection? And for the community he came from? I don't know how I would have possibly coped with something like that.

And I think perhaps the most awful element of these stories for me was not just that they were treated with disdain, but how there were concerted efforts by the powers that be to make sure that what they sacrificed was not recognised. It was all planned. It is surely unforgivable that they were denied the chance to partake in the victory parades.

The trashing of their legacy was deliberate and evil. Even in the brutality of war, they were not given their dues. No acceptance, no recognition, no achievements. But wait, it doesn't end there. There was no memorial placed anywhere in England to commemorate the African-Caribbean soldiers who fought alongside the white soldiers until June 2017. And that came after a memorial to commemorate the animals that had served and died under British military command had been placed in Hyde Park, London, in December 2004. So, the animals were commemorated thirteen years before the Black soldiers who fought for Britain, and anyone with a fleeting knowledge of London will recognise how central and popular Hyde Park is for locals and tourists alike, while the memorial to the soldiers was placed in Brixton, which is a long way from the hot spots. Not much more to say there.

This was a whitewashing of history, of the collective successes and triumphs of Black people and people of colour. Collective is a key word. There was no 'safety in numbers' here in that regard. You might have thought that governments and the military wouldn't have the gall to try to pull off such a stunt considering there were so many who could raise a dissenting voice. But who would hear them? Besides, this was a well-trodden path for the elite. For years and years individual Black people who had achieved extraordinary successes, brilliant minds who had saved lives and managed feats that were considered world firsts, had been airbrushed from history. Lord forbid anyone should get the idea that a Black person was as brave or strong, but as intelligent, too.

The forgotten

I am writing this the day after it was announced that a vaccine was ready, effective and safe to unlock the world from the grasp of Covid-19. Some media organisations called it 'a great day for humanity'. And for sure it was a happy, hopeful day. The stock markets surged, world leaders claimed that a return to normal life – going out for meals with friends, seeing vulnerable family members again, hugging them – was on the horizon and people celebrated (in a socially distanced way, I hope!) that one of the most tragic and tough periods some of us have ever known could soon be over.

Let's think for a second about the achievement of the scientists who made that possible. Heroes and heroines one and all. What a debt each and every one of us owes them. Think of the pride that those people must feel. And the pride of their families. It is enough to bring a tear to the eye. No doubt, in time the brains behind such a scientific breakthrough will be cheered the world over, received by heads of state, given gongs and awards and prizes, one of them maybe with the word 'Nobel' in. They might, even, in time, receive a statue or two.

And, if we're being crude, think of the riches that will come the way of the individuals and companies responsible. Few would begrudge them that. After all, they could well save hundreds of thousands of lives. Grandparents will see their grandchildren grow up. Families will not be ripped apart. Loved ones will not leave us prematurely. The gift of life.

This is, of course, what scientists do. And they have been doing it for years. The history of medicine is a ticker-tape parade of brilliant discoveries by brilliant minds.

But what about the person who discovered vaccines? The very first person to do so in the Western world. Let's think about that brilliant mind. Think of the gift of life that they bestowed on the world. Think of the way they were feted and cheered and remembered. Think of the pride their friends and family felt. And, if you like, you can think of the money that they made.

In 1721, smallpox was running riot through Boston, USA. The disease, one of the most deadly of the era with a fatality rate at 30 per cent, was carried by crew on cargo ships. It arrived in Boston via crew from a British ship docking there. Out of a population of 11,000, 6,000 were struck down and 850 died. It disproportionately affected Native Americans because they had no immunity. The colonialists, who had introduced the illness when the state of Massachusetts became a slave colony in the mid-1600s, were not as badly affected because they had had some previous exposure in Europe.

The local authorities' only hope of controlling the epidemic was to put arrivals in quarantine. They were shut up in houses with a red flag outside and the words 'God have mercy upon this house' painted on the door. Those who could, fled Boston. But the vast majority who remained were terrified.

That was until a man called Onesimus revealed a treatment for smallpox. The problem was, Onesimus was a slave, from Libya. He had told his owner, one Cotton Mather, a Puritan minister, that he had been inoculated against smallpox in Africa. Mather wrote that Onesimus 'had undergone an operation, which had given him something of the smallpox and would forever preserve him from it . . . and whoever had the courage to use it was forever free of the fear of contagion.'

What Onesimus described was the process of pus being

taken from a person infected with smallpox and rubbed into a cut on a person's arm. This triggered an immune response to protect against the disease. Need I point out, again, that African civilisation had been far in advance of the supposedly superior Western super-race?

Despite Mather describing Onesimus as 'wicked' and 'thievish', he asked his other slaves whether the story was true. When they told him they'd had the same treatment and believed they were immune, Mather wrote, perhaps begrudgingly, that Onesimus was a 'pretty intelligent fellow'. However, he had a task to convince the colonialists that it was effective. They refused to believe that a slave could possibly be right. It was no doubt dismissed as some form of witchcraft or quackery. Indeed, there was outrage at the suggestion that white people should take it seriously. Mather became almost a pariah. He was criticised for his 'negroish' thinking. A bomb was thrown through the window of his house but fortunately it did not go off. Mather was a victim of his own prejudice, of course. His beliefs that Black people were inferior or 'devilish', as he wrote, were used against him.

Only one doctor in Boston believed that Onesimus's treatment would work. His name was Zabdiel Boylston. After another outbreak, he inoculated his family and the slaves he owned. In total, he inoculated 242 people. Only six died. Towards the end of the eighteenth century, a vaccination was developed against smallpox thanks to Onesimus's method. Edward Jenner, an English physician, got the credit and was hailed as a pioneer. He was white.

As for Onesimus, no one knows what happened to him. Some historians say he was able to buy his freedom from Cotton Mather. Let's think about that for a second. The man who helped beat smallpox in Boston wasn't even granted his freedom. He was still considered worthless. And, years later, a white man took the credit. To this day, smallpox is the only disease that has been completely eradicated.

It is perhaps not surprising that Onesimus would have been treated this way given the fierce and deep-rooted disease of white supremacy at the time. Slaves had no rights whatsoever. And the idea of a Black man being credited with even the smallest amount of intelligence, skill or craftsmanship – and there were many slaves denied the opportunity to patent the inventions they produced at the time – would have been met with howls of derision. And any trappings, awards or recognition? Unthinkable. Forget it.

White people and colonialists just couldn't possibly countenance the idea that a Black person was capable of such ingenuity or brilliance of mind. But it is surprising that, in the hundreds of years since, the achievements of Black people continue to be ignored or airbrushed from history. On an individual level, Onesimus was something of an unfortunate trendsetter in that regard, as well as being instrumental in saving millions of lives.

I didn't read about Onesimus until I started researching this book. It takes on greater significance because of the Covid pandemic and I can only shake my head at the idea that he was one of the very first Black people – and no doubt there were so many more who have slipped through the white parchment of history – to have their successes ignored or denigrated. I suppose, as part of my 'awakening', I had been for years keeping notes of others who had suffered the same fate, remembering snippets of information here and there which, when put together, grows to a mountain of injustice. People who did brilliant, radical things only to be forgotten or have their achievements stolen by a white person.

Had I known about Onesimus when I had my bit to say on Sky Sports, I would have told his story. Instead, I spoke about another man: Lewis. Howard. Latimer. I write his name with pauses to try to evoke some of the passion and emotion that I felt that day. I can remember the hurt and bewilderment rising up in me as I spoke his name. Who was he? A genius, simply put. But one you will have never heard of because there is probably not a school or college in this world that teaches his name for the simple reason that he was a Black man.

Let's go back to school for a minute. One of the first things you learn, maybe in your second or third year at the latest, is the answer to this question: who invented the lightbulb? To a man, woman and child the answer will come back: Thomas Edison. Of course. Thomas Edison invented the lightbulb. Everybody knows that. It is burned into our memory. Apart from the fact that he didn't. At least, not a functional lightbulb.

Thomas Edison invented a lightbulb with a paper filament. It lit up the room, for sure, but it burned out by the time you clicked your fingers. The man who invented the carbon filament, which burned and burned, allowing us to have a lightbulb lasting years? Lewis. Howard. Latimer. In 1882 Latimer received the patent for that carbon filament. He literally lit up our homes. And our streets – he went on to supervise public streetlight systems in New York, Philadelphia, Montreal, London.

Edison, a genius himself, may well have been the first to actually invent the lightbulb. But which is really significant?

A lightbulb that burns out after seconds or one that keeps going and going, which was and is of use to mankind? I would think the latter, and Lewis Howard Latimer was the one who made it a functional reality.

I tell this story not to try to rubbish Thomas Edison or label him an intellectual thief, because he wasn't, but simply to point out that it was inconceivable for Latimer to be given any credit at the time, or in all the years that have followed, because of the colour of his skin. Had he not been Black, had he not been the son of slaves who had escaped from Virginia and fought for their freedom in a court of law, then his name would have tripped off the tongue in exactly the same way as Edison's.

Nor did he have the same, shall we say, appetite for self-promotion as Edison, it seems. *Time* magazine noted that, although Edison held the record for US patents, he had a habit of exaggeration. A 1979 profile read: 'An incurable show-off and self-promoter who circulated so many myths about his personality and accomplishments that 48 years after his death historians are still struggling to separate legend from fact.'

Latimer didn't stand a chance. During the 2020 US election campaign, Joe Biden was corrected by CNN when he said that Latimer had invented the lightbulb. I can tell you now, I'm with Joe. Who should receive the credit? The person who invents something that doesn't work or the person who corrects the faults of the invention to make it useful? Or, at the very least, how about equal recognition?

Let's keep going. Who invented the telephone? Alexander Graham Bell, right? Well, he takes almost all of the credit. But again, Latimer played a significant role. He was the man who produced the plans and drawing for Bell's idea. Never heard about that either, did you? Latimer's story is not hard to find. He is included in the American National Inventors Hall of Fame. His obituary in the *New York Times* after he died at the age of eighty in 1928 does not stint on his achievements. But none of what he did is taught in schools.

I could have filled this book with other such examples. There are plenty more Black inventors (check the list at the back of this book) whose accomplishments have struck a chord with me but who you won't have heard of. Garrett Morgan invented the three-way traffic signal. Who doesn't see a traffic light when they leave the house? Everybody does. But who knows the name of the man who invented it? Very few.

Morgan was born in Kentucky, USA, in 1877. He had only an elementary-school education and in his mid-teens moved to Ohio, where he took a job as a handyman. He used this money to hire tutors to get a better education and he became fascinated by machines and how they worked. He invented an improved sewing machine and his business was a huge success.

In 1914 he patented a 'breathing device' which protected people from harmful gases. He travelled the country selling it, employing a white actor to play the inventor because he knew fire departments wouldn't buy it from a Black man. Some reports said his gas masks were used by American soldiers in the First World War. I wonder how many lives that saved? Likewise the traffic lights. Morgan was the first Black man in Cleveland to own a car. For all that he did, he should have owned Cleveland, not just a car.

Considering the treatment of Black servicemen during and after the world wars, it is worth pausing for a minute yet again to think about how those men wanted to give their lives just so they could be accepted. And here we are talking about more unheralded Black people who saved lives.

Otis Boykin is another. He was born in Dallas, Texas, in 1920. He invented a wire precision resistor. Now, I'm not entirely sure what that is or precisely what it does, but my research tells me it proved to be useful for radios and televisions. He modified it later so that it could withstand extreme temperatures and so the IBM computer arrived. All of this experience led to him being in demand as one of the brightest electronic innovators and to his greatest achievement: the control unit for the pacemaker. How many lives has *that* saved?

Type into Google 'Who discovered the North Pole?' and the answer will come back as Robert Peary. In fact, there is a chunk of evidence that it was, in fact, a Black man called Matthew Henson.

Henson, who was born in 1866, three years after emancipation, was Peary's team-mate. They shared the dream of being the first humans to stand on top of the world, and together they endured tremendous physical and mental hardship in trying to realise it, spending eighteen years on expeditions all over the world. Seven times they tried to conquer the pole.

The pair had met when Henson was working as a store clerk in Washington, DC. He had previously been a cabin boy after he walked barefoot from DC to Baltimore – about 40 miles – looking for work because he was orphaned (his parents had been sharecroppers). He sailed all over the world on the *Katie Hines*, was educated on board and became a good sailor.

Peary, a US Navy officer, had employed Henson as his

personal assistant. Their first expedition was to the jungles of Nicaragua. They formed a bond which would (almost) last a lifetime. Their Arctic explorations began in 1891 and together they mapped the entirety of the Greenland ice cap. Yet they kept failing in their bid to be the first to the earth's northern-most point. Each time they got closer and today it is recognised that Henson's skills and expertise were crucial. Peary was the frontman, the public face of the excursions. Much of the brawn and brains came from Henson, and it is widely acknowledged that he was of equal experience to Peary.

Their eighth and final attempt came in 1909. Henson believed that learning the local Inuit language could make the difference. He was the only member of the team to do so.

In freezing temperatures, howling winds and a mist that blocked out the sun, navigation was hard. But when the fog cleared Peary and Henson realised that they had overshot the pole. It transpired that Henson, who had been the lead sledge, had been the first man there. Henson said: 'I was in the lead that had overshot the mark by a couple of miles. We went back then and I could see that my footprints were the first at the spot.' Henson had made history.

There would be no triumph, however, for Henson. Peary was furious that Henson had got there first and barely spoke to him again. 'From the time we knew we were at the Pole, Commander Peary scarcely spoke to me,' he said. 'It nearly broke my heart ... that he would rise in the morning and slip away on the homeward trail without rapping on the ice for me, as was the established custom.'

There was no campaign to ignore Henson's achievements. It was considered ridiculous that a Black man could achieve something so monumental. In a book called *The Adventure Gap*, by James Edward Mills, it is noted how strange Peary's reaction was, particularly as, at the outset, he said, 'Henson must go all the way.' The two men had been friends, teammates and adventurers for years. Perhaps Peary's reaction was due to the fact he had discovered incontrovertible proof that Black people were equals.

Even when sceptics raised doubts about the success of the expedition, Henson's view was not worthy. Ironic really, because he was the only member of the crew, remember, who could speak Inuit, and they would have been able to corroborate Peary's story. History remembered the pair differently. Peary was promoted to rear admiral and travelled the world as a superstar, feted wherever he went. Henson took a job as a clerk at the federal customs house in New York and later parked cars for a living.

Peary died in 1920 yet it took another seventeen years before the truth emerged when Henson became the first Black member of the Explorers Club. Peary had two spells as president of the club, 1909–11 and 1913–16. Henson died in 1955. On the seventy-ninth anniversary of the expedition, Henson's body was relocated to Arlington National Cemetery and buried close to a monument erected to Peary. And in 2000 Henson was posthumously awarded the National Geographic Society's Hubbard Medal. The first person to receive it? Peary in 1906.

Read between the lines of that story of 'equality': white man is in charge of Explorers Club, his Black 'rival' only allowed to join after his death. Black man has to die before he receives rightful honour, and is then buried near the white man's *monument*. I guess you could say it is progress of sorts, but Henson's life is an example of how slowly the wheels of change turn.

It also reinforces my point about education. Kids weren't being taught the truth about one of the most significant explorations in history. They were being taught a lie convenient to the status quo, to reaffirm white supremacy. It just would not do that a Black man was equal to a white man in extraordinary feats.

It is rare to find a person of colour being hailed as a hero in the history books you find in schools. Mary Seacole is one example that springs to mind, although for depressingly negative reasons. As I said before, there are so many, but I could not ignore the Jamaican for obvious reasons.

Seacole, as you may know, was recognised for her extraordinary compassion, bravery and skill in caring for British soldiers during the Crimean War. In 2004 she was voted the Greatest Black Briton. There is a statue of her on Westminster Bridge in London. She was added to the British national curriculum in 2007.

But in 2013 a campaign started to have Seacole removed from the curriculum. Michael Gove, the education secretary at the time, said more time should be spent learning about figures like Oliver Cromwell and Winston Churchill. Gove's decision followed a particularly nasty campaign by the media, claiming that Seacole 'wasn't really Black', wasn't 'really a nurse' and was a 'politically correct myth'. It only becomes clear what was at play here when you consider the attack was along the lines of, 'She was no Florence Nightingale.'

Now, what does Nightingale have to do with it? She was white, of course. And kind, caring, wise and, as you would expect, there to be glorified on the curriculum. The idea of a Black woman being considered as her equal? Of being considered as virtuous? And children being taught such things? This raised the hackles of those who felt that their history of superiority was being threatened. The two women were pitted against each other in some sort of bizarre historical nursing play-off. For anyone who had the time to read up on both women, it was patently ridiculous. Nightingale was the mother of modern nursing, Seacole gave solace and succour on the battlefield. Not that this should be relevant, but please let's not compare batsmen to bowlers – they do different things but both are essential.

Few were more hysterical than the Nightingale Association, which seems to exist to rail against comparison of the two women and yet is full of articles doing exactly that, only in grossly unfavourable terms to Seacole. It is nothing short of a character assassination, claiming she was a criminal for wearing war medals which weren't hers, repeating that she wasn't really Black and slyly questioning her motives: 'she missed the first three battles [in Crimea] to tend to her gold stocks'.

It's worth pointing out that Seacole felt she suffered racism in her bid to be taken on as a nurse, first with the Americans and secondly with Nightingale herself. She wrote in her autobiography:

Was it possible that American prejudices against colour had some root here? Did these ladies shrink from accepting my aid because my blood flowed beneath a somewhat duskier skin than theirs? I had an interview with one of Miss Nightingale's companions. She gave me the same reply, and I read in her face the fact that, had there been a vacancy, I should not have been chosen to fill it.

Many of the arguments against Seacole being on the curriculum focus on her colour. That she is a poster girl for the politically correct who desperately need a heroine. Excuse me, but Black people, as I think I have proved in this very chapter alone, should not need some sort of politically motivated campaign to gain recognition. Just don't hide their accomplishments and they will become self-evident. What, precisely, is wrong about championing and remembering Black achievers? It should, in fact, be a matter of championing achievers, full stop. Irrespective of the colour of their skin. And that should be the case with all well-thinking people.

But there are those who say that this is Black people trying to take over, to punish white people and to denigrate their achievements. Give me a break. As I've said before, what is really going on is their belief that they are superior is being challenged and they cannot stand it. So they attempt to continue to whitewash history. Listen, having equal recognition for all achievers does not lessen anyone's achievements. And, surprise, surprise, it came from a government responsible for the Windrush scandal. This was when the UK government deported – and threatened many more – the people, and their children, who they had pleaded with to come over and help rebuild the country after the Second World War. The same political party who relied on and encouraged support from sections of the population who no doubt had some hostility to Britain's diverse racial history.

Why, I wonder, when it has been proved that Black kids do better at exams when they learn about historical figures they can identify with, would they not teach pupils about such people? Is it not time that the lessons taught in schools reflect the multicultural nature of the society being taught? I heard the British prime minister himself say that you can't go back and edit history. Well, I would suggest that history has already been edited and what we're asking is for it to be unedited, to reflect all achievers, not just what suits one set of people.

The beat goes on

Black achievements and sacrifices have been ignored. And every time there have been successful Black expressions, through culture, religion and indeed sport, there has been a move to beat it down, too. I should give my views, mainly, on sport. It is the context of my life, after all. But music moves every man, woman and child more than sport. And without Black people we would not be tapping our feet in the same way.

Because of music's universal appeal it is important to note how Black influence and invention could rate as one of the biggest whitewashes in history. Sure, everyone knows that rap, hip-hop, soul and gospel are what you might call 'Black' music. But blues, jazz, rock and roll, country, funk and house were born back in the plantation fields. Music was escapism from the horrors of slavery.

The blues has its origins in the American South and the first recordings were made in the 1920s by Black women. Elvis Presley, the king of rock and roll, would not have existed without the blues. These days, Elvis would be criticised for cultural appropriation. That's a buzz phrase, among some others, that people get agitated about, but it's not something that bothers me at all. I only mention it to show the origins of the music.

Elvis was deliberately and consciously positioned as an artist who blended Black and white. And it could be argued that the way his music and style did that helped bridge the racial divide. That's not a ground-breaking view, though. But I bet you don't know that 'Hound Dog', one of his greatest hits, was first performed by a Black woman. Big Mama Thornton was one of the most influential blues singers in the 1950s. 'Hound Dog' was written for and inspired by Thornton. And her version sold more than 2 million copies. Of course, Thornton barely made any money, but Presley's version three years later was one of the biggest money-spinners of his career.

Dominic James 'Nick' LaRocca is the composer, wrongly, credited with 'inventing' jazz. He was white. Can anyone really, with a straight face, say that white people invented jazz? Charles Joseph 'Buddy' Bolden was one of the earliest jazz musicians in 1900 and was regarded by his contemporaries as a key figure in the development of a New Orleans style of ragtime music, or 'jass', which later became known as jazz. He was Black, of course. He was barely fifty-four years old when he died in 1931, leaving behind no written scores or recorded music as all his performances were live and full of improvisations, which is exactly what jazz is. LaRocca was born in 1889 and, by the time he formed his Dixieland jazz band in 1916, Buddy had already been going for quite a few years.

Sister Rosetta Tharpe, another forgotten name, was the 'mother' of rock and roll legends like Little Richard, Chuck Berry and Fats Domino. Sister Rosetta was a singer, songwriter, guitarist and recording artist who was popular in the 1930s and 40s, mixing spiritual lyrics and rhythmic accompaniments, which was the precursor to rock.

Country music, however, is supposed to be as white as it gets. Stetsons, pick-up trucks, cowboy boots and white faces dominate. It was, in fact, heavily reliant on African-American culture because of the playing of the banjo by Blacks in the south of America. This can be traced back to the seventeenth-century slave ships, where the captors made Africans bring instruments from their homeland. The 'akonting' was an early folk lute version of the American banjo and came from West Africa. The banjo and the accompanying vocal style were appropriated by minstrel or 'blackface' shows. The 'blackface' image perhaps intentionally or unintentionally showing the connection to the slaves who invented this style of music. This was the beginning of country.

Although musical history is another story that had been whitewashed, I had thought the modern industry was more inclusive. And by that I mean we have visible Black stars, like Beyoncé or Rihanna or Jay-Z. And not just 'stars' in the common sense of the word, but titans who are powerful and influential enough to move into other industries and dominate. That is change for the better. Not since the great man, Bob Marley, was in his prime have we had Black musical artists crossing divides and breaking down barriers.

Country music still has a lot of work to do, though. In 2017 a multiracial artist called Kane Brown was topping all the country charts but was ignored by industry executives at the Country Music Awards. Lil Nas X, a rapper and country music kid from the projects in Atlanta, Georgia, remixed a song with Billy Ray Cyrus, a country music legend. 'Old

Town Road' became US number one on the *Billboard* Hot 100 chart for a record-breaking number of weeks, but it didn't have the same influence on the country music chart from which it was 'dropped' earlier. Note the language, 'dropped' – that means it was originally classified as country. *Billboard* decided that the song did not embrace enough elements of 'today's' country music. Country music radio stations also refused to play the song.

Those who know better say that 'today's' country music has lost sight of its roots, the Black instruments and traditions of its origins. The *New York Times* went a bit further; they translated this as 'the song is too Black for certain white people'.

Sport doesn't have this problem. If you win, you are recognised and revered. If you are good enough, you play, although this tends to apply more to individuals than team sports. In any individual endeavour on the sporting field, there can be no doubt about who is fastest, strongest, fittest or most skilled. The finishing tape does not discriminate. Hence Hitler could do nothing about Jesse Owens showing up his so-called superior race in the 1936 Munich Olympics. Winning margins are difficult to dispute but it can be a bit different when it comes to teams. And I had personal experience of that when playing for the West Indies.

On the shoulders of giants

Maybe you know this. Maybe you don't. The greatest sports team ever was the West Indies cricket team that I was a part of. No team has been so dominant or unbeatable over as long a period. Ever. This is not a boast, or rose-tinted bias.

It is a simple fact. Between June 1980 and up to the start of March 1995, West Indies did not lose a series. We beat everybody for fifteen years, both home and away. No other sporting team, in any discipline, anywhere in the world, dominated for that long, not even domestically, let alone internationally.

Is that West Indies team now revered and recognised? For sure. Books have been written about it, films made and legacies have been long-lasting. I know that without membership of that team, I would not have had a career in broadcasting. But there is no doubt that when we were beating everybody out of sight, there was an effort by some in the cricket establishment and the media to malign what we were doing and how we were doing it. And that's because the story of West Indies cricket is one about a mainly Black team taking on and defeating 'white supremacy'. Indeed, because the Black Power movement had not long since been seen as a destabilising influence in America in particular, one media personality thought it wise to try to throw mud on what we were accomplishing by trying to stick the label of Black Power militancy on the team.

Without slavery, there would not have been cricket in the Caribbean. It's so obvious it doesn't really need saying, but the colonial rulers brought the sport to the islands and the slaves watched and, eventually, learned to play. But they were not allowed to bat. The Black man learned to play cricket because the back-breaking hard work of bowling the ball in extreme heat suited their supposed inferior status. The slave master would bat. The Black man would bowl or be sent to collect the ball.

Batting was also seen as something of an art form,

something beautiful, technical and highly skilled that only the white man could do. Bowling the ball was about being strong and fit. On racial lines, cricket has moved on from those ideas, although to this day the phrase 'it's a batsman's game' probably has a nod to that slice of history. Indeed, that view continued in the Caribbean for many years. In the eighteenth century, Blacks were not allowed to play in official matches. And it wasn't until 1906 that a West Indies touring team included Black players. And only when the natural brilliance of players like Learie Constantine and George Headley became undeniable did attitudes really change. They made their debuts for West Indies close together, Constantine in 1928 and Headley in 1930.

Headley was a trailblazer. He was made the first ever Black captain for the West Indies in 1948, an extraordinary achievement because if folks were stubbornly convinced that batsmanship was for 'whites only', they were practically immovable about who should lead a team. A Black man didn't have the wit, ingenuity or respect, apparently. Headley apart, every West Indies team from 1900 to 1957 was captained and managed by a white person when the white population in the islands was decreasing and the number of Black people playing cricket was rising exponentially. Michael Manley, the former Jamaican prime minister, described Headley as 'Black excellence personified in a white world and white sport'. It was Michael Manley's political party, the People's National Party, albeit in the days of his father, Norman Washington Manley, that pressured the all-white West Indies Cricket Board to make Headley skipper against England in Barbados. It would be only one game. The job full-time was too much ground for them to concede. It would be another eleven years before the West Indies had a full-time Black captain, the esteemed Frank Worrell.

Headley knew what he represented. When he toured Australia in 1930, he wrote 'African' on the immigration form. He was also known as the Black Bradman. This moniker was considered a feat in itself because Don Bradman was regarded as the greatest ever. So, there was a Black man who stood shoulder to shoulder with him in terms of ability – and there was recognition that this was the case, although we West Indians, and Jamaicans in particular, preferred to call Bradman the White Headley. I'm not sure why anyone of colour had to be compared to a white person and called the 'Black whatever'. I have never heard of 'the white Pelé' or 'white Muhammad Ali', 'white Michael Jordan'. I think you get my drift.

This was at a time when cricket was run by the colonial masters, the English, and here was a descendant of slaves showing everybody that equality was possible. Manley summed it up rather well, I thought, with this: 'Headley became the focus for the longing of an entire people for proof – proof of their own self-worth and their own capacity.' That role model theme again – people need to lift themselves.

The teams that Headley was a part of, as well as the ones before and the ones after, were seen as entertainers rather than winners. They could be brilliant one day, and awful for the next four. This was how the term 'calypso cricket' was coined. West Indies were not winners. This made them extremely popular with spectators in Australia and England because it reinforced the supremacy. The West Indies' collective performances were a reminder to Black and white that the status quo remained. When the West Indies eventually won their first Test match on English soil in 1950, it was a source of inspiration for all West Indians. That they went on to win the series meant unadulterated joy.

My first tour as a West Indies player was to Australia in 1975/76. And it was a wake-up call. We were abused on and off the field but, I repeat, I heard nothing derogatory from the cricketers themselves. I want to keep making this point clear. We were given a terrible beating (5-1 in a six-game series) by the Australians.

I had been taken aback by the hostility of the Australian team. Maybe it was just my naivety. They did not give an inch. They had two terrifying fast bowlers in Dennis Lillee and Jeff Thomson, who peppered our batsmen with bullets to the body, leaving them bruised and broken. Not that we complained about that. It was part of the game. 'Lillee! Lillee! Lillee! *Kill-kill-kill*,' the crowd would chant. That wasn't a white versus Black thing. The Aussies would shout that at their grandmother if she was batting. But there was racist abuse, too, on the field of play. Some of my team-mates have since said that the colour of their skin was brought into it. Gordon Greenidge said he felt humiliated by the abuse. Viv Richards was targeted from the stands, too. 'Fans' would shout at him, 'You Black bastard!' Viv said, matter-of-factly, 'I'm not a bastard.' It was a degrading experience as a human being and a cricketer.

The abuse aside, that defeat by Australia sowed the seed for the rising of the greatest team. It was the fast bowlers who had done the damage. Our captain, Clive Lloyd, knew that and thought, *How would Australia fare it we had fast bowlers of our own?* So he set about building a fast-bowling unit as lethal and as terrifying. I was one of them. My nickname was 'Whispering Death'. This was because I was light on my feet and the umpire, who always had his back turned to me, of course, as I ran in to bowl, could not hear me coming. The 'Death' bit? Well, I could kill at the speed that I bowled, at least that's what Dickie Bird, the very good and famous umpire, thought anyway. At speeds upwards of 90mph, a blow to the head from a cricket ball could be fatal. Andy Roberts was called 'The Hitman'. Colin Croft was the 'Smiling Assassin'. Both were as fast as me.

We also had our own George Headley. Viv Richards was one of the all-time great batsmen. But he was an extraordinary man, too. He lived and breathed the Black man's heritage. He knew where we had come from, where we were going and, more importantly, how we were going to get there. On the field of play he was aggressive. He would swagger to the wicket with his head held high. He stared down the bowlers and the fielders. He chewed gum in defiance. He refused to wear a helmet to protect his head and at all times wore his wool maroon West Indies cap. It was a deliberate performance, a show. He personified Black power without uttering a word. 'Aggression meets aggression,' he said. 'If you're going to fight me, I'm gonna fight back. We were as good as anyone. *Equal*, for that matter.'

The combination of terrific fast bowlers and a talismanic Viv dovetailed with a movement in the Caribbean. We came together as young men at a time when the Caribbean islands were growing up, too. It was the time of independence. Many of us had been born on colonial islands but we were becoming men on independent nations. It was a get up, stand up moment all over the region (no pun intended referencing the great Bob Marley song). For us as cricketers and our supporters back home, cricket became an expression of Black rebellion. Previously it had been about imparting British values and a way of disciplining the Black man or keeping him in his place, such as having no Black captain or, years before, not being allowed to bat. We were restoring a dignity that had been taken.

Some of the guys I played with lived and breathed that every single day. Gordon Greenidge had moved to England at the age of fourteen. He was called a 'wog' in the street. The anger of those experiences came out in the way he played. I think Viv was like that. As he said years later, he 'felt the pain of the brothers and sisters' during the civil rights movement in America. He saw cricket as a way that we could have a true level playing field. And every match he would wear a wristband of green, gold and red. Green for the colour of the African plains, gold for what was stolen and red for the blood that was spilled. In Viv's pomp, they used to sell those wristbands to kids in English sports shops. I wonder how many mums and dads would have bought them if they'd known what they symbolised?

We were one people. One nation. For me, I wasn't thinking every single minute of the match that 'we must have equality' or 'Black power' as I knocked over a batsman. That was emotional and it couldn't get in the way of me doing my job. I felt that I had to be in control and to be rational if I was going to get batsmen out. If I roared in as an angry Black guy, I wouldn't have done so well. So, was it a motivation for me? Absolutely, but I think the impression that as a team we were obsessing about an ideal was off the mark. Our intensity didn't alter whether we played against cricketers of colour or white cricketers. Most of us were trying to do ourselves and our families justice.

And we did that. As I said, we beat everyone. And when we were beating everyone it sure got interesting. A bunch of Black guys coming together and dominating was unprecedented. And the old colonial powers didn't like it. The status quo was under threat. We attacked teams with sheer pace. A battery of fast bowlers that had never been seen before – and rarely since. We scared teams. Once you have that capability to hurt someone, the batsman is preoccupied with self-preservation.

Despite the fact that the Aussies and the Lillee–Thomson axis gave Clive Lloyd the idea, the authorities, the scared and the weak tried to use it against us. We were terrorists. We were bringing the game into disrepute. There was even the ludicrous assertion in the press corps that, if the rules were not changed, ten batsman would be killed in one English summer. When we went back to Australia and gave them a taste of their own medicine, the same crowds that chanted 'Kill!' booed when one of their players got hit.

The press, all over the world, parroted the angst of the establishment. And often in a racist way. 'Stop this mayhem!', 'Clamp down on bullies', 'The Hate Brigade', 'All bouncers and bongos', 'Coconuts!' were just some of the headlines. What these people wanted was a return to the old West Indies teams, the entertainers or the calypso cricketers. They were happy with us winning every now and again but we weren't meant to dominate. They wanted us to lose with a smile and say, 'Thank you for the opportunity.' No way. Nothing could stop us. So many ideas were being bandied about to try to limit our success. There was talk of drawing a line across the middle of the pitch and calling no-balls for any deliveries pitching short of that line. They couldn't whip us or 'put us in our place' any more, so they had to find a way to stop us. Maybe they didn't realise what they were doing and that it was their deep-seated subconscious screaming, 'You are superior, this cannot happen.'

Let me pause here for a minute, though, to make it absolutely clear that at no point did I think that attitude was universal. I am well aware of the fact that many white folks enjoyed and loved our cricket. We made great friends on and off the field in Australia and England. You see, just like today, there is a difference between the ordinary man and woman on the street and those in authority.

And while we're on the topic of how the game should be played, let's cast our minds back to the 2005 Ashes series. It was one of the best Test series I was fortunate enough to commentate on. England won with four outstanding fast bowlers in their line-up. When Steve Harmison hit Australian captain Ricky Ponting on the cheek at Lord's, drawing blood, the crowd bellowed approval and cheered. There was not a word about intimidatory bowling or too many bouncers.

One of West Indies cricket's fiercest critics was David Frith, editor of *Wisden Cricket Monthly* (*WCM*). Before the West Indies tour of England in 1991 he wrote this: 'Another invasion is upon us by a West Indian team that is the most fearsome, the most successful and the most unpopular in the world. Their game is founded on vengeance and violence and is fringed by arrogance. The only mercy is that they're not bringing their umpires with them . . . these matches have long since become manifestations of the racial tensions that exist in the world outside the cricket gates.'

Four years later with West Indies in England again, Mr Frith got himself into trouble for publishing views on those racial tensions. He was sacked as the editor of *WCM* after he published an article by a writer called Robert Henderson entitled 'Is it in the blood?' It was a racist analysis of supposed 'foreigners' playing cricket for England and there was an outcry, even making front-page news.

Henderson wrote: 'An Asian or negro raised in England will, according to the liberal, feel exactly the same pride and identification with the place as the white man. The reality is somewhat different. It is even possible that part of a coloured England-qualified player feels satisfaction (perhaps subconsciously) at seeing England humiliated because of post-imperial myths of oppression and exploitation.'

Phil DeFreitas, an England player at the time, who had moved to the country at the age of ten from Dominica, and Devon Malcolm, the Jamaican-born England fast bowler, successfully sued. Chris Lewis, an all-rounder who played eighty-five times for England and was born in Guyana, received damages. I note that David Graveney, CEO of the Professional Cricketers' Association, suggested DeFreitas and Malcolm should not sue. Graveney led a rebel cricket tour to apartheid South Africa in 1989/90.

It is also worth noting, with Frith's 'racial tensions' comment in mind, that the English summer of 1995 was a period when Black people in England were once again being victimised, abused and killed, as I was reminded by a friend who sent the following passage from a book by Mike Marqusee, an American author, called *Anyone But England*:

In May, Brian Douglas, a Black man, died after being struck on the head by police using new US-style batons in Kennington, not far from The Oval. In June, Asian youths in the Manningham district of Bradford took to the streets for three days following the wrongful arrest of teenagers playing a noisy game of football. An enquiry later blamed the riot on the 'arrogance and ignorance' of local police. In July, the Commissioner of the Metropolitan Police singled out Black youths as 'muggers', relying on statistical evidence nearly as spurious as Henderson's [the author of the *Wisden* article], and launched Operation Eagle Eye – a police sweep explicitly aimed at a particular section of the community, defined by colour. The Tory Government announced yet another crackdown on illegal immigrants and launched their Asylum and Immigration Bill, which sought to deny welfare benefits to asylum seekers. According to the British Crime Survey, there had been a 50% increase in racial incidents over the previous five years. A TUC report revealed that Blacks with university degrees remained twice as likely to be unemployed as whites with the same qualifications, and that 66% of Black employees were being paid a lower hourly rate than white workers doing similar jobs. Another report showed that Black children were being excluded from state schools at a rate six times that of whites. Meanwhile, Childline, the children's charity, revealed that racial abuse was a common experience for children from ethnic minority backgrounds, and a major cause of mental illness.

During that summer of 1995, the West Indies bowlers were called 'savage' and 'muggers' in British newspapers. That use of language was deliberately derogatory and used to reinforce the stereotype that people with Black skin should be feared. On a purely sporting level that was okay for us. We wanted the batsman to be frightened. But, unfortunately, the inference was not limited to sports.

That West Indies team had the opposition in a psychological vice, I guess. We had them every which way. Given what had come before in history and what was happening in the world at the time with apartheid and West Indians being treated as second-class citizens in Britain, me and my teammates were their worst nightmares realised. Black people showing that they were equal in mind, body and spirit. So it was no wonder that West Indians in England and other foreign lands who felt oppressed drew strength from the performances of our team and started to demand equality in day-to-day life.

But we were the lucky ones. We had strength in numbers. Many of the Black sportspeople who were doing it on their own, who had come years before, are only now being recognised. And it wouldn't be right if I didn't spend some time paying homage to a guy I read about, and was wowed by, during Black History Month. His name was Fritz Pollard. He was a pioneer for Black sport. And, hopefully only until now, had been largely forgotten. Pollard was the American football player who took the sport by storm at a time when his fellow African-Americans were being lynched in alarming numbers.

American football is a sport that I love because of the nuances of the game and its complex tactical strategies. And it is one where Black athletes are given their dues. They are equal and leading the way. Pollard was way ahead of his time. He was the best player for the champions in 1920, the first Black coach in 1921 and the first Black quarterback in 1923. A Black coach telling white players what to do in the US in 1921! It blows the mind. Likewise, Pollard being a quarterback, the most coveted position in the team and, since him, until only recently, the domain of the white college superstar.

Pollard's story gives another insight into what life was like for a Black man in America in that period. He was born in 1894 and named after the abolitionist Frederick Douglass. He earned the nickname 'Fritz' because he grew up in Rogers Park, Chicago, where there was a strong German community. His family had moved from Oklahoma. They wanted to get away from the South and the oppressive laws of segregation.

What's interesting about Pollard's early life is that he actually wanted to be a baseball player. But Blacks were banned from that sport. So he adapted. He launched himself into American football instead. His brothers all played. They had adapted. And he would have to do the same. Keep quiet. Don't retaliate. Bite your lip. Pollard did more than that.

After earning a scholarship to Brown University – an Ivy League college – Pollard sought out the football trials. Well, surprise, surprise, the white kids didn't want a Black guy in the team. So they set out to make his life a misery. The racist abuse was nothing new to him but the brutality was. It wasn't just one guy who'd tackle him, but five or six. Pollard laughed. He smiled. The racists were the ones who quit in the end in their quest to break him. They also soon realised he was their best player, their fastest player, their cleverest player. He had a low centre of gravity so he was incredibly hard to stop. He played in the Rose Bowl in 1916, the ultimate for a college footballer.

Not that he was treated the same way. He had to be smuggled into the stadium for fear of verbal and physical assaults. The hotel the team were staying at in Los Angeles initially refused to give him a room, until his team-mates, the same ones who had abused and targeted him, said they would walk out if he was not treated the same. Brown became the first team to beat Harvard and Yale in the same season. And Pollard, with his lightning feet and brain, did it almost on his own. He was selected for the all-America team.

His professional career began in 1919, the year of terrible race riots. He played for Akron Pros. He was abused by his team's supporters. He was abused by other players of colour. Jim Thorpe, a Native American who had excelled in football and won gold in the 1912 Olympics at decathlon and pentathlon, called him 'nigger'.

Akron won the first ever championship, going the entire season undefeated. When the team was awarded the trophy, Pollard was not allowed to attend. Remember, this was an era when a Black person couldn't eat in the same restaurant or sit in the same train carriage as white people. The following year Pollard was player-coach. There wouldn't be another Black coach in the NFL (the competition changed its name in 1922) until 1985. In 1923 he became the first Black quarterback when he played for Hammond Pros. It would be almost fifty years before another Black man played the same role for a team.

A certainty for the NFL's revered Hall of Fame, then? Of course not. This was believed to be largely the work of George Preston Marshall. Marshall was the owner of the Washington team, which he nicknamed with a racist slur – Redskins. Marshall was instrumental in the Black player ban because in the Great Depression he said it wasn't right to pay Black footballers. In July 2019, the Redskins revoked the name and a statue of Marshall outside their stadium was taken down.

After retiring from football Pollard founded the first Black investment fund in America. He started the first Black tabloid newspaper. He became a theatrical agent for Black talent, demanding equality for his clients. He died in 1986, aged ninety-two. It took another nineteen years for Pollard to be inducted into the Hall of Fame. When his family began a campaign, those who made the decisions about who was recognised said, 'We can find no record of his achievements.' They were looking in the white-owned newspapers and periodicals of the time.

Pollard's story is moving and hopeful. It neatly encapsulates so many of the themes of this book. Without people like him, Black sportspeople and Black teams would have been set back decades from their rightful path to a level playing field in their own sports. But we can also say that if his accomplishments had been highlighted at the time, that playing field could have been levelled a bit earlier. That role model theme once again.

There are many others like him, of course. Jack Johnson, a Black boxer, endured such abuse and anger for the seven years that he held the world championship title from 1908 that he had to escape America. Johnson is the reason the phrase 'great white hope' exists. The supremacists were desperate to find one of their own to beat him and reclaim superiority. In the end they settled for a trumped-up criminal charge. He was convicted of 'transporting a white woman across state lines' in 1913. For many years this was what he was reminded of, instead of his 'first' – the first Black heavyweight champion. He wasn't pardoned until seventy-two years after his death. Donald Trump signed the declaration. His family must surely hope Jack Johnson's pardon is not compared with and lumped into the same category as some of the disgraceful pardons given by this president.

Then there is Althea Gibson, the first Black female winner of a tennis Grand Slam title in 1956, winning the French Open, crossing the colour lines to do so. In 1957 and 1958 she did the double – Wimbledon and the US Open. The great Venus Williams said: 'I am honoured to have followed in such great footsteps. Her accomplishments set the stage for my success, and through players like myself and Serena and many others to come, her legacy will live on.' Need I say it again? Role models!

Venus Williams and her sister Serena are household names the world over. But Althea Gibson isn't. And, of course, Learie Constantine and George Headley. Truly the Black stars that followed her, Constantine, Headley, Johnson, Pollard and the many others, stand on the shoulders of giants.

What all the achievers listed and discussed in this chapter proved is that people of colour can be accepted and they can be equal. They destroyed the stereotypes. We're not lazy, stupid, incompetent, weak. We are as good as anyone. All the rubbish that was spouted by those pseudo-scientists, who classed people by colour, or the great brains like Voltaire who argued we were lesser beings? Those athletes put it in the trash can. So we take a knee to remember the history of dehumanisation and to raise awareness that it is still happening. But these folks, and what they did, allow us to get up. They have inspired so many heroes of the present day and in their stories and experiences we can learn how more of us can rise.

HOW WE RISE

CHAPTER 10

Progress

With Thierry Henry

'My colour came back, Mikey,' Thierry Henry tells me, wide-eyed, gesticulating, a blur of movement on the WhatsApp screen. 'You know what I'm saying? And I was like; "Whoa", I remember *this*. I was just a Black guy again.'

It's winter 2020. And Thierry and I are catching up on how 'the movement' is going. Progress since we last spoke in the summer when he was one of the first people to get in touch with me, saying, 'We need to talk.' Progress in his lifetime. Progress since whenever.

We can both see that, in the context of sport, Black athletes get the respect they deserve. They can be as revered as white sportsmen or women. On the field, on the track, in the ring, they get their dues. Look at Usain Bolt. And, of course, Thierry himself.

And when athletes of colour get that recognition and they are put on a pedestal, quite rightly, for their brilliance, something interesting happens. They are shown what it is like to be accepted by the majority of people. They are not followed in shopping malls. Because, 'Oh my God, it's Thierry Henry.' They are not told they can't afford a watch. 'Everyone knows Thierry Henry.' They can hail a cab: 'All right, Thierry, how's it going?' A nice friendly greeting from the cabby.

Why is that? Well, if you want me to be blunt, the security guard, the shop assistant and the cab driver don't feel threatened by that Black face. It's Thierry Henry, for goodness sake!

The Black superstar has just suddenly found out what it's like to be white. They only had to become world-famous to leave the category of 'other'. Unless, it's a mirage. And that's what Thierry was telling me about. Because that glimpse into white privilege only works if that person knows who you are. If they don't recognise you, watch out, here comes 'other' again!

'In Europe, people know me,' Thierry continues, 'and I don't say that in an arrogant way. I am recognisable. I've got a funny face. Big forehead.' He laughs. 'But when I went to America, whoosh . . . I am not known. I was just a Black guy. My colour never left me but I was reminded.

'It was New York City. I like wearing my tracksuit, I like wearing my hoodie, I like wearing my hat because, as a culture, I grew up with that, but I'm waiting for the Uber to arrive. It's not raining. And this is not hailing a cab. It's booked. My name. The driver sees me. I waved. And he went like . . . *Zooooom!* I was like, "I'm sure that was my car, the number plate matches."'

Ouch. I wince yet again but I am not shocked. I could relate to so many stories like that but this is Thierry's time to talk, so I ask: 'Did it sting? Did you dwell on that? Were you surprised?'

'No, you know why? Because I got the vaccine a long time ago.' He laughs again. 'So I'm immune and, you know, it came back quick. I was back to the past. I was like, "That again? *Still? Now? Before!*" You feel a bit embarrassed because you've avoided moments like that for so long. Now it's just like, that's just sad for you, man. Wow. That's me at thirty-eight, me at thirty-seven, thirty-five and so on. It took a long time for me to digest it, understand it, and know that those people are morons. And you just look at the guy and you're like, "Your mind is so little."'

Like Thierry, I have said the same thing in my mind when I've had those experiences, but nonetheless it still hurts, and I can detect in his voice, vaccine or no vaccine, it touched a nerve.

'Before I played football, if I walked into a shop with a tracksuit, straightaway the security guard is following me. That's a given because that's the norm. I go with the same tracksuit after I score a hat-trick for Arsenal, it's, "Mr Henry, how can I help you?" When I first got a bit of attention, Mikey, I *liked* it. Because I was like, "Oh! They're helping me. I might be someone."'

Well, there's no denying that. Thierry Henry sure is someone.

He is considered one of the greatest strikers of all time. He scored 360 goals in league and cup matches, 228 of them for Arsenal as he became their leading goalscorer. He won the Premier League Golden Boot a record four times, two FA Cups and two Premier League titles. He won the treble with Barcelona. He played for New York in Major League

Soccer. This was when the Uber incident occurred. Oh, and he also won the World Cup with France, the European Championship and is the national team's record goalscorer with 51 goals.

That's the sort of honours board you're going to need if you wanted to be treated right as a Black person. And, even then, you can still be cut down. 'You're made to feel sub-human,' Thierry adds.

Look, Thierry wasn't being naive. He wasn't telling that story to complain that people didn't recognise him. He was telling it to highlight how ludicrous it is how 'protected' – the word I used with Usain – you have to be to get a fair shot.

This isn't breaking news but people do treat you differently if you are 'famous' or well-known. And I use that in the context of famous to the person you might be talking to. Whatever the colour of your skin. In the past, I have been sometimes naive about that. A few years ago, my wife Laurie-Ann warned me about a white friend, saying, 'He only treats you well because you're on the TV . . . he treats other Black people badly.' I didn't believe it and thought it was a figment of her imagination. But I decided to pay more attention to see if it was true. Needless to say she was right. I just needed to be more aware.

Thierry has seen and heard it all. His dad is from Guadeloupe and his mom from Martinique. 'I had a tough but fair upbringing with my parents,' he says, 'probably like you. They did a good job, with the tools they had.' He grew up in a block of flats in the tough Paris suburbs, known as *banlieues*. His patch was Les Ulis. The *banlieues* are a hotbed of footballing brilliance because of their diverse population and they have produced many football stars. Kylian Mbappé, seen as something of a Thierry Mark II, grew up in one, too.

'I come from a neighbourhood where we were French, right? And some guys were from North Africa. Some were from Western Africa. Some were from Central Africa. Some were from the West Indies. Some had Italian roots. I learned about culture there. I travelled without moving because on the first floor it was Portuguese, second was Spanish, third was Senegalese, fourth was a guy from the Gambia, a guy who was Russian. That was so rich for me. That education showed me the way.'

His first awareness of racism is a familiar story. He left the community he was used to. Football took him to a smaller town in France when he was in his early teens. He was with team-mates from Nigeria and Senegal and they were warming up for the game. And suddenly . . .

'Silence. Nothing. Even the wind stopped. I can remember the look on the faces now but I didn't know that look so I was like, "What is wrong with these guys?" And then it's, "Go back to your own country" and, "Black this, Black that. Arab this, Arab that." Why?'

Thierry soon realised that his way out of a life where that sort of reaction was a constant was football, to play it and to be good at it. 'The only way out, always,' he says. 'And it was my dad who told me that; my dad always said to me, "Be you, be yourself. Don't try to fit in, you need to belong."

'My playing generation in France? There were more Black players in the national team, in the youth team as well, so my generation created this shift. And that shift also, you could see that sometimes people were like, "Wait a minute, is this the

French national team or is it Senegal's? What are we watching?" You could hear that sometimes.'

So the noise came from outside. And I can relate to that with the West Indies team. We were doing our own thing, beating everyone, but remember, those not inside our team or, as Thierry would put it, some of those not from our community, they weren't so happy about that. And I remember that World Cup-winning team of 1998 that Thierry was involved with. There was a lot of discussion in the French media about the number of Black players. When they won the World Cup in 2018? That had disappeared. Thierry says that preconceived ideas about Black players have probably changed. And we know those well-worn phrases; too lazy, too ill-disciplined, etcetera.

'I saw it as, "Thierry, you need to do everything right. Don't be late, work hard, do this, do that." Give no excuses. You need to make sure that it's perfect, because you are representing a community. And like you did, Mikey. You were the West Indies, so it's one team. I have a friend who is an Arsenal fan, he is from Jamaica. You know how many times he talks about your team, your cricket team? He does my head in. *All the time.* Trust me, if you didn't do it right, we would have known about it.'

Doing it right, though, doesn't stop the morons. Nor does being one of the all-time greats. He had to face things that I didn't. At least not at close quarters. The manager of the Spanish national team called him a 'Black shit'. He suffered racist abuse on the field when he was playing in Spain, too. 'My way to answer was to beat them through football without reacting to what they were saying. I used to look at them in a cocky way. Because that was my only way to show them.

To answer with a smile and go, "Hey, I'm better than you; you can talk or do whatever but *I'm better.*" And most of the time, you know what happened? People come up after the game and go like, "Yeah, you're good."'

You can't get away from the fact, though, that he had to be good. As I have been writing this book and reading and researching, it has been hard not to get a little down at times. And one thought did creep in. I wonder if sport is a true barometer for progress in terms of Black people being accepted in society? I ask the question but I know the answer. It's no. Late 2019 I came across an article stating that England had recorded more than 100 non-white footballers, mostly Black, who had represented the country. Think about it. More than a hundred and yet football still has its racist elements. But there are certain things that are inarguable. First over the line is the best. The guy who scores most goals is best. Sport is measurable in a way other industries are not. There can be no denying that Usain Bolt is the fastest man in the world or that Thierry Henry has scored the most goals for France. So maybe you have to be the best. Or good, or great in your sport to be treated better.

I shared this with Thierry. And I make a specific point harking back to what Hope Powell said about Black coaches in football. We see so few and it kind of backs up that idea that it's okay for Black people to be physical and strong and fast. But, hey, you don't have the brains for the 'important' jobs. The decision-making. Also, 'good management' in sport is not so easily measured. You are only considered good if you win trophies, but there are so few of those to actually win that it is just not as clear.

Thierry is someone in that regard, too. He is a coach

now. One of the very, very few Black coaches in a white-dominated area of the sport. He was manager of Monaco and, since 2019, was in charge at Montreal Impact in the MLS, leading them to the play-offs for only the second time in their history in the particularly trying circumstances of the coronavirus pandemic – Montreal had to play all of their remaining matches away from home.

Thierry listens intently, nodding, before answering. And from there the conversation just rolls along as we try to pick it apart. It was fascinating to me (and I still think it's pretty interesting having read it back) and it gives an insight to Thierry's honesty and energy.

'It is still annoying that we get recognised only for physical attributes,' he says. 'Rather than mental ones. You have a lot of the generation in the 1980s or the 1990s that could have been coaches. They had everything. But they didn't even bother, because they knew they wouldn't get the job. They couldn't even dream of the job because they were like, "Why am I going to bother?" A lot of Black players didn't even want to take their coaching exams.

'But there are two sides of the story, the one that the door will never open for you. Or, you need to find a way to open it. The generation of the 1990s cracked it a bit, the generation of 2000 a bit more and so on. And hopefully I can crack it even more.

'We have lost a lot in the process. I always say one name when I think of this. Ashley Cole. One of the best ever players in England's history, 107 caps. Went unbeaten with Arsenal, won two league titles with Arsenal, one with Chelsea. Won a Champions League. Do you ever hear anyone talk about him? The guy was a great player, and I can give you other names. But I go back to the why?'

I tell him why I think that is. Because when you promote people like that, you're defeating the argument of white supremacy. And that is not something that people want to do. A lot of people believe that equality means they lose something. If we get equality, they're losing their white privilege, although many will tell you there is no such thing. And it comes back to the theme so far – you're acceptable on the pitch, but not off it. They cheer for you on the pitch, but on the street you can be abused. The media has a big role to play here. Look at how Black footballers are treated in the British tabloids. When Marcus Rashford, the Manchester United and England striker, took on his government to reinstate free school meals in the school holidays for impoverished children during a pandemic, one paper saw fit to run an article about his own wealth, strongly hinting that he was some sort of hypocrite. Raheem Sterling, the Manchester City and England player, is another who has made 'news' for supposedly flaunting his wealth. The biased coverage is obvious to those who want to see. Black footballer buys a home for his mother, he's showing off. White footballer buys a home for his mother, he's a good son. Those stories encourage people looking for an excuse to dislike Black people away from the sports stadiums. What they do in them, or on the pitch, is fine and the back pages give them the credit, but there are two sides.

The media's treatment of people of colour is dubious to say the least. I remember seeing a video of Akala, the British rapper, journalist, author and activist, talking about its influence on a political television show. And how the media is obsessed with a person's otherness, so long as they are not white, if they have done something wrong. 'I've lost count of the number of times I've read "Pakistani man does blah" . . . but when Jimmy Savile [is mentioned] are his ethnicity or religious beliefs put forward as the primary reason for committing an offence? No. We stoke the flames of bigotry and then act shocked.'

A friend of mine who works in the media tells me that journalists in Britain are almost trained to be racist in their reporting. A lot of national newspapers use what are called 'news agencies' for stories in parts of the country where they do not have their own journalists based. For example, if the *Daily Mail* wants to cover a story about the Bristol protestors removing a statue of the slave trader Edward Colston, they could ask a Bristol news agency to cover it for them.

In turn, these news agencies also find stories in their local area to sell on to national newspapers. One of the very early lessons a journalist will learn at a news agency is that Black does not sell. If you have a story about someone who has done something positive or good and they are white: fine. It will be sold. But if they are Black? Or Muslim? Or 'other'? No. They don't even bother to begin the process of covering that story. If that Black person or Muslim or 'other' has done something wrong? Hold the phone.

'What's difficult is not knowing, at times, who is stopping the progress of someone,' Thierry says. 'That's why now, for example, you have Black ex-athletes who are still in the game, because now you have Instagram, a platform where you can voice your opinion. People are listening. I know it's possible, Obama was president. And before, I was like, "That will never happen." If anyone had asked me if that could happen, I would have said, "Please, don't be stupid."

'Now I see more and more people from my community

on TV, having a voice that people listen to. So I know it's possible. So maybe if you change the hierarchy and who is at the top to younger, fresher, community-minded people, maybe it will be different. We will always be the reflection of the education of your parents. If you have an open mind and you read well and travel then you are moving away from what your parents told you. It takes time for people to accept something.'

He's right, of course. And we know. This is learned behaviour. But I'd also add that learned behaviour won't be such a big roadblock if white and Black come together to beat this thing. The BLM demonstrations show us that. Look at how many young white people, brown people, Black people were on the street together and all over the world. Not just in America where the most high-profile killing of a Black man had taken place. Years ago, in the 1960s, when Martin Luther King was leading the civil rights movement in America, the crowd was 99 per cent Black and the marches and demonstrations were limited to the streets of that country. Now you see the young people all over the world recognising that things aren't right (well, a big chunk of them anyway). And they're willing to come out to say that things are not right. So, one would hope that when these young people start getting into positions of influence, things will slowly but surely change, and that is why I tell people that I am hopeful. As the world becomes a smaller place and more information is freely available and the re-education gets rid of the old brainwashed thoughts, progress is being made.

Sometime in the middle of 2020, I saw a story about a bloodstock agent who had posted some racist comments on his social media platform. He was immediately banned from operating at the upcoming Kentucky yearling sales, which was a big thing. His son then posted on social media that he was glad his dad got banned because he had wanted to have a conversation with him for years about his attitude to Black people and now it had given him the opportunity to have that conversation. Wonderful! Thierry nods in agreement as I tell him this story.

'The new generation coming in with a different type of vision, a different type of education means we'll be in a multicultural place, we'll be more open than the previous generation, because they were brainwashed in a particular way. And it's very difficult when you pass a certain age to change your habit.

'I don't understand why those older people, from other communities, don't want to talk about it. It seems like a taboo. "I don't know what it is to be Black, I don't want to talk about it." I was talking to a journalist one day, they were asking me, would I walk off the field if I was insulted? I said, "Why are you asking me that question? Ask the white player if he's gonna leave the field." Asking a white player that question, let me tell you, is a big step towards any improvement.

'Some people don't want to elaborate on the Black subject. But they can elaborate about sexuality and women in football. And it's great we talk about that. You're a human being, no problem. You ask anyone about Black people? "Oh, I don't know what I can say."'

Progress, then? Where are we? It is heartening to hear that Thierry is positive. He talks with such enthusiasm and energy. And during the call he continues to be a blur on the screen to the extent that sometimes I worry that it's going to just freeze. I am very conscious that at this stage of the story we need to be looking to the future, to be talking about change, to be talking about good things.

'I'll tell you why we made progress,' he says. 'I think what has happened this past year after what happened to George Floyd is . . . people want to know. Before it used to be our community that was crying and trying to make people understand, "Hey, it's hard, right? I'm here! Hello, we're suffering!" So people didn't feel our pain. They didn't feel my pain. Because as much as you want, if you don't live it, you can't see it.

'It's like when you're about to become a parent. And people who have kids say, "You're gonna understand *something* when that baby arrives." And you're like, "Nothing's gonna change, I'll still do what I want to do." No! So once you live it, you understand. I saw all the communities caring about our community. That's where I think the progress has been made.

'And also, Mikey . . . this is weird what I'm gonna say but I know you'll get it. So, the way we dress, what we eat, our music, the way we dance or whatever it is, that was more accepted than the human being. They don't like the human being because of your look and colour, but they like the culture. You like to come on holiday. You like the sea, you like the sun, you like the food, you like the camaraderie, you like the fun of it, you like your rum. You like whatever it is. But yet, you don't like the individual. That is a big change that needs to happen right there.'

Let me just make a point here about cultural appropriation, because that's what I hear some people complaining about when one culture adopts or copies another. It can be controversial when it is done to mock people from another culture and I think we can see clearly when that is the case.

But I have no problem with people trying to adopt a culture because they admire it. I have always believed that imitation is the sincerest form of flattery. When Thierry played football, kids wanted to be him, to copy him.

'It will always come back to a need to belong,' Thierry says. 'I have to force those people to accept me the way I am. And sport is an easy way to do that. It is easy to convince people. It's easy for people not to see your colour any more if you do the right thing because you give them emotion. Then suddenly, Mikey, and I bet this was the same with you, people see your heart, they don't see your colour any more. They see your heart. They see your passion and don't care where you are from. When someone sees your heart, they can relate. They can relate because when people go to a stadium after a week of a miserable job that they don't like, they want to live through you for one and a half hours. That's what sport gives to people.'

I think that's true but with a slight reservation. At the moment, it is still easy for some fans to flip to being racist haters. But, as I said and accept, it's not a short journey. Thierry, as he says, 'can talk about this all day'. And he has. All over the media in the days since George Floyd was murdered. On newscasts, newspaper web chats, telling folks that, despite everything, he really feels that he belongs and he's not just seen as a Black athlete. That's really something. Two Black guys talking about how things are changing for the better? That's progress. I would echo his thoughts that people can now see the pain in our communities. And people are asking questions about racism. I think back to the emails and text messages I got on that rainy day in July.

One in particular is important to me. It was from a Sky

cameraman. His name is Ian Dicker and he wasn't even working on the game but was watching the broadcast. I've reproduced it with his permission.

> I was inspired by what you said about BLM on Sky which I thought was spot-on. I want to say that I've never thought twice about my position of white privilege. Though I always treat anyone I meet of any race, colour, or creed exactly the same, I have come to realise listening to yourself and others how lucky I have been to be free from the shadow of racism my whole life. I also wanted to tell you that my grey Confederate cap has been consigned to the bin. I liked the shape of the hat but I was never comfortable with the politics and history associated with it. I will not wear it again.

Hopefully, like Ian, others will come to the realisation that white privilege doesn't mean you're getting a free ride; it just means that whatever hurdles you have to cross are not put there because of the colour of your skin.

Soon after Ian's message, I had the shock of Thierry calling me up, encouraging me to talk, to speak up. And change will keep coming.

'Exactly,' he says. 'And it will be because of what I've done, not because of who I am. So now we need people to listen to us or hear us for who we are instead of what we've done.'

And that brings him back again to Black coaches. Positions of responsibility. The next big leap forward. And he has one last important point to make.

'I'm a winner,' he says. 'I'm a competitor. So don't give me a free ride. Don't give Black people jobs because it's a good thing to do. I want a fair call.'

We can talk all day. And I know, and am grateful, that someday soon I will do so again with Thierry. But he gave me an idea with those parting words. There's someone else I need to talk to.

CHAPTER 11

The Blueprint?

With Makhaya Ntini

Change does not happen overnight. There is no magic wand. No quick fix or back route to equality. I wish there was. Change happens over generations. And I think we have shown that in this story so far. Black athletes now get the recognition they deserve. In the past, they didn't get the opportunities needed to show what they were capable of.

But the question no athlete – Black or white – wants to be asked is whether they have succeeded because of an unnatural attempt to speed up the process of equality. That they have been picked for the team because of the colour of their skin, rather than the mental, physical and technical ability they possess in their chosen sport.

Meet Makhaya Ntini. He knows what I'm talking about. Makhaya played 101 Test matches, the pinnacle of cricket, for South Africa. He took 390 wickets. Like me, he was a fast bowler. He is retired now and I have had the pleasure of getting to know him in the commentary box. Only two other South Africans have taken more wickets than Makhaya for South Africa. He is a legend, a true great of the game and the personification of Black talent. He was also the first Black person to represent South Africa in cricket.

So get out of the way, and I say that nicely, if you suggest that Makhaya was only picked to tick boxes about what a post-apartheid South Africa team should look like. 'It should be on merit,' he bristles as he sits talking to me from his kitchen at his home in East London on the Eastern Cape. 'Don't tell me that I am a quota player after fifty or sixty matches. Or that I started because of the quota system.'

Let's come back to that and take a second to explain what the quota system is. After apartheid, the South African government drew up what was called a 'transformational' charter that demanded national sports teams pick a certain number of 'people of colour'. In cricket it has been broken down to two Black African players and four players of Asian or mixed-race heritage. In rugby, the target for the most recent World Cup – which South Africa won – was 50 per cent of the starting team. Cricket and rugby are front and centre for this rule because, traditionally, these are sports that have been dominated by white people because of the powerful South African public school system.

It comes from a good place, no doubt. But Makhaya disagrees with it in cricket and the rugby World Cup-winning captain Siya Kolisi also disagrees with it. Kolisi said that he believed the great Nelson Mandela would have been against it too. He is probably right. To paraphrase that other great man, Martin Luther King, he said Black people deserve not to be judged on the colour of their skin but the content of their character. As Black people, we have to be true to that. We can't have it both ways – complain about inequality but then accept it if it suits.

Maybe you're thinking, *Surely you want this visibility for Black people? To inspire others? These are role models.* Believe me, I understand that argument. Throughout this book I harp on about that theme, but discrimination – positive or negative – to my mind does not work. What if that Black person who gets picked purely because of the colour of his or her skin, rather than his or her ability, is shown up to be hopelessly out of their depth? And this goes for any industry – not just sport. It is counterproductive. If you start filling positions in sport, business, industry or whatever because you need to tick a box based on ethnicity, gender or age, instead of employing the best person for the job, you don't solve a problem, you create one. In fact, you create lots of problems. For a start that person might not be capable of doing the job and, in a high-profile area like sport, that person is embarrassed. How is that good for inspiring someone or being a role model? It will also embolden the racists who can stoke resentment, arguing, 'Told you they shouldn't be there' or shouting, 'Look, they're taking our jobs and they can't do them.'

Makhaya told me that he had to deal with this sort of negative fallout from quota systems during his career. Despite his undoubted natural ability, there were those who would always question him or use it as a stick to beat him with. Luckily, Makhaya is a confident man and was always secure in his sporting prowess, but what he described to me also runs the risk of chipping away at a person who is capable and turning them into something less capable.

'I think it was at a time when I already had 200 wickets

to my name,' he says. 'And I was still being called a quota player. Excuse me? I don't think so. In any other team in the world I would have been a senior player, a decision-maker. A guy who was there at all the meetings, having a say, being a leader.'

In cricket – and most sports – there are meetings held between senior players to discuss things like strategy and discipline, much like businesses hold board meetings. Makhaya was the equivalent of a chief executive with all of his experience. Yet he was treated like an associate and not invited to the meetings. But the guy who has played only a handful of games and is white?

'He becomes a senior player because he's not Black. Straightaway he gets called to the senior meetings. That meeting has to be white people only. So those are the things that we had to go through even though this system was supposed to help. And if we say something? All of a sudden, we are ungrateful.'

And just like what has been said on so many other occasions or about other scenarios, if a Black man tries to 'forcefully' object to an unfair situation, that man immediately is the latest 'angry Black man'.

So you see, change takes time. Only white players at the senior meeting? Those are deep-seated views. Hardly surprising considering South Africa's history. And it feels unfair to criticise South Africa, because they are trying their best to ensure their nation is fairly represented, but, as we've seen, unconscious bias dies hard. I suppose the powers that be consider it important to try to legislate equality and perhaps they hope that eventually the legislation won't be needed and can be done away with. It is a Black-dominated country (a 2011 census showed that 76 per cent of the population was Black African) and it has, shall we say, a difficult history to overcome.

Apartheid only ended in 1994. It was a system of racial segregation straight out of the colonial playbook. South Africa had been colonised by the Dutch and the British. And the indigenous people were, as you won't be surprised to read by now, treated like sub-humans. When the all-white National Party won elections in 1948, apartheid was two years away. It was a party comprised mostly of politicians descended from those colonialists. Laws were brought in to separate white from Black and ensure white supremacy. There were 'mandated' residential and business zones for each racial group and other races could not live in or own land in those areas.

How was it decided where you were allowed to live and work? The National Party divided South Africans into one of four groups based on appearance, socio-economic status and culture. White, Black, Coloured and Indian. Between 1960 and 1983, 3.5 million Black people were thrown out of their homes and off their farming land. It was one of the largest mass evictions in history, creating widespread poverty among the community and simultaneously enriching white people. In less than ten years, 80 per cent of the land was owned by whites (because the National Party made it law), and non-whites had to carry documents allowing them to go into restricted areas.

By 1960 Black protestors were being mass-murdered by police. In Sharpeville, a Black township, police opened fire on a group of unarmed Black people who were protesting against the government. At least 69 were killed and more than 180 were wounded. I fleetingly remember hearing about Sharpeville when I was six years old, before any thought of what took place was overtaken by more important things like running out to play with my friends for the entire day. As I got a bit older and noticed the grown-up members of my family, and in particular my mother, paying attention to events in South Africa, I began to take notice of the images emerging from there. Police officers with dogs and shooting unarmed Black folk made an impact. Looking back, I guess that must have been one of the first moments in my life when I had an inkling – and I say an inkling because, at that young age, I would have soon become engrossed in play and making mischief – that something wasn't right with the world.

Something else happened in my early days that I did not wholly understand until I got older. I do not remember how old I was but I remember us having a dog called Biko that got killed by a car and my mother weeping. I had never seen my mother cry and it wasn't the first dog that we had lost in that way, as the yard did not have a front gate and the dogs would at times just go wandering off. She showed grief before but not tears. It wasn't until many years later that I worked it out. That dog was named after Stephen Biko, the South African anti-apartheid activist who died in police custody, and that was her connection to the struggle in South Africa.

Mr Mandela, whose party, the African National Congress, was a political rival to the National Party, was imprisoned three years after the Sharpeville massacre. And that's where he would remain until 1990. Imprisoned purely because he wanted equality for people of all colours and creeds in South Africa and was seen as a threat to white supremacy. Today, we can recognise that the National Party's decision to lock him up was one of their biggest mistakes because it enraged fair-minded folk all over the world. And Mr Mandela's mainly South African movement was globalised. But in my opinion that seemingly didn't trouble certain powerful nations enough to try to do something about the injustices. Was that unconscious or conscious bias because the oppressor was white and the oppressed non-white?

Importantly, sport played a huge role in raising awareness. Sporting organisations took up the mantle and acted while governments sat on their hands. Football's world-governing body, FIFA, suspended the South African football federation in 1963, the country was banned by the International Olympic Committee in 1970 for refusing to pick multiracial teams and the International Cricket Council followed suit. Rugby was a little slower to act; South Africa were barred from the first two World Cups in 1987 and 1991 but remained as a member of the International Rugby Board. Sports saying, 'We're not playing against you because you are racist' made people sit up and take notice. And it made governments sit up and take notice. The American and British governments, under Ronald Reagan and Margaret Thatcher, had been largely supportive of apartheid. They had considered Mandela a communist and terrorist. But when people began to understand apartheid through a sporting perspective, it's my belief that it helped to really pressurise the powers that be to do something. Remember that the next time you hear someone say that taking a knee is virtue signalling or 'woke'. Give me a break. It raises awareness, it keeps the conversation going and reminds people that things have got to change. And what is wrong with being 'woke'? It seems people don't quite understand what woke means. The *Oxford English Dictionary* defines it as being 'alert to injustice in society, especially racism'. Please call me woke for ever.

Cricket had a particularly interesting role to play. The South African government tried to legitimise their racist endeavours by inviting what were known as 'rebel' tours to the country, and also to satisfy a sports-mad white public's thirst for high-level competition. Most of these tours were organised in secret and the public only found out about them when the players arrived at the airport. An England team was the first to tour in 1981/82, followed by another tour in 1989/90. Two Australian teams went, in 1985/86 and 1986/87. The first England team was led by Graham Gooch. Geoffrey Boycott, the leading batsman at the time and only until recently a commentator for the BBC, was also on that tour. There was, unsurprisingly, a huge row about it. The English players had been paid big money to go and effectively sanction the apartheid regime. A player who agreed to go on such a tour had to be either ignorant or uninterested in the plight of people of colour in South Africa. The phrase 'selling your soul' comes to mind.

One would have thought that taking 'blood money' would have damaged their reputations. Despite the players being banned from international cricket for three years, Gooch would go on to captain England and retired as a legend. Boycott was a sought-after media personality. Bob Woolmer would go on to get the coaching job of South Africa. Mike Gatting, a former England captain, led the second tour. Gatting became president of the Marylebone Cricket Club, better known as the MCC. It is considered the moral authority of the sport. David Graveney, who was a player-manager on the tour, was made a chief selector of the England team. He is now national performance manager. It is probably a sign of progress that you can look back at those tours, remember that people were paid money to help keep the Black man down and reckon that it wouldn't happen today.

Still, it was not the most shocking moment of that period of cricket's history. Two West Indies teams took the 'blood money', too. And they included people who were friends and team-mates. You can see why a white English player would not bother to do his research or just purely be thinking how much money could be made, but a West Indian? It beggars belief that Black people, whose ancestors had suffered in the same way that the South African people were suffering, took that money. And some of them did it twice. There were tours in 1982/83 and 1983/84.

I was angry and felt betrayed. I made my feelings known to those players I knew who decided to put greed ahead of their culture and people. I also gave an interview to a journalist in Australia and that experience taught me to never again speak to a journalist while angry. I said some things then that were very harsh. They were true but not everything that is true needs necessarily to be exposed in public. But we learn.

Apparently, the tour organisers had asked Sir Viv Richards to name his price. Let me tell you, they didn't know Viv very well. He wouldn't have gone there for anything, but I suppose they figured they had to try. Getting such a huge name in West Indies cricket would have been a massive coup for them.

These tours were all done in a very hush-hush way. I remember before the first tour I was playing a match for Jamaica against Barbados in Barbados. I had left the hotel with Big Bird (Joel Garner) for some reason or another.

When I came back there were a lot of players on the balcony. And as soon as I approached all the conversation stopped and there was an uncomfortable atmosphere. When that tour was announced my mind flashed back to that moment in Barbados and I'm pretty sure they must have been talking about it.

Was I asked to go? Yes. I was in Australia playing domestic cricket before the second tour and Lawrence Rowe, who was a good friend of mine, called me to ask if I would be interested. He probably thought he was helping me. I had a knee injury; he may have thought my career didn't have many years left and that I could do with the money. I tried to explain to him why I wouldn't do it, that the apartheid regime was wrong and I couldn't support a government that dehumanised Black people in that way. In my opinion, going there was support-ing the regime, telling them you saw nothing wrong with what was happening there. I mean, the players on those West Indies tours were given 'honorary whites' status. I kid you not. Lawrence told me he didn't think South Africa was as bad as had been made out because he saw a Black guy driving a Mercedes-Benz! I give him the benefit of the doubt and am 100 per cent sure Lawrence, in his mind, was trying to help me. But he obviously didn't see the big picture.

The contrast between what happened to the England players who went and the West Indies players couldn't be more stark. And that tells a story. The West Indies players returned to their homelands in the Caribbean to find out they had become pariahs and their lives, mostly, went to hell. People at home thought, *How could they?*, but I say 'mostly' because the players from Barbados generally didn't suffer to the same degree socially as the Jamaicans, for instance. Most of the Jamaicans, if not all, lost their jobs and whatever social standing they had on the island. Some left the country and those who stayed fell on very hard times. One, Richard Austin, died of a drug overdose; another, Herbert Chang, suffered a nervous breakdown. I am sure those guys regretted their decisions in the end and it is a shame they couldn't see beyond making a fast buck. And I am happy to forgive anyone who makes a mistake in life, we all do. But not everyone shows remorse and they will be remembered differently.

It's a terribly sad story. And there is certainly something depressing about the English reaction, as I can't remember hearing too many apologies being issued, but maybe they see no need to apologise. All manner of cushy jobs handed out. The arrogance, the hypocrisy, the, let me think . . . there must be a phrase for it? Oh yes. White privilege.

But what did Makhaya remember of those rebel tours? He was born in 1977 so would have been a young boy through that period.

'No, no,' he said. 'We had no television. I knew nothing.'

Of course. Why would Makhaya have known? The rebel tours were not staged for his benefit and apartheid ensured that people like him led completely different, separate lives from white people. The end of apartheid, however, would change Makhaya's life.

He was born in a small village called Mdingi in Cape Province. He was a cowherd and he spoke fondly about the community spirit of people in the village, sharing food, helping one another with their smallholdings and animals. 'We were all together, it was the greatest time ever.' It is particularly poignant and moving to hear Makhaya say that because, at the age of fifteen, he was spotted by cricket talent scouts. Nothing would be the same again; his life changed – and in many ways for the better – but there is no doubt in my mind when hearing him talk all these years later that throughout his professional career he would pine for that feeling of belonging and community.

He was packed off to Dale College in King William's Town, which had a renowned cricket programme. He couldn't speak English. 'I just had a plastic bag with my clothes in,' he said. 'Nothing else.'

Apartheid may have been over but he was still an outsider. At school, because he couldn't speak English or understand what was being said, his classmates thought they could be racist without him knowing. But he knew. And he had his way of getting his own back.

'Being the only Black guy was always gonna be a big issue,' he says. 'But I had one good friend. And he would tell me what was said. So, at the next training session I would say to the coach, "Give me the ball when that guy comes in to bat – I bowl at him." And I bowled fast, at his body and head. He understood after that. Word got around.'

During his international career with South Africa, Makhaya was always revered for his skill and dedication to his fitness. Or at least what they thought was his dedication to his fitness because of one particular story. Every morning before the match, he would run to the ground instead of taking the bus with other members of the team. People were wowed by that. What a professional. And Makhaya was like that, don't misunderstand me.

The truth, however, was sad. Makhaya didn't want to take the team bus because he was an outsider and he knew the white players would not sit with him, talk with him. It was the same in the hotel dining room.

'You get to the breakfast and you're the first there. Two guys walk in, they sit someplace else. And then the next person walks in, he goes and sits with them. And so on. You try to turn a blind eye, say to yourself, "They have things they need to talk about." But in the end, you find out that this is normal, this is how they do things. They forget that you exist until we are on the field. And this became life.

'It is easy to see, actually, when you look at someone's face, that the person doesn't want to look you in the eyes – might be your coach, your captain. It tells you straightaway that they don't really appreciate you being there.

'They are thinking I was not being selected on merit. Every game for me felt, it's almost like there was a trial of some sort. And you will hear remarks from your own colleagues, that you don't belong here, you don't deserve to be part of our team.'

Is this racism or the quota system? Probably a bit of both. And although I understand why positive discrimination exists, and the South African government introduced it because they were so keen to demonstrate to the world that they were going to bring about change, Makhaya's experience shows that it's not necessarily the right way to go about things.

'You've got to do it at grassroots level,' he says, 'at a provincial level. That's good. Give those people the opportunities. But when it comes to the top level, international, it has to be all on ability.'

In sport there should be an infrastructure introduced all over the country so kids aren't picked up and moved to another place where they feel like aliens, reinforcing the 'outsider' mentality. And Makhaya agrees with me that this should be the case in every industry. If you want to bridge the gap between the haves and have-nots, look at apprenticeship schemes, mentoring, training and education. That's where it should start, not at the very top of the ladder.

In South Africa they have also introduced a rule whereby companies have got to have a certain number of Blacks on their board. But what that can lead to is companies having Black people on their board, drawing a salary, but not actually being involved in the decision-making. It satisfies the law but doesn't really lead to eventual empowerment of the masses in the country.

But don't get me wrong – I think South Africa is showing the way forward. It has come an extremely long way in a short space of time. And there are always going to be things that don't work out, bumps in the road and challenges. But having spent a lot of time in South Africa post-apartheid I am hopeful. I don't want to say the country is a blueprint for the way to do things, but with Black leaders making decisions, making the laws and educating the young as to what has gone on in the world and what is going on, the country – and the people – have a chance.

'That's my wish,' Makhaya says. 'If it does not start from our schools, it will never work. Treat people equally, it will change right through to the sport, schools and everything. My son, he has white friends and they come over to the house. That is progress, you know? We are seeing each other's ways and cultures. Embrace it because before we were not able to expose our children to that. Our kids are united, they are able to wrap their arms around each other. That for me will be the turning point.'

Makhaya just enforced my thoughts on the problem. Each

sport or industry can try to put their house in order, but the message has to reach the society at large or no real meaningful change can take place. Fingers crossed. South Africa is a young country. And in ten or twenty years' time it will have leaders who were not even alive during apartheid. That's some thought. It will take time and it cannot happen overnight. And, as they say, the children are the future.

CHAPTER 12

A New Generation

With Adam Goodes

It's a bright, perfect Sydney morning just before Christmas. Adam Goodes is talking to me on his phone via Zoom. Adam is one of the most celebrated Australian Rules players ever and an Aboriginal icon. He's sitting on the grass, baseball cap and shades on, talking matter-of-factly about deeply distressing moments in the history of his family and Australia while watching his 18-month-old daughter, Adelaide, toddle around a play park, eating a rice cracker. Occasionally she comes over to say 'hello' before wandering off again.

'To think in three and a bit more years, someone could come into my house and take Adelaide away from me,' Adam sighs. 'You know, I'd go to jail stopping people doing that.'

Most parents have had that irrational fear of their child being abducted. But for Adam it is not irrational. A generation ago it happened to his family. His mum, Lisa, was five when she was snatched away.

'My nana was saying, "Hide the kids, hide the kids,"' Adam says. 'Mum remembers hearing those boots on the floorboards walking towards her. She started crying under the bed and saw this white hand reach underneath the bed and grab her and my auntie Joy. They dragged them both out. And Mum's screaming and looking at my nana, saying, "Why aren't you helping me? These people are taking me away." And that was the last time my mum got to see Nana.'

If you're confused, you should be. Adam's family, as incredible as this sounds, were not victims of a crime, you see. They were the victims of state-sponsored abduction. From 1910 and into the 1970s, the Australian government forcibly removed children of Australian Aboriginal and Torres Strait Islander descent from their families to be adopted by white families or placed in institutions. Why? To purge Australia of people of colour. It happened to one in three indigenous families. One in three.

They are known as the Stolen Generations. If you've not heard of them, or what they endured, then that's probably because Australia's PR machine is very effective. Things that come to mind when most people think of Australia might be a sun-filled paradise, boundless opportunity and a no-worries culture. And, of course, in many respects Australia is like that. Unless you are indigenous and you are the victims of the dirty, big secret that Australia wants to keep under wraps.

I know about it because when I was touring Australia in 1975 I met an Aboriginal family in Perth, and over the years they became great friends with my family and some members even came to Jamaica and spent time at my mom's house. One of the boys visited me in Derbyshire when I was playing county cricket. And over the years they educated me to what the indigenous people of Australia had been through. We remain friends to this day.

It is that history to which Adam has dedicated his post-playing life. As trophy-laden as Adam's career was (highlights include two player of the year awards, two league titles, named in the Indigenous Team of the Century), he is perhaps now best known in and outside of Australia for his work not just in highlighting discrimination towards his people and his culture, but in doing something about it. Adam is now giving back generously to the country that stole from him. And, to be frank, treated him appallingly during his career when he dared raise his voice to say, 'This isn't right.'

While playing for Sydney Swans in 2013 at the MCG against Collingwood on a weekend of matches dedicated to celebrating indigenous people, he heard a voice scream: 'Goodes, you're an ape!' It was from a 13-year-old girl. Adam pointed her out to security and she was removed. It was the first time he had been the target of a racial slur for eight years. He escaped to the dressing room and broke down in tears.

The girl's mother, perhaps providing the best interpretation of racism in these pages, said: 'She's a 13-year-old girl, from a small place in the country, who doesn't get out much.' I don't think you need two guesses to figure out where she got that idea from. Adam did not condemn her and instead reached out to her and her family. He offered her support, education. Because it was a young girl, conversations started all over the country – why would she think it's okay to use that word?

The Collingwood president, Eddie McGuire, apologised to Adam immediately after the match. But four nights later he went on a Melbourne radio station and compared him to King Kong. Suddenly, the story began to change. Why was

Adam picking on a girl? Why couldn't he handle a bit of name-calling? The media started to portray Adam as a bully. His social media accounts were riddled with the same slur. Adam was being framed as the villain.

So he was vilified as that PR machine whirred into action again. Despite being named Australian of the Year in 2014, the fact that he continued to have his say, to not quietly toe the line and instead criticise a country that had bestowed one of its highest honours upon him, was not 'fair dinkum', you might say. He said Australia had a problem with racism. With those words Adam had committed a cardinal sin – the Black man who complains. Cue Colin Kaepernick in the USA taking a knee during the national anthem. Just like Colin, it would end his career, too.

Adam was booed and abused week in and week out for the rest of his career. He was a 'jerk', according to a former AFL player, Sam Newman. Remember that name.

The girl's mother showed her true colours. 'If he hadn't have carried on like a pork chop it wouldn't have mattered. I don't think he should retire, he should man up and just take it.'

That abuse ended Adam's career early. He felt that he had given racists a platform. His last game was in 2015. 'The booing was like a howl. I felt like an absolute piece of crap. I was an emotional wreck. I didn't want to go to training. I never had that feeling in eighteen years of playing. I called the coach and he brought around my best mate and I broke down. I was like: "I can't do this any more."' Today he can't even bring himself to watch the sport.

These days, the media like to report this as an incident that 'divided the nation'. And that's probably true. On one side you had people who were embarrassed about their nation's past, present and future, so liked to pretend it was just Adam picking on a teenage girl. On the other were those who said it was time Australia faced the uncomfortable truth.

It was nothing new, though. In 1993 an indigenous player called Nicky Winmar had done something similar to Adam. In a match, also against Collingwood, Winmar, who grew up in an iron shack with no running water in Western Australia, had been targeted by racist fans, calling him, among other things, a 'Black cunt'. At the end of the game Winmar lifted up his jersey, pointed to his Black skin and said, 'I'm Black and I'm proud to be Black.' A similar period of national soul-searching was supposed to have followed, although it was hijacked by the same sort of folks who thought it was overblown. The Collingwood president said: 'As long as they conduct themselves like white people off the field, everyone will admire and respect them. As long as they conduct themselves like human beings, they will be all right.' Wow.

Winmar received death threats. His club, St Kilda, banned him from talking about what happened. Five years later Sam Newman (yep, him again) 'blacked up' on television to pretend to be Winmar when he didn't appear as a guest. Winmar, by the way, was at the MCG the night Adam was abused.

Time away from the sport gave Adam clarity and purpose. He could see that casual racism was alive and flourishing. And that the population was ignorant. Did Australians even know what racism was? Could they ever know?

He was an agent of change, a man who would transcend his sport, hold up a mirror to Australia and force people to look. What they saw wasn't pretty. Maybe that's what upset so many people. Adam spent plenty of time looking in the mirror, too. He asked himself difficult questions. Should he have just kept his mouth shut, let it all die down and lived a peaceful life? After all, look at Nicky Winmar, who ended up working in a mine and as a sheepshearer. As I make the finishing touches to this book, Eddie McGuire and Collingwood are facing the same accusations of racism over their treatment of another Black player, the Brazilian-born Héritier Lumumba. No apology, just promises to 'fix' the problem. What has changed?

'I talked to those indigenous leaders that have been doing this stuff for fifty-plus years. I said, "Man, is anything gonna change?" They stopped me in my tracks and said, "Look what's changed in my generation of living." We used to be living on reservations, we weren't allowed to get educated, we weren't allowed to vote. We're now seeing our grand-children get an education, going to university, owning their own businesses, building wealth – don't tell me that nothing's changed. It's changed a lot in that one generation and is going to change again in another generation. So be optimistic, be forward-thinking, don't be angry, be positive, that this is an opportunity now, more so than ever." If Adam could get an opportunity to talk to the indigenous people of America, he would realise even more how far his people had come.

I, too, want to be forward-thinking and positive and I say as much to those who have serious doubts. But all in good time. Before we can understand what is changing and how, we need to understand what the situation was in the past. It's another section which, alas, makes for grim reading. But before we can see the light, we have to deal with the dark.

The estimated number of children who were stolen? Give or take . . . One. Hundred. Thousand. Indigenous people on average die ten years before white Australians. Those two statistics are linked. Cause and effect. Right there in black and white. I can also tell you that indigenous people are forty times more likely to experience domestic violence, ten times more likely to die from those experiences and fourteen times more likely to go to jail. There is a heavy price to pay for history (as we have already described post-slavery) and, unfortunately, the indigenous people in Australia have also paid. If you subjugate and terrorise an individual or a group of people, they suffer.

People's children being wrenched from the grasps of their parents is going to hurt. And it's going to hurt when people find out why it was done. The 'European Australians' called it, with unsurprising coldness, 'assimilation'. This government policy reckoned that Aboriginal people and Torres Strait Islander people, also known as First Nations People, should be allowed to die out through a process of natural elimination or be 'assimilated' into the white community. Particularly vulnerable were children of a combination of First Nations and white parentage. Adam's mum was Aboriginal but his father had Celtic ancestry.

These poor folks were classified by the colour of their skin. The categories were typically derogatory – half-castes, crossbreeds, quadroons and octoroons. And there were task-forces roaming the country to find children who needed to be assimilated. This is why many First Nation folks talk about moving around a lot when they were growing up as kids. They were on the run. The police were often tasked with rounding up victims and they were given titles like, wait for it, Aboriginal Protection Officers. It's like something out of a George Orwell novel. Oh, the officer who is supposed to protect me is going to snatch me away from my mother? Again, wow. A Dr Cecil Cook, who was the Northern Territory's Chief Protector of Aborigines, said: 'Everything necessary must be done to convert the half-caste into a white citizen.'

The seed of that barbaric ruling came, of course, from supremacy. First Nations were considered inferior. They were considered to be a threat to the white ruling class's way of life. But guess what? When First Nations people were being assimilated into white families, the white Australians didn't like that, either. They were worried they would be outnumbered. So many children were instead placed in 'compounds' or religious missions. Physical, mental and sexual abuse was not uncommon in those places. They had a lot stolen from them. They were lost, too. They were forced to adopt a white culture which was, frankly, alien to them. Their names were changed to make them more acceptable and they were forbidden from speaking their native tongue. Sound familiar? Cue African slaves in America and the Caribbean.

Australians Together, an organisation that catalogues the abuses and stories of the Stolen Generations so that indigenous people can fill in the blanks about what happened to them as kids and why, lists the effects of assimilation. Here are some of them . . .

Efforts to make stolen children reject their culture often created a sense of shame about being of Indigenous heritage. This resulted in a disconnection from culture, and an inability to pass culture on to their children.

Many children were wrongly told that their parents were abusive, had died or had abandoned them. Many never knew where they had been taken from or who their biological families were.

The children generally received a very low level of education, as they were expected to work as manual labourers and domestic servants. This has had lifelong economic implications and means many who are now parents are unable to assist their children with schoolwork and education.

Of course this should all sound familiar. People stolen from their homes, families split apart, denied their culture; organised abuse, violence and forced labour. But surely the European Australians didn't just wake up one day and decide to dehumanise an entire race? Of course not. These were entrenched views being borne out. At least Christopher Columbus had nothing to do with it. The culprit here is another false hero from history: the Briton Captain James Cook.

Cook was another who 'discovered' the fabled 'southern continent' when landing at Botany Bay on 29 April 1770. The fact that the indigenous people had been there for 60,000 years, one of the oldest and most established peoples in the world, is an inconvenient truth. Cook claimed *terra nullius* – a Latin phrase for 'empty land' – to set in motion the hundreds of years of disregard for indigenous life and culture. But even before setting foot on Australian soil he shot an Aboriginal man, wounding him. It was a warning shot for sure. The British would bring disease and genocide. Eighteen years later, Captain Arthur Phillip returned to Botany Bay to set up a penal colony. A fleet of eleven ships arrived on 26 January 1788. This is known as Australia Day. Indigenous people call it Invasion Day. 'We were murdered and you expect us to celebrate that day,' Adam says. 'We don't celebrate the Holocaust.'

What followed was 140 years of massacres of indigenous people by the invaders, starting in 1791. And, of course, there was rape and enslavement into the bargain. Man, woman or child were not spared. In September 1794 the British suspected an indigenous boy of being a spy and he was burned in a fire, thrown into a river and shot dead. There were at least 310 massacres until the last recorded one in 1928, when at least thirty-one Aboriginal people were murdered in Coniston by a mob led by a Northern Territory police constable, seeking revenge for the death of a white man.

That organised violence is no longer happening. But state-sponsored dehumanisation has continued to occur in my lifetime, when the homes of indigenous people were destroyed and their land was taken from them. Naturally, the daily abuse, that 'drip, drip' effect, continues. Derogatory names, being followed in shops by security guards, assumptions about your status. 'Every indigenous person has a story to tell about being vilified,' Adam says. 'We're made to feel we're not worthy.'

And would you believe that it was only in 1967 that Australia actually recognised indigenous people as human beings, as part of the population? Prior to a referendum – yes, Australians actually had to be asked the question – they were classed as flora and fauna.

What you will notice again is how the dehumanisation of Black people in America was being repeated in the exact same way on the other side of the world. And that's because it was learned behaviour, deeply entrenched and passed down from generation to generation, that people of colour were inferior.

And so we are back to those phrases again. Post-traumatic stress disorder. Or post-traumatic slave disorder. Or trans-generational trauma. People of colour have been oppressed for hundreds of years and no one has got over it. Not white, not brown, not Black. Because they don't know about it and some don't want to know about it.

So has that true history been taught in Australia? Has the government made a commitment and said, 'Okay, we will try to level the playing field where that is concerned'?

'No, not at all,' Adam tells me. 'What they have done is allowed teachers to teach Aboriginal history but without supplying them with the references that they need to be able to do that properly. So if I was a non-indigenous person at primary school or high school, how comfortable would I feel teaching history that I've never learned, never been taught, to students? You just wouldn't have the confidence to do that or to do it respectfully. Saying, "Yes, you can go out and teach it", with no guidance or reference to be able to do so, it's really hard for them to confidently go out and do that.'

There is a knowledge gap. And that gap is filled with all sorts of rubbish. Jeff Harriott, my Australian headteacher friend from Manchester, knows all the stories about indige-nous people. He grew up in a town with a large population of indigenous people and he was afraid of them. They were drunks, they were violent, they stole. That's what he was taught. Now he has educated himself he knows the truth. It is easier for Australian society to generalise about the indige-nous population, and to treat them all as troublemakers, than to face up to their history. 'Why does no one ask, "Why?"' Jeff said. 'What have we done to these people over 200 years?'

Adam makes the same point in a slightly different way.

Even if there was education reform and an environment for those conversations to take place, there would still be people not willing to listen. Getting people to understand the concept of trauma passed down is hard. Too hard.

'It's not only on a colour side, but a non-colour side as well, that intergenerational [understanding] of white privilege and white supremacy. People who don't get that it means they've lived a very privileged life and that they've lived a life that we all hope for our future generations. So, for me, my role is not about educating people about intergenerational trauma; people either want to get it or they just don't.' Adam and I hope those who don't will grow smaller and smaller in number until they just don't matter.

And round and round we go. This is why a 13-year-old girl abused Adam Goodes. But thank goodness he made his stand. That is not an easy thing to do. Believe me. Because I didn't do it. I was abused in a similar way when I toured Australia. But I didn't say anything. And I can say that I was being selfish by not doing something about it. I knew I could go home and I wouldn't have to face it.

'But also you wanted to protect yourself from it, Mikey,' Adam says when I shared my experience and my reaction with him. 'Racism is something that really affects you and then it made you feel so much more comfortable when you did get home to be surrounded by your people. And I think, for me, my mum told me very early that when people call me names to walk away, because they're saying these names to get a reaction out of me. And if I didn't react, they'd stop calling me that. And it worked and it was a way that my mum was able to protect me. But when I then learned about my history and my culture that I was part of, I was like, "No way, you're not gonna call me these names, and try and degrade me of something that I'm so proud of." And that's where it was a real turning point for me after being educated in my culture, and that connection to my spirituality. That changed everything and gave me a voice to be able to stand up to these people, whether they're 13-year-old girls, or whether they're people working in the media, or nine people on the football field from opposition teams, I call them out. Because it was time that I had the courage to do that. And it needed to stop.'

Since retirement, Adam has been working to do that. To redress the balance, to educate and to fill in the knowledge gap. Adam founded the Indigenous Defence and Infrastructure Consortium. It assists indigenous businesses in gaining access to markets which, in the past, might have been closed to them, helps businesses grow and mentors indigenous entrepreneurs.

'It's a way of saying: this is what our community wants. We just want the same as you. To be equal. Not more. It's like welfare dependency. Governments will say, "We'll just give you a little something, we'll just keep giving you enough, enough to survive and do what you choose to do." Now, that, to me, is suppression. And it's been happening for a very long time.

'We want indigenous people to believe they can achieve anything they want to achieve. In the past we've been seen as athletes, artists. And that's great. But we can be doctors, engineers, lawyers, scientists. We're now finishing high school and going on to university, like never, ever before in the history of colonisation. So we're self-educating, we're taking it upon ourselves to break down those barriers so that, in the next generation, we have more indigenous leaders owning their own businesses, and sitting on boards, running companies – that's where true power is. And that's where true change will come, I think.'

The biggest thing that's happening is called the Indigenous Procurement Policy, which the government created in 2015. It forces government agencies to procure through indigenous businesses. In that first year about AU\$268 million was being secured by indigenous businesses. Now, if you go back to the previous twelve months, what did the same government agencies spend with indigenous businesses when this policy wasn't around? Just \$6 million. And, right now, the government agencies have to spend about 3 per cent of the total contracts with indigenous businesses across those government agencies. Nearly a billion dollars a year are now being spent with indigenous businesses.

'So that economic resilience, and also the power that comes with that, is finally happening for indigenous people,' Adam says. 'And with that economic growth and connection for those indigenous people, they're now deciding where to live, where to put a roof over their head, what schools they want to send their children to, and, more importantly, what sort of health cover they want for their children and family. These are the three key areas that create so much disadvantage for indigenous people here in Australia.'

There are works in progress too. And the biggest issue remaining, of course, is re-education. Adam is involved in getting government recognition about what happened to the indigenous people and what is now the priority for their community. It is called the Uluru Statement of the Heart. And it's a collaboration because the government actually reached out and said: 'What should we prioritise?' How's that going?

'We want a nation of truth-telling, and telling the truth about history, and being able to do so with a voice to parliament written into our constitution,' Adam says. 'Right now, we're not acknowledged in our constitution. There are no laws, there's no reference to any indigenous people ever being in Australia before it was colonised – and we want to rectify that. We believe that we should at least have a referendum on this and give the Australian people that opportunity to vote on whether or not they think it's important.'

And just as Adam is talking, his daughter Adelaide appears again to give me a wave and a 'hello'. He beams at her. And in that moment you can see that she is his motivation. That he can do something to help the next generation. It is as the indigenous elders said to him: 'Be optimistic, be forward-thinking, be positive, that this is an opportunity now, more so than ever.' His daughter can be all of those things, in large part thanks to her father, who is doing a great job for his people and pressuring the government to level the playing field.

'I'm very hopeful about the future and the opportunities I can provide for her. She's already miles ahead of where I was as a kid. I didn't know about my Aboriginal history. My mum didn't know about it. Adelaide is already engrossed in her culture. She's already learning about language, about our people. And that's a gift.'

CHAPTER 13

We've Got a Chance

I am making these final notes at home in Miami at the start of 2021. All around me are boxes for the removal men. The walls are bare and much of the furniture has gone. I am moving on. I have 'lived' in Miami for more than twenty years, splitting my time between here and Newmarket in England, escaping the cold winters for the Florida sunshine. I put 'lived' in quotations because although I have had a house there for that length of time, I only became a permanent resident in 2011, previously requiring a visitor's visa because of my constant travelling for work. Early on in 2019 I decided that I didn't want to live in America any more. There were plenty of reasons for that decision and most of them were completely irrelevant to this story. But one wasn't.

The atmosphere in the country had changed. It wasn't immediate. It happened slowly and surely. And it is difficult to explain but I felt less safe as a Black person than I had done previously. Not that I was exactly gallivanting about the place. I rarely left the house, preferring to stay in and watch the horseracing from the UK on my computer in the mornings and local television in the afternoons. I had friends there of course and caught up with them on occasions but, to be honest, I wasn't there that much anyway because of the reasons stated above.

Maybe my attitude was (is) to be blamed for my uneasiness. I don't know as I haven't lain on a couch for a psychiatrist to tell me what's going on, but what I do know is this: speaking to Hope, Adam, Ibtihaj and others who were born and grew up in that kind of atmosphere made me appreciate their strength even more. Those who know me are aware of my travels all over the world (Australia, England, India, Pakistan, South Africa) and I have friends of all races and creeds, but I just felt *different* in America as time passed by. Maybe things will change, but at the moment, I need to spend even less time there.

Michael Johnson's words struck a chord as you would expect. 'We've had a president who has stoked this racism and who said the things out loud, and wasn't afraid to say out loud, what a lot of conservative politicians have always worked for underneath the surface.'

I don't want to spend too much time on Donald Trump. But it is no coincidence that, during a presidency that focused on hate, fear and division and resulted in white supremacists rioting in an attempt to get his election defeat overturned, Black people have felt more threatened than they have for years. And that's saying something. Why would I want to live in a country that could put a guy like that in the highest office in the land? Why would I want to run the risk of him getting another four years? I was getting out of there.

Thank goodness he lost. What could have happened

in another Trump term doesn't bear thinking about. And already – Joe Biden has only just been sworn in as I type – the streets feel safer. This might be more wishful thinking than reality but in the past few days, when I've ventured outside, it seems people *saw me* when I went out. I actually existed. A white gentleman held the shop door open for me before it closed. A small thing. But it stopped happening under Trump.

What I like to think about Trump's legacy – because I'm sure he'd hate it – is that he will be remembered as the president who unintentionally forced America and the world to finally recognise the fact that white supremacy is a dangerous problem. And one that we need to start solving. For a man who wanted to empower and embolden the racists, it's good that, seemingly, the people have said 'enough'. 'We can thank him for that,' Michael Johnson told me. 'I think that it has woken up a lot of us.'

Yes, maybe America has woken up. Maybe the world has woken up. I think about a line in 'The Hill We Climb', the poem by Amanda Gorman at Joe Biden's inauguration, which says: 'we've learned that quiet isn't always peace'. A lot of folks have been asleep at the wheel. In small moments like me finding my voice, or Michael finding his, the message is being passed on and people are learning. The Black Lives Matter movement has told people that it is okay to speak up and out. And it has educated people to what is really going on. It shows no sign of slowing.

That's progress. Perhaps in the past when there was an incident – thinking back to Rodney King's beating in 1991 and the riots that followed in Los Angeles – there would be an outcry. But it was fleeting. People moved on, they forgot about it, too busy with their own personal worries and issues.

I remember another poster carried by a young woman at a BLM protest which read: 'Everyone is saying this is America's wake-up call, but this is not the first, you all just keep hitting the snooze button.' This thing has real momentum now. So hopefully no snooze button this time around.

When I started writing this book, I was worried that it would just be a hashtag movement, something that was popular on social media for a few weeks before disappearing because people were outraged by something else. I don't think that has happened. It has gone on and on. And, unfortunately, that is true because of the political situation in the world. Tragedies have kept on happening to keep it relevant. But I also like to think it has remained relevant because folks are really listening for the first time.

I am positive that progress has been made. But we have to keep going. And in these final pages I think it is worth really trying to reiterate the key points about how we rise. How do we make sure that folks don't just slip back into their old habits? Or politicians don't just pay lip service to an issue? Naturally, I'll do that with a little help from the friends I have made along the way. At the end of each interview, I asked the same question: how do we rise? Each athlete I interviewed said the answer was education. But we will expand a bit on that.

We have to educate people. As Louis Farrakhan said: 'If they don't treat you right, why do you expect them to teach you right?' The decolonisation of the curriculum is the single most important change that we need to see. The true history of the world needs to be taught for there to be equality. And, as I've said, that will benefit people of all colours. Black people will realise that they are not just descendants of slaves. We come from some of the earliest and greatest civilisations. We have a history that we can be proud of rather than be cowed by.

If you teach a young Black kid about Septimius Severus, the first Black emperor of the Roman Empire, or show them how the Moors educated and enlightened Europe, or describe the bravery of the Black Rattlers or the brilliance of Lewis Howard Latimer, what do you think happens to their self-esteem? They walk taller and feel good. That person values themself. Just as the West Indians living in England did when their cricket team won Test matches. But what if they only learn about how they come from folks who were treated like cattle and were stripped of their identity? That is not very uplifting.

The impact is two-fold. White kids are in the same class. And they're learning about all these great things that Black people did. They're learning they are as smart, as important, as innovative as themselves. And those early seeds of white being superior to Black are never given the chance to grow into something ugly. What happens if nothing changes? The white kids continue to leave that class having been taught that all Black people ever did was be enslaved.

If that change happens, everybody benefits. That vicious cycle that destroys Black lives stops turning. We get educated, we get jobs, poverty decreases, we own homes, the prison populations shrink and, guess what, police forces don't need so much money any more and it can used for other things. And round and round we go. But this time in a positive way. And everybody rises.

'We have to educate people that to be different is okay, to have a different skin colour is okay,' Hope Powell said to me.

'We're not stupid people, we're intelligent. We have offered lots and have lots more to offer if you're prepared to have a difficult conversation about racism. Fifty years from now, we don't want to be having the same bloody conversation. It is about educating the next generation to ensure that another person doesn't have to write a book, another person doesn't have to bare their soul and say, "Look, this is an injustice."'

But, as I acknowledged that morning on Sky, this is a challenge. There has been huge resistance in America and Britain to teaching the truth. And, as the BLM movement has gathered pace, it has become almost weaponised by those who want the status quo to remain.

Before leaving office, Trump tried to rewrite America's history curriculum. With this in mind, he set up an advisory committee called the 1776 Commission to support his idea of a 'patriotic education', while railing against 'decades of left-wing indoctrination'. Trump said: 'Our youth will be taught to love America.' It attempted to downplay the horrors of slavery by excusing the American founders for owning slaves and defending the law that Black people counted as only three-fifths of a person. The commission said that law was necessary.

Within days of Joe Biden taking over, the 1776 Commission was dissolved. And, of course, that's great. But let's not rest on our laurels here. Trump gained just over 10 million more votes in the 2020 election than he did in 2016. In total, 74,222,958 Americans thought Trump should be president. That is a big problem. And anyone who thinks that just because he is no longer in office the division and hate and racism he gave legitimacy to are going to go away is destined to be disappointed. Barack Obama was president for eight years but the system was still in place when he was done. And, unfortunately, the fact that he held that position so enraged the white supremacists that Trump was able to come in and be at his absolute worst. That's a lot of education needed right there.

In Britain, the Conservative government launched a 'war on the woke' in early 2021, just when you thought things couldn't get much worse. I suppose it would be 'woke' of me to point out that Britain has the worst Covid death rate in the world, and the majority are people of colour, because of their policies?

What sort of government wants to demonise people who are alert to injustice and racism? Well, it's one that, for the first time, did not hold a reception in Downing Street for Black History Month in 2019. It's one that came up with the 'hostile environment' as an immigration policy. It was as nasty as it sounded and aimed to make life as unpleasant as possible so that people would want to leave. It's one that deported, detained and denied legal rights to members of the Windrush generation. One that employed an aide who believed that Black people are genetically predetermined to be less intelligent than white people. The press secretary of Prime Minister Boris Johnson was asked thirty times for Johnson's views on that one. And thirty times refused to answer. But maybe that's because we already know. Johnson has called Black people 'picaninnies . . . with watermelon smiles'.

He has been very vocal about the real history of Britain being taught. 'We cannot now try to edit or censor our past,' he said. 'We cannot pretend to have a different history.' I have dealt with this earlier in the book but I will repeat: no one is asking for history to be edited. It has already been edited to suit a particular narrative. We need the unedited version. In 2014 there was a petition to update the curriculum in the UK to better reflect Black achievements, their history and the role of empire. It was rejected.

I think I've largely proved that much of the British education system is based on lies, disinformation and bias to prop up racial hierarchy, the legacy of empire and white supremacy. And why not? It is all that people like Johnson have known themselves. And he is terrified, just like all politicians, of the truth coming out.

Populist politicians, like Johnson and his ministers, know perfectly well what they are doing. It is a scheme, a ploy. It is deliberate distortion, misrepresentation of facts and straight out of the populist playbook. It doesn't actually matter what is true to these people. What matters is what lies they can get away with, who they can enrage or make feel threatened to preserve and enhance their position and ambitions.

The row over the tearing down of statues is a good example. Politicians will argue that removing a statue of a slave trader is rewriting history. No. The statue being there in the first place is rewriting and whitewashing history. What other conclusion could you come to when the murder of Black people is something to be celebrated? In the summer of 2020 protestors in Bristol toppled a statue of Edward Colston. Colston was part of the Royal African Company which sold about 100,000 slaves from West Africa to the Caribbean and Americas. They were branded with the initials 'RAC' on their chests.

Quite a few people are now aware of who Edward Colston was and what he did. Why? Was it because there was a statue in Bristol praising him? Or was it because that statue was torn down and pushed into the nearby docks? Who is trying to rewrite history there? And how on earth can you possibly be offended by such an act? I want them all removed from public places. Place them in a museum if you like, so those who may want to learn their history can go and get themselves educated on the subject. I am not telling anyone to forget but please, in these enlightened times, don't tell me you think those people should still be honoured.

This is serious stuff. These are dark and dangerous tactics by politicians. In my opinion it is the new form of brain-washing. They can see how their modus operandi has been challenged and they are desperately trying to provoke a sort of culture war, portraying people who just want education, equality and justice as traitors. That may sound strong but that is exactly where these politicians want this to go. They want to divide and rule.

They are trying to get into people's heads and fill them with more rubbish. They are trying to continue the same story, or learned behaviour, which has been passed down for hundreds of years. They can no longer, unhindered and on a mass scale, physically abuse Black people, they can't take away their rights, segregate them or deny them freedom, so they use this new method. It is a major concern that there is an evolution to the dehumanisation. Look at the insurrection at the Capitol in Washington. People carrying Confederate flags in the home of America's democracy, for goodness sake.

The same people who are up in arms about history being rewritten are the people deliberately misunderstanding the term white privilege. The same people who retort 'all lives matter' in the face of the BLM movement. Or who claim that being woke – which, it seems to me, is being a human being of compassion – is a bad thing. That is how low they will go.

To combat that, people of all colours have got to come together. And, as I've said quite a few times in these pages, through the discussions with the icons who agreed to talk with me, nothing can be achieved unless white people and people of colour are hand-in-hand in this thing together. I think back to that white kid and Black kid playing together in New York City when I was young and my mom saying: 'Mikey, we've got a chance.' What she didn't take into consideration was the age of the kids. No one is born a racist and those two kids hadn't yet been influenced by the society they were about to grow up in. But things are changing. And the multicultural representation on the marches and protests proves that.

On that point, when I asked Adam Goodes about how we can bring about change, he turned the question round, asking not what people of colour could do but what their friends and neighbours from a different creed or culture could do.

'How can you help your fellow countrymen and women, Black people, minorities in our community rise?' he said. 'Well, first of all, for me, it's about understanding our differences. And noting that those differences, well, we may have a lot. And that's okay, it's okay to be different to other people and speak to a different God that has a different name. We love different people and the way that they love.

'We have to acknowledge that we're all different, but also that we're all bonded by one thing, and that is we are humans, and we should want to see the best of each other and not the worst. And we need to celebrate that.'

Indeed, what was striking to me when talking to these

athletes was how often they would have been brought up in multicultural environments, only to suffer racism as soon as they left. Thierry Henry didn't see it in his community, nor did Michael Johnson. There's a lesson there. If people from different backgrounds and cultures and countries can mix well, then multiculturalism works. Now, does it work because those folks are all in the same boat, united by their status? Possibly. But at the same time there is no 'otherness' there holding back those communities. As Thierry said, he 'travelled without moving'. He could well have said that he learned to be open-minded and accepting of people who are different.

For Thierry, it was important for Black people to have role models. To have someone to look up to and aspire to be like. And I think education is wrapped up in that.

'We do rise because we need heroes, we need examples,' Thierry said. 'We need guys who are going to be at the top for us. That's why you stand up again – to try to reach the top. Because if you kneel, you know exactly what kneeling means. We need people from our community to be able to represent our community in business, in politics. That's why we rise and we fight in an intelligent way. It's not about how you fall; it's about how you get up.'

Thoughts and feelings have to be backed by real action, though, from the power brokers in the world. And that means big business has to start behaving like activists, donating money, putting pressure on politicians to end the cycle of racial injustice.

'We're going to need help from the corporations and institutions because big money around the world makes a difference,' said Ibtihaj Muhammad. 'You ain't gonna change it just on the streets.

'If we think of it as a fight, I think that that can be a deterrent for people. This is a marathon. This has taken hundreds of years to get to where we are today. And it'll take time to dismantle this system of oppression that exists, and big corporations are going to be a major part of that.' There is good news on that front. JP Morgan committed $30 billion to advance racial equality for five years from 2020. That's the largest bank in America, right there. In real terms, that money, they claim, is going to be used as loans for Black people, to fund community projects, build more affordable housing and help grow businesses. Remember redlining? Remember how Black folks could not get the financial support they so desperately needed to rise? Well, that's a huge step in the right direction. Citibank and Bank of America have each pledged $1 billion for the same.

Nike has donated $40 million up to 2024 to support the Black community in the US. Apple plans to give $100 million to racial equality initiatives, Amazon $27 million and Sony $100 million. These numbers show that protest works. People walk, money talks. Adam Goodes spoke about money for indigenous businesses in Australia. We can't get anywhere without that sort of financial support. It comes with a warning, though. Consumers are watching you, just to check it's not being done for good publicity. Michael Johnson was clear on that.

'I think we have to remember that they're not just doing these things out of a moral obligation or because it is the right thing to do,' he said. 'They're doing it because it hits the bottom line. And I'm fine with that. I don't care how we get them there as long as we get them there, and I'm going to always assume that it's because they want to do the right thing but it has to be economically advantageous to them. Whether that's because it's helpful to them, or because doing nothing is hurtful to them.

'Racism didn't all of a sudden just start happening with George Floyd. It's been happening for hundreds of years, which just got highlighted in the moment. And you could turn on your television and not see major *Fortune* 500 companies with all these heartfelt, beautiful messages about their commitment to equality, and acknowledging the inequality in our systems and all of these sorts of things. Well, we're not seeing any of that any more. In the moment you were, we were flooded with that. They've gone back to their same advertising, pushing their products, pushing their services.

'A good friend of mine just went over to JP Morgan to run the programme that you're talking about. Bank of America are trying to get financial institutions to loan to Black families and Black businesses for homes and mortgages and that sort of thing. So there are a lot of companies doing a lot of good, but let's be clear that it's our job to continue to hold them accountable.' I suppose you could compare this situation to what the South African government legislated regarding inclusivity at the end of apartheid. Hopefully what these companies are doing will soon not be considered extraordinary but what socially responsible companies do.

I think the message here is 'don't let up'. I know I won't be. And that's something for me to recognise. In that summer of 2020, I stood up and said something. And as soon as I did, I thought, *Uh-oh! I didn't expect this reaction.* I thought I would be able to slip back into a quiet life. I know I have to keep talking, keep trying to get people to listen to the truth. That's progress for me, a guy who, when he encountered racism as a young man, turned the other way and thought, *Not my problem.* Then, as an older man, shrugged and grimaced inside without really doing anything about it. I have been on a journey myself.

And I am fully aware that for the words I have put together in these pages there will be a backlash. People will reckon I hate white people – I don't (unless they reckon I married my wife to punish her!). Or that I don't think 'all lives matter' – please, not again. And I'm ready for that. We can't change the minds of those people. We can't waste our time on them. But if we focus on those people who have open minds and are willing to learn and be taught new things, then we will continue to make progress. Bit by bit.

One day, people of colour might have equality. It will be the generation, young and hopeful and fierce, who marched together in 2020 that will propel us to that point. They are smart enough to see through the lies and the schemes and the tricks. They are smart enough to go online and educate themselves and educate others through social media. And as time goes by and those people rise themselves into positions of power, still teaching, still changing, progress will be accelerated.

And, listen, I don't expect to be around to see the fruits of that labour and love. I will be long gone by the time we have a genuine level playing field, a day when the Black person is not stuck on first base and the white person is on third. It is going to take time. Maybe as long as my 6-year-old grandson getting to the ripe age I am now. But like my mom said to me, I think I can safely and happily say to him, and to you: 'We've got a chance.'

Still I Rise
By Maya Angelou

You may write me down in history
With your bitter, twisted lies,
You may trod me in the very dirt
But still, like dust, I'll rise. [. . .]

Just like moons and like suns,
With the certainty of tides,
Just like hopes springing high,
Still I'll rise.

Did you want to see me broken?
Bowed head and lowered eyes?
Shoulders falling down like teardrops,
Weakened by my soulful cries? [. . .]

You may shoot me with your words,
You may cut me with your eyes,
You may kill me with your hatefulness,
But still, like air, I'll rise. [. . .]

Leaving behind nights of terror and fear
I rise
Into a daybreak that's wondrously clear
I rise
Bringing the gifts that my ancestors gave,
I am the dream and the hope of the slave.
I rise
I rise
I rise.

A *WHY WE KNEEL, HOW WE RISE*
BLACK HISTORY TIMELINE

AD 1–33 Life of Jesus Christ; born in the Middle East and certainly not white as portrayed.

193–211 Septimius Severus, the Black emperor, serves the Roman Empire. A military garrison is set up by Severus at Burgh by Sands, near Hadrian's Wall, with the African auxiliary unit Numerus Maurorum Aurelianorum stationed there. One of the first examples of Black people in Britain.

440 The Kingdom of Ghana. One of the earliest and most advanced civilisations in history. The kingdom had its own trade networks and its capital, Koumbi Saleh, had a population of more than 30,000.

620 The beginnings of African–Indian trade. Chinese coins found on east coast of Africa.

668 North African-born scholar Hadrian becomes an abbot in Canterbury Cathedral. He rejected the opportunity to be made Archbishop.

711 The Moors conquer Spain and Portugal and rule until 1492. The Moors' advances in mathematics, astronomy, art and agriculture would help propel Europe out of the Dark Ages and into the Renaissance.

800 African presence in the 'New World'.

890–992 Trade routes in West and East Africa to Indonesia as African kingdoms proliferate.

1100 Stone structures are proof of an early civilisation in what would become Rhodesia and later Zimbabwe.

1241 Earliest image of a Black person in Britain found in Domesday Book.

1400 Bronze statues produced in Benin, West Africa.

1460 Slaves are taken from Africa by the Spanish to Europe. Ten years later sugar plantations in Italy emerge with labour done by Africans.

1492 Christopher Columbus 'discovers' the New World. Two years later he claims Jamaica for the Spanish.

1518 First slaves arrive in West Indies.

1562 Admiral John Hawkins leads first English slave-trading voyage from West Africa.

1619 Slaves arrive in the English colony of Virginia.

1623 Britain annexes St Kitts as their domination of the Caribbean begins.

1652 The Dutch establish a white colony in
South Africa.

1660 The British take control of Jamaica.

1672 King Charles II gives his Royal African Company
exclusive rights to take slaves to the Americas.

1721 Black slave Onesimus introduces inoculation
to America.

1780 132 slaves thrown overboard on the ship *Zong*.

Sugar becomes Britain's dominant import.

1781 Los Angeles is founded by fifty-four settlers
including twenty-six of African ancestry.

1791 The Haitian Revolution begins, the only
successful slave uprising.

140 years of massacres of indigenous population of
Australia begin.

1804 Haiti becomes first independent Black republic
in the Americas. The reparations it must pay to
France cripple the country.

1807 British slave trade is abolished but not until
reparations are paid in 1834 – the equivalent of
40 per cent of Britain's annual income – does it
actually cease.

1838 Law enforcement officer Bass Reeves is born.
He will be the inspiration for the Lone Ranger
character. He was Black but because of white
supremacy he could not be portrayed as such.

1839   Edmond Berger invents the spark plug.

1844   Elijah McCoy is born. The man who coined the term 'the real McCoy' because of his invention to stop steam-train wheels sticking. Other companies tried to copy him but the railways only wanted his invention.

1849   Harriet Tubman, an escaped enslaved woman, becomes a 'conductor' on the Underground Railroad, leading enslaved people to freedom before the Civil War.

1852   Frederick Douglass, the most influential civil rights campaigner in the nineteenth century, gives his acclaimed Fourth of July speech.

1855   Mary Seacole opens the 'British Hotel' in Crimea.

1863   Abraham Lincoln issues the Emancipation Proclamation.

1864   George Washington Carver is born. He will develop revolutionary farming techniques that help former slaves in Alabama become self-sufficient.

1865   The Jim Crow laws era begins. It lasts until 1965.

1867   Alexander Miles patents the electric elevator.

1870   Bill Pickett is born. He will become one of the most well-known rodeo stars at a time when one in four cowboys was Black.

1872   Thomas Marshall patents the fire extinguisher.

1877   Charles Joseph Bolden is born. He will be one of the very first jazz musicians.

Lynchings begin in America.

1878   Osbourn Dorsey invents door knob.

1882   Lewis Howard Latimer patents the carbon filament for lightbulbs.

Thomas A. Carrington invents the stethoscope.

1885   Africa is carved up by the European powers. Some borders are decided by a ruler. King Leopold of Belgium acquires the Congo as his personal possession. His rule will kill up to 10 million Africans.

1887   The Black nationalist and Jamaica icon Marcus Garvey is born.

1888   Slavery is abolished in Brazil.

1889   W. A. Martin patents the lock.

1890   Walter B. Purvis patents his improved fountain pen design.

1892   Alice Ball is born. She developed a herbal remedy for the treatment of leprosy and was the first woman to earn a master's degree from the University of Hawaii.

1898   Lydia D. Newman invents a new practical hairbrush.

1899   Boer War begins. The British imprison more than 100,000 in concentration camps and up to 30,000 die.

J. A. Burr patents his rotary-blade lawnmower.

1906   A West Indies cricket team includes Black players for the first time.

1908   Jack Johnson becomes the first African-American world heavyweight boxing champion.

1909   Matthew Henson discovers the North Pole.

1910   Australian government begins forcibly removing indigenous children from their families. 'Assimilations' last another sixty years.

1914–18 The First World War. The British West Indies Regiment and the all-Black 369th Infantry Regiment of the New York Army National Guard serve with honour.

1914   Garrett Morgan patents his 'breathing device', predecessor of the gas mask. Later he invents the three-way traffic light.

1915   US President Woodrow Wilson screens a Ku Klux Klan film at the White House.

1918   Katherine Johnson is born. She will be a mathematician whose calculations of orbital mechanics as a NASA employee were critical to the success of the first and subsequent US crewed spaceflights.

1919   Race riots in Britain with Black sailors and Black businesses targeted.

British murder at least 400 protestors in Amritsar, India.

Gandhi begins campaign to end British rule in India. His passive resistance movement inspires Martin Luther King.

American footballer Fritz Pollard begins his professional career.

1920   Inventor Otis Boykin is born.

1921   At least thirty-six African-Americans die in white violence in the Tulsa Massacre.

1922   Marie Van Brittan Brown is born. She will invent the first home security system and lay the groundwork for the modern closed-circuit television system.

1924   James Baldwin, novelist, is born.

1928   Learie Constantine makes his West Indies debut. He will become a racial equality activist and the first Black governor of the BBC.

Poet and writer Maya Angelou is born.

1929   Martin Luther King is born.

1930   George Headley makes his West Indies debut.

Betty Boop, the cartoon character, is introduced to the world. She was inspired by African-American jazz singer Esther Jones.

1932   Black sharecroppers are used in a medical experiment for syphilis.

1936   Jesse Owens wins four gold medals at the Berlin Olympics in front of Adolf Hitler.

1938   Kofi Annan, who will become secretary general of the UN, is born.

1939–45 Soldiers of colour play huge role in the Second World War.

1940   Frederick Johnson invents the portable air-conditioning unit. He also patents the thermostat control.

1942   Muhammad Ali, the greatest, is born.

1943   Winston Churchill diverts food to British soldiers, causing the Bengal famine. Four million die.

1945   Bob Marley is born.

1947   British partition of India results in religious genocide.

1948   Apartheid begins in South Africa.

         The *Empire Windrush* arrives at Tilbury docks.

1950   The Red Cross recognise that all blood is 'equal' after Charles Drew, who developed the first large-scale blood banks and blood plasma programmes, resigned from a 'segregated' blood policy.

1952   Big Mama Thornton records the original 'Hound Dog'.

1954   Philip Emeagwali born. He will be known as 'the African Bill Gates' for his innovation in computer processing.

1955   Civil rights movement in America begins after the Rosa Parks bus boycott.

1956   Sisters Mary and Mildred Davidson invent the sanitary belt.

         Althea Gibson becomes first Black woman to win a tennis Grand Slam at the French Open.

1957   Ghana becomes first African nation to be independent.

1960   Sixty-nine Black protestors against apartheid are murdered by police in Sharpeville, South Africa.

         Frank Worrell becomes first West Indies Black captain for an entire series.

1962   Jamaica gains independence.

         Commonwealth Immigrants Act is passed in Britain to reduce immigration from former colonies.

1963   Nelson Mandela is imprisoned.

         Martin Luther King delivers his 'I Have a Dream' speech.

1964   America's Civil Rights Act comes into force.

         Martin Luther King wins Nobel Peace Prize.

1965   Racial equality activist Malcolm X is murdered.

The Voting Rights Act is passed in America.

1967   Indigenous people of Australia are formally recognised as human beings.

1968   Martin Luther King is assassinated.

Tommie Smith and John Carlos raise a black-gloved fist at the Mexico Olympics to protest racial inequality in America.

Enoch Powell delivers his 'Rivers of Blood' speech.

1971   Richard Nixon's 'war on drugs' deliberately targets Black people.

Bernard Coard's exposé of British school system discriminating against West Indian children is published.

1973   Dr Shirley Jackson receives her PhD from Massachusetts University. She helps to invent the touch-tone telephone, the portable fax, caller ID, call waiting, and the fibre-optic cable.

1974   Kissinger Report states aim to slow population growth in Africa.

1976   Negro History Week, founded in 1926, is replaced by Black History Month in the US.

The novel *Roots*, by Alex Haley, is published.

1977   Steve Biko, anti-apartheid campaigner, is killed in police custody.

1980   White rule ends in Rhodesia, later
becoming Zimbabwe.

Burning Spear releases the song 'Columbus'.

West Indies cricket team beat England 4–0. They
will not lose a series for fifteen years.

1981   Brixton race riots.

1982   First English rebel cricket tour to South Africa.
Two West Indies teams tour in 1983 and 1984.

1990   Nelson Mandela is released from prison.

1992   Riots in Los Angeles after four white police
officers are acquitted of charges for beating
Rodney King.

1993   Teenager Stephen Lawrence is murdered
in London.

1994   Apartheid in South Africa ends. Nelson Mandela
is elected president.

1998   Makhaya Ntini becomes first Black African to
play cricket for South Africa.

Hope Powell becomes first Black coach of an
English national sporting team.

Christopher Alder dies in police custody
in England.

2000   Michael Johnson wins his fourth Olympic gold
medal in Sydney.

2002 Thierry Henry wins first of two Premier League titles.

2005 John Sentamu becomes first Black Archbishop of York.

2008 Barack Obama is elected first African-American president of the USA.

2012 Trayvon Martin is shot dead, aged seventeen.

2013 Adam Goodes is racially abused at an Aussie Rules match.

2014 Tamir Rice is murdered, aged twelve.

12 Years a Slave wins Oscar for Best Picture.

Michael Brown is shot dead, aged eighteen.

2015 Nine African-Americans are shot dead by a white supremacist while at church in South Carolina.

2016 Donald Trump is elected president of the USA.

Usain Bolt becomes first sprinter to win 100m and 200m gold at three consecutive Olympics.

Ibtihaj Muhammad wins bronze medal at Olympics.

Colin Kaepernick takes a knee for the first time.

2018 Windrush scandal. Britain wrongly deports or detains at least eighty-three people of West Indian heritage.

2020   Breonna Taylor is murdered, aged twenty-six.

Ahmaud Arbery is murdered, aged twenty-five.

Naomi Osaka wins second US Open title.

Covid-19 spreads, disproportionately killing people of colour.

George Floyd is murdered, aged forty-six.

Jacob Blake is shot and paralysed, aged twenty-nine.

Black Lives Matter protests sweep the world.

Joe Biden defeats Donald Trump to become the 46th US president.

SOURCES

Black Clouds

'New transcripts detail last moments for George Floyd',
New York Times, 11 August 2020

'This is the toll that everyday racism takes on Black men in
America', WeForum.org, 2 July 2002

Melanie Morris, Laura M. Woods and Bernard Rachet,
'A novel ecological methodology for constructing
ethnic-majority life tables in the absence of individual
ethnicity information', *Journal of Epidemiology and
Community Health*, April 2015

'America has an infant mortality crisis', *The Guardian*, 25
November 2019

'Number of people shot to death by the police in
the United States from 2017 to 2020, by race',
Statista.com, accessed: 5 January 2021 and
3 February 2021

'Black people are up to 6 times more likely to be killed
by police, Harvard study says', MarketWatch.com,
28 June 2020

'George Floyd death: How many black people die in police
custody in England and Wales?', BBC, 3 June 2020

'Black people dying in police custody should surprise no one', *The Guardian*, 11 June 2020

'Britain doesn't care about health inequalities', *The Guardian*, 23 April 2020

A Sheltered Start

'Barbara Blake-Hannah: how Britain's first Black female TV reporter was forced off our screens', *The Guardian*, 7 January 2021

Black Lives Matter, Too

'Naomi Osaka made sure Black lives mattered at the US Open', The Undefeated, 12 September 2020

'Leading by example: How Naomi Osaka Became the People's Champion', *Vogue*, January 2021

'Naomi Osaka in no mood to back down on support for Black Lives Matter', *Japan Times*, 11 June 2020

Living It

'Cherry Groce: Mum's police shooting "robbed me of my childhood"', BBC News, 30 June 2020

'They used to tell us, "go back home"', *The Independent*, 14 June 1998

'How Caribbean migrants helped to rebuild Britain', British Library, 14 October 2018

Like the Roman: The Life of Enoch Powell, Simon Heffer
(Orion, 1999)

'In 1968, a British politician warned immigration would
lead to violence. Now some say he was right',
Washington Post, 24 November 2015

'How racist is Britain today? What the evidence tells us',
The Conversation, 1 July 2020

Natives, Akala (Two Roads, 2019)

Black and British, David Olusoga (Picador, 2016)

Dehumanisation

'Father of modern gynaecology performed experiments
on enslaved Black women', *USA Today*,
June 2019

'The dark side of Thomas Jefferson', *Smithsonian* magazine,
October 2012

'The long history of how Jesus came to resemble a white
European', The Conversation, 17 July 2020

'Jesus wasn't white: he was a brown-skinned, Middle
Eastern Jew. Here's why that matters', The
Conversation, 28 March 2018

'Did race and racism exist in the Middle Ages?',
NotEvenPast.org, 1 March 2018

'Humans did come out of Africa, says DNA', *Nature*,
7 December 2000

'Recalling Africa's harrowing tale of its first slavers as UK
Slave Trade Abolition is commemorated', *New Africa
Magazine*, 27 March 2018

'The *Zong* Massacre', BlackPast.org, 11 October 2011

Dr Hakim Adi, 'Africa and the Transatlantic Slave Trade', BBC History, October 2012

'The "father of modern gynaecology" performed shocking experiments on enslaved women', History.com, 29 August 2017

'Discrimination against Blacks linked to dehumanization', Stanford News Service, 7 February 2008

Post Traumatic Slave Syndrome: America's Legacy of Enduring Injury and Healing, Joy DeGruy (Uptone Press, 2005)

Breaking Rank, Norm Stamper (Nation, 2006)

'Georgia police chief, officer ousted after video of racist remarks on slavery, Stacey Abrams', NBC News, 1 February 2021

American Slavery, American Freedom, Edmund Morgan (Norton and Company, 1975)

'Covid: Ethnicity vaccine gaps in over-70s', BBC, 18 February 2020

'It's true: 1 in 1,000 Black Americans have died in the Covid-19 pandemic', Vox.com, 29 September 2020

'Access to health care for ethnic minority populations', A. Szczepura, BMJ, Vol. 81, Issue 953, 2005

'American slavery, reinvented', The Atlantic, 21 September 2015

Examples of Jim Crow Laws, Ferris State University Archive – Jim Crow Museum of Racist Memorabilia

'Redlining's legacy', CBS News, 12 June 2020

Touré, 'Slavery in America reminds us: Trump is far from an aberration', The Guardian, 16 August 2019

Joe Hopkinson, 'Racism and the misconceptions around it', hud.ac.uk, June 2020

'Jim Crow Laws created "slavery by another name"',
  National Geographic, 5 February 2020
Nancy O'Brien Wagner, 'Slavery by Another Name', Twin
  Cities, 2012
'Institutional racism explained through a Michael Jackson
  song', TRTWorld.com, 11 April 2018
'How a Psychologist's Work on Race Identity Helped
  Overturn School Segregation in 1950s America',
  Smithsonian magazine, 26 October 2017

Show of Strength

'US Olympic fencer Ibtihaj Muhammad: "I'm just your
  basic Hijabi Zorro"', ESPN, 15 July 2016
J. Danny Hays, 'What does the Bible say about race?',
  Ouachita Baptist University Archives, 23 June 2020
'Ibtihaj Muhammad has a calling', Unicefusa.org, 20
  February 2019

History Lesson

'They came before Columbus', Africa Speaks Archives
'We came before Columbus', OurTimePress.com, 4
  September 2017
'Pre-Columbian Black presence in the western hemisphere',
  Negro History Bulletin, Volume 38, Number 7,
  October/November 1975
'Columbus was a mass killer and the father of the slave
  trade', IrishCentral.com, 12 October 2020

'British Empire: Students should be taught colonialism "not all good", say historians', *The Independent*, 22 January 2016

'The Truth about Christopher Columbus', *The Progressive*, 9 October 2017

'Winston Churchill has as much blood on his hands as the worst genocidal dictators, claims Indian politician', *The Independent*, 8 September 2018

'The history of the British Empire is not being taught', *New Statesman*, 12 June 2020

'What They Don't Teach at School', Bustle.com, 8 February 2021

'Black British history: The row over the school curriculum in England', *The Guardian*, 13 July 2020

'How Britain is facing up to its hidden slavery history', BBC Culture, 3 July 2020

'Which UK cities most benefited from the slave trade – and how can you tell?', *The Week*, 11 June 2020

Bernard Coard, 'Why I wrote the "ESN book"', *The Guardian*, 5 February 2005

'How Black Working-Class Youth are Criminalised and Excluded in the English School System', Institute of Race Relations, 28 September 2020

'Teachers' implicit bias against Black students starts in preschool, study finds', *The Guardian*, 4 October 2016

'For Black kids, the school-to-prison pipeline opens the second they start pre-school', Splinter News, 6 August 2018

'Florida couple says home was appraised 40 percent higher after removing Black relatives' photos', The Hill, 26 August 2020

'Remembering the conference that divided Africa', Al Jazeera, 15 November 2019

The Wonderful Adventures of Mrs Seacole in Many Lands, Mary Seacole (Penguin Classics, 2005)

Black Victorians, Gretchen Gerzina (Rutgers University Press, 2003)

'*Mary Seacole* by Jane Robinson', *The Independent*, 21 January 2005

Tan-Feng Chang, 'Creolizing the White Woman's Burden', *College Literature*, John Hopkins University Press, Volume 44, Number 4, Fall 2017

Fear

'Olympian Michael Johnson on Ahmaud Arbery: "This is not about running"', The Undefeated, 15 May 2020

Acceptance

'Black culture appropriation', *New York Times Magazine*, 14 August 2019

'Black Artists Built Country Music – And Then It Left Them Behind', *Time* magazine, 11 September 2019

'Black people invented music: a historical overview', ForgeToday.com, 7 July 2020

'The Quintessential Innovator', *Time* magazine, 22 October 1979

'Lewis H. Latimer dead: member of Edison Pioneers drew

original plans for Bell phone', *New York Times*, 13
December 1928

'The Fight Over Inoculation During the 1721
Boston Smallpox Epidemic', Harvard University
Archives, 2014

'Mary Seacole to be removed from national curriculum',
The Voice, 18 November 2020

'Mary Seacole: Myths in the Making of the Nursing
Profession', NightingaleSociety.com

Matthew Henson profile, Diversityinc.com, 8
February 2020

Otis Boykin profile, Biography.com, accessed: 12
January 2021

Garrett Morgan profile, Biography.com, accessed: 5
January 2021

Henry Louis Gates, Jr, 'Who Were the Harlem
Hellfighters?', PBS.org

'Black Americans in the US Military from the American
Revolution to the Korean War: World War One', New
York State Military Museum Archives

Black Soldiers of New York State: A Proud Legacy, Anthony
Gero (State University of New York Press, 2009)

'A WWI-Era Memo asking French officers to Practice Jim
Crow with Black American troops', Slate.com, 27
April 2016

'Remembering Fritz Pollard', Brown University Archives

Anyone But England, Mike Marqusee (Aurum, 2005)

Fire in Babylon, documentary by Stevan Riley (Cowboy
Films/Passion Pictures, 2010)

A New Generation

An Account of the English Colony in New South Wales, David
    Collins (T. Cadell and W. Davies, 1804)
Donald McRae, 'Adam Goodes: "Instead of masking racism
    we need to deal with it day-to-day"', *The Guardian*, 2
    March 2020
'Viewers unload on Eddie McGuire for DEFENDING
    Sam Newman over his blackface stunt in footage aired
    during a polarising documentary featuring AFL great
    Adam Goodes', *Daily Mail Australia*, 26 February 2020

We've Got A Chance

'Who was Edward Colston and why was his Bristol statue
    toppled?', *The Guardian*, 8 June 2020
'Boris Johnson says we shouldn't edit our past. But Britain
    has been lying about it for decades', *The Guardian*,
    16 June 2020
'Racism has cost America $16 trillion this century alone',
    CNN.com, 24 September 2020